D0849787

Bloom's Modern Critical Views

Bloom's Modern Critical Views

Bloom's Modern Critical Views

DAVID MAMET

Edited and with an introduction by
Harold Bloom
Sterling Professor of the Humanities
Yale University

CHELSEA HOUSE
PUBLISHERS
A Haights Cross Communications Company

Philadelphia

Library of Congress Cataloging-in-Publication Data

David Mamet / edited and with an introduction by Harold Bloom.
    p. cm. -- (Bloom's modern critical views)
Includes bibliographical references. and index.
   ISBN: 0-7910-7660-1
1. Mamet, David--Criticism and interpretation. I. Bloom, Harold. II.
Series
   PS3563.A4345Z656 2003
   812'.54--dc21
                                        2003011517

Chelsea House Publishers
1974 Sproul Road, Suite 400
Broomall, PA 19008-0914

http://www.chelseahouse.com

Contributing Editor: Pamela Loos

Cover designed by Terry Mallon

Cover photo © AFP/CORBIS

Layout by EJB Publishing Services

Contents

Editor's Note

My Introduction meditates upon *Sexual Perversity in Chicago* as David Mamet's *Inferno*, a vision of the damned.

Anne Dean sees *Sexual Perversity in Chicago* as a satire upon American *praxis* of the 1970's, while Douglas Bruster deftly invokes the city comedies of Ben Jonson as antecedents to Mamet's charlatans and gulls.

The complexly Jewish strain in Mamet's work is illuminated by Toby Silverman Zinman, who emphasizes the Talmudic mode of answering questions with another question.

Male bonding, another source of complex anguish in Mamet, is judged by David Radavich to catch the Spirit of the Age, where male identity feels threatened by the supposedly new assertiveness of women.

In an overview, Edward J. Esche attempts to apply aspects of Shakespeare's darker, more problematic comedies, to our quest for appreciating Mamet, after which Michael L. Quinn relates Mamet's expressionistic "realism" to the paradoxical American exaltation of an artist's "creative rejections."

Howard Pearce develops Mamet's idea of the artist-as-"freak" confronting a tinsel reality, while Leslie Kane returns us to Jewish identity and its discontents in Mamet.

A comprehensive account of Mamet is given us by the vastly informed critic of contemporary drama, C.W.E. Bigsby, who bluntly remarks: "His plays feature man as an endangered species."

Oleanna is contrasted with Lillian Hellman's *The Children's Hour* by David Kennedy Sauer, for whom "the system" is to blame, rather than the man or the woman.

Richard Brucher turns back to *Edmond*, in order to uncover yet once more the pervasive influence of Thorstein Veblen upon Mamet.

In a brilliant reading of *The Cryptogram* (considered by Tony Kushner to be Mamet's best play so far), Linda Dorff analyzes the dramatist as being victimized by the male mythology he seeks to parody and overthrow.

HAROLD BLOOM

Introduction

V ery few contemporary dramas of authentic eminence depress me quite so much as does *Sexual Perversity in Chicago*, whether I see it at a theater, or reread it in my study. Doubtless, Mamet wants that affect in auditor or reader. I have encountered only one photograph of Mamet, the Brigitte Lacombe shot of the playwright as Groucho Marx that adorns the paperback of *SPC* (a short version of the title). One could argue that Groucho is more of an influence upon Mamet than are Beckett, Pinter, and Albee, since *SPC* seems (to me) best acted as parodistic farce. T.S. Eliot, still the major poet who makes me most uneasy, had a great regard both for Groucho and for Marlowe's Jew of Malta, Barabbas. I cannot read *The Jew of Malta* without casting Groucho in the role, and sometimes I wish I could direct *SPC* with Groucho playing Bernie and Chico as Danny.

The epigraph to *SPC* might be Marlowe's Mephistopheles cheerfully answering: "Why this is Hell, nor am I out of it." Though Douglas Bruster usefully compares Mamet to Ben Jonson of the City Comedies, I suspect that Mamet actually resembles Marlowe more than Jonson. The savagery of Mamet's stance towards his protagonists, particularly in *SPC*, is Marlovian, as is Mamet's fierce obsession with hyperbolical rhetoric. Here is Bernie, wildly prevaricating, and approaching the vaunting terms of Sir Epicure Mammon in *The Alchemist*:

> *Bernie*: So wait. So I don't know what the shot is. So all of a
> sudden I hear coming out of the phone: "Rat Tat Tat Tat
> Tat. Ka POW! AK AK AK AK AK AK AK *Ka Pow!*" So
> fine. I'm pumping away, the chick on the other end is
> making airplane noises, every once in a while I go
> BOOM, and the broad on the bed starts going crazy.

1

> She's moaning and groaning and about to go the whole
> long route. Humping and bumping, and she's screaming
> "Red dog One to Red dog Squadron" ... all of a sudden
> she screams "Wait." She wriggles out, leans under the
> bed, and she pulls out this five-gallon jerrycan.

Danny: Right.

Bernie: Opens it up ... it's full of gasoline. So she splashes the
> mother all over the walls, whips a fuckin' Zippo out of the
> Flak suit, and WHOOSH, the whole room is in flames.
> So the whole fuckin' joint is going up in smoke, the
> telephone is going "Rat Tat Tat," the broad jumps back on
> the bed and yells "Now, give it to me *now* for the love of
> Christ." (*Pause.*) So I look at the broad ... and I figure ...
> fuck this nonsense. I grab my clothes, I peel a sawbuck off
> my wad, as I make the door I fling it at her. "For cab fare,"
> I yell. She doesn't hear nothing. One, two, six, I'm in the
> hall. Struggling into my shorts and hustling for the
> elevator. Whole fucking hall is full of smoke, above the
> flames I just make out my broad, she's singing "Off we go
> into the Wild Blue Yonder," and the elevator arrives, and
> the whole fucking hall is full of *firemen*. (*Pause.*) Those
> fucking firemen make out like bandits. (*Pause.*)

Bernie is confidence man rather than gull, so that we dislike him,
whereas the outrageous Sir Epicure Mammon is weirdly endearing. And yet
Bernie's obsessive rhetoric has an hallucinatory quality that is more than
Jonsonian enough. No audience easily tolerates Bernie, whose final tirade
manifests what could be called a negative pathos, which involuntarily
expresses a desperate sense of damnation:

> *Bernie*: Makes all the fucking difference in the world. (*Pause.*)
> Coming out here on the beach. Lying all over the beach,
> flaunting their bodies ... I mean who the fuck do they
> think they are all of a sudden, coming out here and just
> flaunting their bodies all over? (*Pause.*) I mean, what are
> you supposed to think? I come to the beach with a friend
> to get some sun and watch the action and ... I mean a
> fellow comes to the beach to sit out in the fucking sun,
> am I wrong? ... I mean we're talking about recreational

fucking space, huh? ... huh? (*Pause.*) What the fuck am I
talking about?

The fear of female sexuality hardly could be more palpable, and a new
kind of Inferno beckons in: "What the fuck am I talking about?" Hell,
according to Jean-Paul Sartre's *No Exit*, is Other People. Like Rimbaud's
Hell, Bernie's Inferno is not less than the existence of women as such.

ANNE DEAN

Sexual Perversity in Chicago

Like most of Mamet's plays, *Sexual Perversity in Chicago* is set in a desensitized society. The characters inhabit a cheap and fraudulent world in which standards decline daily and sexual intimacy seems to have become public property. Language is often used shoddily and obscenities are commonplace—their sexual connotations have, through overuse, become dulled, rather like their users' consciousnesses. Human relationships have become attenuated to the point at which men and women view each other as little more than media-created stereotypes, and millions of people watch television soap operas sincerely believing that their convoluted plots reflect real life.

In the mid-1970s when the play was written, what Mamet calls the "jejeune super-sophistication"[1] of the American populace was at its height. The "Swinging Sixties" had come and gone and, in their place, was a cynical, rather detached society that plundered the most negative aspects of the previous decade's sexual revolution, emphasizing promiscuity and irresponsibility to the detriment of its emotional sanity. Because of the dominating influence of all things sexual, erotica flourished, pornography boomed, and sex could be found in the unlikeliest of places. It was—indeed, it still is—used to sell clothes, food, cars, books, and toothpaste. Such an emphasis upon the nonemotional aspects of sexuality was bound, sooner or

From *David Mamet: Language as Dramatic Action.* © 1990 by Associated University Presses, Inc.

later, to result in a deleterious blunting of the nation's consciousness. This is precisely what has happened to the four young people portrayed in Mamet's play. For them, sex really has become a dirty word, a sniggering pastime for the easily bored. Rather than fulfilling its original function as an integral part of an emotional relationship, sex is for them little more than a cheap thrill, something that men "do" to women and for which women should be grateful.

Mamet's view of such a society is bleak; his characters are alienated in every sense of the word. Alienation, as Marx observed, is descriptive of more than people's sense of estrangement from the result of their labors. Marx wrote, "What is true of man's relationship to his work, to the product of his work, and to himself, is also true of his relationship to other men, to their labor, and to the objects of their labor ... each man is alienated from others, and ... each of the others is likewise alienated from human life."[2] As a result of this sense of alienation, human relations come to rest on what Christopher Bigsby describes as "an exploitation that is not necessarily of itself material but is derived from a world in which exchange value is a primary mechanism. One individual approaches another with a tainted bargain, an offer of relationship now corrupted by the values of the market ... people become commodities, objects."[3]

The characters in *Sexual Perversity in Chicago* are, in common with many others in Mamet's drama, emotionally adrift in a world where the second-rate has been accepted as the norm. They occasionally glimpse the possibility of something other than the tawdry lives they endure, but these momentary revelations have no chance of taking root in the febrile atmosphere in which they exist. With no real moral base upon which to pin their ideas, their lives are shapeless, distorted, and corrupt. As Richard Eder points out,

> the characters speak as if calling for help out of a deep well. Each is isolated, without real identity. They talk to find it—"I speak, therefore I am"—and the comic and touching involution of their language is the evidence of their isolation and tracklessness.... Their world is full of.... lessons learned but learned of the unreasonable ferocity, the lack of shape or instruction of middle American life.[4]

Sexual Perversity in Chicago is replete with dialogue powered by a pulsatingly neurotic energy. Its urban rhythms are merciless and relentless; its movement is conveyed by Mamet's rapid sentence structure and the fast-paced episodes. The frenetic verbal affrays that the characters indulge in are their way of concealing the vacuum that exists at the root of their lives; the abandon with which they bounce wisecracks and platitudes off one another only partially conceals their desperation. So long as they can continue to joke, criticize, and fantasize, they can delude themselves that they are happy.

Structured in swift, short scenes that rise, like dirty jokes, to punchlines, the play examines the void at the heart of contemporary sexual relationships. Life for Mamet's characters is as shallow as the fictional lives of their soap opera heroes and incorporates many aspects of an obscene joke; their exploits are crude, debased, and usually over very quickly. The form and shape of the play are themselves reminiscent of such jokes, and so the very structure of the piece enacts its meaning. The parallel is carried one stage further with Mamet's Bernie constantly spouting his elaborate and ludicrous sexual fantasies. These are reported to Danny as fact, but are little more than routine dirty stories that have been opened out into mini-dramas in which Bernie himself is the chief protagonist. Sex dominates all their conversations, just as work dominates those of the salesmen in *Glengarry Glen Ross*. Such characters have only one subject at their disposal and they must discuss it exhaustively in an effort to conceal their insecurity and loneliness. Their relentless bragging is intended to impress, but underneath the cool bravado lies a desperate vulnerability. Mamet has commented upon this aspect of the work: "Voltaire said words were invented to hide feelings. That's what the play is about."[5]

Bernie is an excellent example of a man who uses language to conceal his insecurity. He urges Danny to view women as he does—as sexual objects that can be picked up and discarded at random. He does his very best to impress his friend with his callous insouciance and contemptuous reductivism but, in fact, he is terrified of women. There is no evidence to suggest that he has ever had a satisfactory relationship, in spite of all his masculine posturing. Bernie is, literally, "all talk." In order to assuage his fears, he constantly reduces women to the most basic physical level. For him, they can be succinctly summed up in the following crude jingle:

Tits and Ass. Tits and Ass. Tits and Ass. Tits and Ass. Blah de Bloo. Blah de Bloo. Blah de Bloo. Blah de Bloo. *(Pause.)* Huh? (scene 30, p. 47)

The opposite sex is thus described in purely sexual terms, which are debased further still by occurring alongside a string of nonsense words designed to convey Bernie's apparent casual contempt. By saying the words aloud, he can wield his spurious power over women. However, his final "Huh?" suggests his weakness and need for approbation and concurrence from an easily swayed friend.

In *Sexual Perversity in Chicago*, Mamet looks at the ways in which language can contribute to the formation of sexist attitudes. His characters employ a kind of subtle linguistic coercion as a means of influencing and persuading their companions to concur with their way of thinking. Consequently, barriers are erected that are then exceedingly difficult to penetrate. Bernie's relentless chauvinism filters through to Danny, who is influenced by and in awe of his ostensibly suave friend. As a result, he eventually becomes as coarse and offensive as his mentor. Mamet points out that the play is much concerned with

> how what we say influences what we think. The words that Bernie Litko says to Danny influence his behavior; you know, that women are broads, that they're there to exploit. And the words that Joan says to her friend Deborah: men are problem-atical creatures which are necessary to have a relationship with because that's what society says, but it never really works out. It is nothing but a schlep, a misery constantly.[6]

Partly because of the pressures of language exerted by their companions and partly through cultural fiats, any relationship formed between Mamet's male and female characters is doomed to failure. The men are unwilling—or unable—to view women as anything other than sex slaves and receptacles for their pleasure and, not surprisingly, the women regard men as natural enemies and emotional cripples. The reductive and crude exploitative images of women that are daily emblazoned across tabloid newspapers and broadcasted in countless films and television programs have perverted the perception of their audience. In such a society, women have only two choices: they can try to emulate the ideal feminine stereotype pushed forward by the media and craved by unimaginative men like Bernie and Danny, or they can turn to feminism with a vengeance. Those who choose the former are satirized by Tom Wolfe in his essay, "The Woman Who Had Everything." In this work, Wolfe writes of the trouble to which some women will go in an effort to conform to a popular (and desirable) stereotype:

> Women [engage in a ceaseless quest to] make themselves irresistibly attractive to the men of New York ... coiffeurs ... The eternal search for better eyelashes! Off to Deirdre's or some such

place, on Madison Avenue—moth-cut eyelashes? Square-cut eyelashes? mink eye-lashes? ... Or off to somewhere for the perfect Patti-nail application, $25 for both hands, $2.50 a finger, false fingernails ... [then] the skin ... that purple light business at Don Lee's Hair Specialist Studio ... [7]

Desirability often depends therefore upon as much artificial assistance as can reasonably be applied—and at a price. Wolfe exposes the obsession with public myths of beauty and sexuality for the absurdity it undoubtedly is. Good sense and dignity are overridden by a desperate need to conform.

Although women are without question the most offensively exploited of the sexes, men do not escape the pressures of the media. They, too, must manufacture a false image and endeavor to live up to it in order to attract the equally false objects of their desire. It is little wonder that love should so infrequently enter such relationships; they are superficial in the extreme, with both parties acting out a fantasy ideal of what they imagine the other craves. Mamet blames the mass media for much misery and heartache, observing that *Sexual Perversity in Chicago* is, "unfortunately, tales from my life."[8] He explains,

My sex life was ruined by the popular media. It took a lot of getting over. There are a lot of people in my situation. The myths around us, destroying our lives, such a great capacity to destroy our lives.... You have to sleep with every woman that you see, have a new car every two years—sheer, utter nonsense. Men who never have to deal with it, are never really forced to deal with it, deal with it by getting colitis, anxiety attacks and by killing themselves.[9]

Certainly Bernie seems to be desperately trying to live up to a stereotype; his adopted persona suggests that he is something of a "super-stud." What is so tragic about a man like Bernie is that he is, at base, painfully aware of his own inadequacy and fear, and that is why he must behave in the overtly masculine fashion that has become his trademark.

The "perversity" of the title is not, as one critic ironically observes, "a misprint for perversion"[10] but is entirely intentional. Mamet's characters are indeed perverse, but not in the sense that might be expected—although one of them does observe that "nobody does it normally any more" (scene 1, p. 13). The perversity Mamet has in mind emanates from his characters' diminished perception of each other, their lack of understanding, and the cold, inhumane manner in which they conduct their lives. What is crucially missing is any real sense of value beyond the material, or an awareness of any need unrelated to immediate sexual satisfaction.

Sexual Perversity in Chicago was voted the best Chicago play of 1974 and, in 1975, won an Obie for its off-Broadway production. There have been a number of productions of the work, both in the United States and England and, in 1986, a filmed version was released under the title of *About Last Night*.

The first scene sets the tone for the play: it is fast, funny, and outrageous. In this episode, Bernie lovingly outlines for Danny the details of a ludicrously unlikely story about a recent "erotic" exploit. Bernie's tale is something of a tour-de-force of sexual fantasy, and the longest and most involved of a number of stories he relates throughout the play. What is ironic is that he wants Danny to believe every word he utters. This hymn to sexual excess is hypnotic not only for Danny but for Bernie as well; so involved does he become in the sheer force of his narrative that he appears to believe it himself. This early conversation establishes Bernie as the character with the "knowledge" and Danny as his eager ingénu and is reminiscent of the power plays of language frequently found in the work of Harold Pinter:

> *Danny*: So how'd you do last night?
> *Bernie*: Are you kidding me?
> *Danny*: Yeah?
> *Bernie*: Are you fucking kidding me?
> *Danny*: Yeah?
> *Bernie*: Are you pulling my leg?
> *Danny*: So?
> *Bernie*: So tits out to here so.
> *Danny*: Yeah?
> *Bernie*: Twenty, a couple years old.
> *Danny*: You gotta be fooling.
> *Bernie*: Nope.
> *Danny*: You devil.
> *Bernie*: You think she hadn't been around?
> *Danny*: Yeah?
> *Bernie*: She hadn't gone the route?
> *Danny*: She knew the route, huh?
> *Bernie*: Are you fucking kidding me?
> *Danny*: Yeah?
> *Bernie*: She *wrote* the route. (scene 1, p. 7)

Bernie's responses to Danny's initial questions are intended by him to be rhetorical; answering a question with another question is his way of emphasizing just how incredible a time he actually enjoyed the previous evening. He works Danny up into a kind of verbal frenzy merely by refusing to give him anything other than strongly implied hints of sexual success. Mamet captures perfectly the grammatical anarchy of idiomatic conversation in the repetition of "building" words like "so" and "yeah" and the abbreviation of a sentence such as "Twenty, a couple years old." The age of the girl is left totally ambiguous, which is just as well since, shortly after its initial mention, it moves from about eighteen to over twenty-five, depending upon whether Bernie currently favors the idea of corrupted naïveté or well-seasoned maturity. Bernie encourages Danny's lasciviousness through his carefully constructed routine; Danny's breathless "Yeah?" increases in intensity until one can almost hear his jaw drop open in erotic anticipation. Exactly why Danny finds it difficult to believe that the girl should have been "Twenty, a couple years old" is unclear. His incredulity is possibly due to the fact that Bernie's success with such a young woman seems unlikely; although Bernie's age is unstated, it is clear that he is considerably older than his friend. Perhaps the woman's age, referred to by Bernie, most potently symbolizes female sexual rapacity for the two men. Or perhaps Danny's incredulity is his way of encouraging Bernie into new areas of excess.

In an effort to make his fantasy sound as realistic as possible, Bernie takes pains to establish the correct location and timing. Danny enjoys the detail, no matter how irrelevant, and incites his friend's erotic imagination still further by uttering neat, monosyllabic asides that will not interrupt the flow of things too much:

Danny: So tell me.
Bernie: So okay, so where am I?
Danny: When?
Bernie: Last night, two-thirty.
Danny: So two-thirty, you're probably over at Yak-Zies.
Bernie: Left Yak-zies at one.
Danny: So you're probably over at Grunts.
Bernie: They only got a two o'clock license.
Danny: So you're probably over at the Commonwealth.
Bernie: So, okay, so I'm over at the Commonwealth, in the pancake house off the lobby, and I'm working on a stack of those raisin and nut jobs ...

Danny: They're good.
Bernie: ... and I'm reading the paper, and I'm reading, and I'm
            casing the pancake house, and the usual shot, am I right?
Danny: Right.
Bernie: So who walks in over to the cash register but this chick.
Danny: Right.
Bernie: Nineteen, twenty-year old chick ...
Danny: Who we're talking about.
Bernie: ... and she wants a pack of Viceroys.
Danny: I can believe that ... Was she a pro? (scene 1, pp. 8–9)

Bernie still plays cat and mouse, keeping Danny in suspense until the last possible moment. He wants to paint a picture of the events that will accurately reflect his "experience" in all its glory and he makes Danny work for the trifles he offers. Bernie creates an atmosphere of Yuppie-style establishments, where neon lights and potted palms endeavor to give some class to what are, essentially, late-night pickup joints. The slightly sleazy sounding bar and restaurant names add to the aura of Bernie's sexual adventure: "Yak-Zies" and, especially, the onomatapoeiac "Grunts." Danny's responses to the more prosaic aspects of Bernie's tale add immeasurably both to the humor of the scene and to our understanding of him. The banality of his reactions is absolutely hilarious. Despite Bernie's linguistic game of suspense and titillation, which both men clearly relish, Danny unfathomably wishes to hear even mundane details. Whatever the input, he exhibits no impatience and enjoys the opportunity to comment on (and become vicariously involved in?) Bernie's "adventure."

  Danny is also obsessed with establishing if the girl was, in fact, "a pro" (pp. 9–10 and 14), that is, a prostitute. At regular intervals, he repeats the question: "Was she a pro?" as if this fact would somehow add to the spiciness of Bernie's tale. As far as Bernie's fantasy is concerned, this information is— at least for his present purposes—irrelevant. He has not yet made up his mind whether she should be a sexually voracious virgin who has been deranged by his charms, or a hard-nosed trouper to whom such exploits are routine. He stalls Danny's tireless questions by responding with variations on the theme of "Well, at this point we don't know" and "So, at this point, we don't know. Pro, semi-pro, Betty Co-Ed from College, regular young broad, it's anybody's ballgame" (scene 1, p. 9).

  As Bernie's story progresses to the ridiculous point at which the girl dons a World War II flak suit before allowing him to make love to her, so Danny's ingenuousness similarly reaches new heights:

Bernie:	... From under the bed she pulls this suitcase, and from out of the suitcase comes this World War Two Flak suit.
Danny:	They're hard to find.
Bernie:	Zip, zip, zip, and she gets into the Flak suit and we get down on the bed.
Danny:	What are you doing?
Bernie:	Fucking.
Danny:	She's in the Flak suit?
Bernie:	Right.
Danny:	How do you get in?
Bernie:	How do you think I get in? She leaves the zipper open. (scene 1, pp. 11–12)

Bernie is clearly getting carried away with his fantasy. He no longer wishes to hear Danny's questions and inane remarks, but wants to get on with the action. As Bernie moves further and further into the ecstasies of libidinous fantasy, Danny remains down-to-earth, questioning details that had at first acted as spurs to give the story depth and realism, but now serve only as interruptions and irritations.

The fantasy eventually ends with Bernie's "recollection" that the girl telephoned her friend during their lovemaking, asking her to make "airplane noises" over the telephone, and then set fire to the hotel room in an orgy of abandon:

Bernie:	... Humping and bumping, and she's screaming "Red dog One to Red dog Squadron" ... all of a sudden she screams "Wait." She wriggles out, leans under the bed, and she pulls out this five gallon jerrycan. ... she splashes the mother all over the walls, whips a fuckin' Zippo out of the Flak suit, and WHOOSH, the whole room is in flames. So the whole fuckin' joint is going up in smoke, the telephone is going "Rat Tat Tat," the broad jumps back on the bed and yells "Now, give it to me *now* for the Love of Christ." *(Pause.)* So I look at the broad ... and I figure ... fuck this nonsense. I grab my clothes, I peel a saw-buck off my wad, as I make the door I fling it at her. "For cabfare," I yell ... Whole fucking hall is full of smoke, above the flames I just make out my broad (she's singing "Off we go into the Wild Blue Yonder")....
Danny:	Nobody does it normally anymore.

> *Bernie:* It's these young broads. They don't know what the fuck
> they want. (scene 1, p. 13)

Bernie concludes his imaginary exploit without his having reached orgasm: it is as if, even within the realms of a dream, to submit to such an action is to acknowledge some form of commitment. As he imagines his "lover" lying amidst the smoke and flames, his fear of and sheer contempt for women become the uppermost emotions in his mind. Rather than complete the sexual act he has begun, he prefers to turn on the girl, flinging money in her face as if to suggest that she is nothing more than a common prostitute and he a disgusted client. For such deep-seated contempt to manifest itself within the safety of a sexual fantasy suggests Bernie's very real sexual problems. He tells Danny that, having set the room aflame and produced her quota of sound effects, the girl begged him to bring her to orgasm. By denying her that satisfaction, Bernie likewise denies himself. His language takes on the coldness of a character like Mickey Spillane's Mike Hammer; his terminology owes more to fictional cops and robbers than to real life. He evidently sees himself as the cool-headed, although rather misogynistic, stud who has been represented by countless film and television heroes. Bernie has been acting all the time, but perhaps nowhere so purposefully as here; he strives to give Danny the impression of his supreme control over the situation and, in so doing, verbally reenacts what has never taken place. By saying the words aloud, Bernie enjoys a frisson of excitement over an event that had only ever existed in his mind.

Bernie's contempt for women is consolidated as he blames the imaginary girl for her perversion: "It's these young broads. They don't know what the fuck they want." This is patently untrue since, if nothing else, the girl in his dream exploit knew *exactly* what she wanted. Symbolically, Mamet has suggested Bernie's inability to have a satisfactory sexual relationship with a woman, and does so within the first few minutes of the play. Finally, Danny finds out if Bernie's "lover" was indeed "a pro":

> *Bernie:* A pro, Dan ... is how you think about yourself. You see
> my point? ... I'll tell you one thing ... she knew all the pro
> moves. (scene 1, p. 14)

Sexual Perversity in Chicago has much in common with Jules Feiffer's *Carnal Knowledge*, which was filmed in 1971 by Mike Nichols. In fact, Mamet's play has been directly compared with Feiffer's work: in his book, *The Literature of the U.S.A.*, Marshall Walker observes that it is "a set of clever variations on material ... treated in Jules Feiffer's screenplay for Mike Nichols's *Carnal Knowledge*,"[11] and John Elsom likens it to "Feiffer's cartoons, but less acid and more human." [12] *Carnal Knowledge* concerns the changing fortunes of two young men from their college days through to their early forties. The film version was a great success; Jack Nicholson starred as the sexually predatory Jonathan and Art Garfunkel as his more reserved friend, Sandy. Like Bernie, Jonathan spends his time trying to convey a sense of knowing sexual expertise to his eager, and sexually curious, younger friend. Also like Bernie, Jonathan is unable to sustain a satisfactory sexual relationship. At first, in an effort to retain a feeling of superiority over Sandy, he steals Susan, Sandy's girlfriend, and later becomes involved in a love affair with a stereotypical "dumb blonde" who wants to be loved for more than her body. Jonathan is capable of being aroused only by the most buxom—and passive—of women, is incapable of treating them as individuals, and refers to them always in demotic terms that relate to their physical characteristics. Early in the screenplay, Jonathan and Sandy discuss the ideal woman. Like Bernie and Danny, the two men at first differ from one another in their crassness:

Sandy:	You want perfection.
Jonathan:	What do you want, wise guy?
Sandy:	She just has to be nice. That's all.
Jonathan:	You don't want her beautiful?
Sandy:	She doesn't have to be beautiful. I'd like her built, though.
Jonathan:	I'd want mine sexy-looking.
Sandy:	I wouldn't want her to look like a tramp.
Jonathan:	Sexy doesn't mean she has to look like a tramp. There's a middle ground.... Big tits.
Sandy:	Yeah. But still a virgin.
Jonathan:	I don't care about that.... I wouldn't mind if she was just a little ahead of me—with those big tits—and knew hundreds of different ways ... [13]

Just as Danny is the character in Mamet's play who actually manages to sustain some kind of sexual relationship, however, brief, so it is the naïve Sandy who first attracts the beautiful—and sexually experimental—Susan. Like Bernie, Jonathan resents the relationship and ignores any emotional involvement that may exist, reducing it always to a sexual level. The truth of the matter is that Jonathan feels excluded. In an effort to put his own "stamp" on the proceedings, he notes how Susan's "tits were too small," how "her legs were great" and (with great generosity!) declares that he "wouldn't kick her out of bed."[14] Bernie, too, realizes that he may be losing his hold over Danny and so tries to influence (and diminish) Danny's view of Deborah:

> *Bernie:* So what are we doing tomorrow, we going to the beach?
> *Danny:* I'm seeing Deborah.
> *Bernie:* Yeah? You getting serious? I mean she seemed like a hell of a girl, huh? The little I saw of her. Not too this, not too that ... very kind of ... what? *(Pause.)* Well, what the fuck. I only saw her for a minute. I mean first impressions of this kind are often misleading, huh? So what can you tell from seeing a broad one, two, ten times? You're seeing a lot of this broad.... I mean, what the fuck, a guy wants to get it on with some broad on a more or less stable basis, who is to say him no. *(Pause.)* Alot of these broads, you know, you just don't know. You know? I mean what with where they've been and all. I mean a young woman in today's society ... time she's twenty two-three, you don't know *where* the fuck she's been. *(Pause.)* I'm just *talking* to you, you understand. (scene 14, pp. 30–31)

Bernie includes Danny in his plans for "the beach" without hesitation; to admit the possibility that there may be other parties who have a claim on his friend's time is unthinkable for him. His reaction to the news that Danny is "seeing Deborah" is to try to diminish Deborah's importance in the scheme of things while carefully avoiding outright criticism—at least at first. Lest Danny suspect his motives, Bernie must take care not to appear too jealous or resentful so he begins by praising Deborah. However, he then moves rapidly into another phase wherein she becomes just another "broad" who might have a very dubious sexual history. After his initial statement, "she seemed like a hell of a girl," he undermines his approach by adding, "The little I saw of her" and "first impressions ... are ... misleading." He goes on to infer that men can never know women, even if they meet them on numerous occasions, thus suggesting that Danny's relationship with Deborah must be of the most shallow kind. He acknowledges that his friend is "seeing a lot" of the woman but infers that whatever may be between them can only be sexual. Bernie gradually moves toward the final phase of his verbal destruction of Deborah; almost imperceptibly, she has become just another "broad." He takes on the attitude of an older brother, an experienced and trusted giver of advice to one who needs assistance; "Alot of these broads, you know, you just don't know. You know?" He brings Danny, unwillingly or otherwise, into the conversation, involving him, making him collude with him, never pausing to allow time for any response. He begins to talk about Deborah as if she were something dirty, or diseased: "where [she's] been and all." Double standards are rife here. It is perfectly acceptable for Bernie and Danny to have had numerous sexual encounters—indeed, they believe this makes them attractive catches—but women are not allowed similar experiences.

Bernie's repetition of "what the fuck" also adds to the coarseness of his innuendo and serves as a means of grounding the conversation at the most basic sexual level. By now, there is the suggestion that Deborah is unworthy of any serious consideration, and is probably not unlike the "pro" in his initial fantasy. This latter insinuation is given further weight by Bernie's echo of the indeterminate age of his "pro"; Deborah, like the fantasy girl, is aged about "twenty two-three." His concluding assertion that he is merely *"talking"* to Danny about Deborah anticipates Moss and Aaronow's notable linguistic distinction between "talking" and "speaking" in *Glengarry Glen Ross*.

Bernie and Jonathan are excellent examples of what Colin Stinton calls the "Teach-like character";[15] both men are, essentially, full of hot air and have very little genuine knowledge to impart, but they nonetheless see themselves as instructors and mentors. Stinton comments upon the specific type of "teaching" that occurs in *Sexual Perversity in Chicago*. He notes that Bernie's "Teach-like quality is really bullshitting ... sexual bullshitting of the type that men usually engage in most. The whole idea of the conquest—this is one of the things that identifies such men in their pathetic little way. The likes of Bernie use this built-in tendency to influence and persuade those around them."[16]

Because of the extremely coarse, sexist language used in the play, Mamet has sometimes been accused of being deliberately outrageous and misogynistic. Although there may be some truth to criticism that the playwright courts outrage, Mamet does not do so in order to score cheap laughs out of obscenity and sexism. Connie Booth, who has appeared in two of Mamet's plays, speaks specifically about the playwright's use of obscene and scatalogical language: "He is anything but arbitrary.... It would be interesting for those who believe his work to be obscene to take out all those words and see just how much their absence would affect both the sense and rhythm of the piece."[17]

As far as accusations of misogyny are concerned, *Sexual Perversity in Chicago* could, in some ways, be viewed as a feminist play in that it is so very critical of its male characters; Mamet examines what he sees as the deplorable state of sexual morality in modern urban America and, in so doing, illuminates inadequacy and ignorance. His female characters are so disenchanted with the men they meet, and so resentful of the pressures put upon them to form heterosexual relationships, that they appear to have retreated into lesbianism!

Colin Stinton asserts that, although Mamet portrays chauvinistic, sexist, or violent men in his plays, it does not mean that he is in some way advocating their behavior:

> A lot of criticism of [Mamet's] work—especially from women—emanates from the rather incredible notion that he is somehow advocating sexist men! If anything, he is calling attention to the fact that there *are* sexist men and this is why they are that way, this is how their minds work. He then subjects these characters to some scrutiny.... Perhaps more than other writers, he takes to heart the maxim that you should only write about what you personally have experienced, and [Mamet's] experience is definitely not having been a woman! ... He feels happier writing from the male viewpoint, but the male viewpoint doesn't have to be a sexist viewpoint. One of the things that is always illuminating is to talk to [Mamet] and to see him in action with his family and you realize what a caring kind of person he is. You begin to see that his plays always deal with the obstacles to the kind of care, kind of love and affection he wishes were there. Some people feel that because he has portrayed the world in this negative, tragic way he is somehow saying that this is how it should be. This is really ridiculous. In fact, what he does is to bemoan the fact that there is not a better world ... he is in fact a feminist writer in that sense because he is very, very critical of males.... He depicts such characters to show up their fragile egos, to show them struggling to find out who they are. He tries to provide some insight into how their minds work.[18]

Similarly, Miranda Richardson believes that

> Mamet is documenting what he has heard other men say. The fact that he *does* it is instructive. He is not suggesting that this is the right way to behave.... He might be writing from his own experiences, but I still enjoy what his experience is. I certainly

don't think he's a sexist writer ... he still manages to spark one's imagination, even if there are only ten lines to go on in his script. There's a deep sensitivity in his writing.[19]

Of the allegations of sexism in *Sexual Perversity in Chicago*, Mamet says: "There's a lot of vicious language in the play.... The real vicious language is the insidious thing, calling somebody a little girl or this girl. That's a lot more insidious than calling somebody a vicious whore—which is also insidious but you can deal with it."[20] C. Gerald Fraser notes that Mamet's play is about "the myths that men go through"[21] and that Mamet "credited the Women's Liberation movement with 'turning [his] head around a lot.' He added: 'Women have babies, have the menstrual period, for God's sake, they have something to do with the universe.'"[22]

The women's roles in *Sexual Perversity in Chicago* are quite substantial but, again, it is the male characters who enjoy many of the best lines. Mamet is only too aware of this imbalance and is anxious to correct it and thus alleviate some of the criticism. While writing the play, he remarked, "I kept getting huutzed by the director and the women in the cast, you know, to write parts for women. I said I don't know anything about women, they said 'Well, you better find out, you're getting too old'—so I tried. The fleshier parts are the male parts. I am more around men; I listen to more men being candid than women being candid. It is something I have been trying to do more of."[23]

Colin Stinton feels that those who urge Mamet to write more parts for women are, in some respects, asking for the wrong thing; he believes that the writer goes to such pains to be truthful in his work that if he should begin to try, self-consciously, to write in a women's voice, he may be doomed to falsity and failure. Mamet is concerned about the imbalance of male/female roles in his plays to the extent that during the writing of *The Woods*, Stinton was told (albeit apocryphally) that Mamet had given some of Nick's lines over to Ruth to make their dialogue more even in terms of volume. Stinton said that this was exactly the sort of thing that Mamet would do and that the story is probably absolutely genuine. Similarly, the role of John, the clairvoyant in *The Shawl* was obviously written for a male actor, but since the play has been performed, Mamet has considered changing the homosexual pair at the center of the work to a heterosexual couple. Thus, John could, without much hindrance, become Joanne! Mamet retains some doubts, but it is a mark of his desire to appease criticism that he has considered the transition at all.

From my own reading of Mamet's plays and from comments made by him concerning women, I feel that the school of opinion that brands him sexist is completely wrongheaded. Quite clearly, many of Mamet's male characters are hardly admirable or self-assured; there is little in them to suggest that the writer is in some way condoning their behavior. His female characters, on the other hand, often seem to represent Mamet's own wish that the world were a nicer and more caring place. In *The Woods*, Ruth and Nick try to come to terms with their rather precarious love affair. Their propinquity in the weekend cottage serves to underline Ruth's need for love and affection and Nick's reticence and anxiety. Ruth's main concerns are romance and love, whereas Nick's are far more sexually oriented. For Ruth, sex is important only when it is a part of love; for Nick, love can often be an obstruction to good sex. In *Speed the Plow*, it is the temporary secretary who comes to work for Gould, the film producer, who injects compassion and warmth into a sterile and ruthless environment. Whatever Karen's ultimate motives prove to be, she brings peculiarly feminine vigor and energy to the proceedings, causing the mercenary Gould to reevaluate (at least temporarily) his opinions on what is worthy and what is not. Her idealism and fecund creativity leave their mark on an otherwise barren and arid play.

Deborah and Joan in *Sexual Perversity in Chicago* also appear to be idealistic but, as the play progresses, their disappointment with what they are offered becomes almost tangible. By the end of the work they seem to have concluded that affection is often more genuine and freely forthcoming from members of their own sex, and that the whole fabric of heterosexual pairing is something of a confidence trick. Indeed, Joan laments:

> *Joan:* ... and, of course, there exists the very real possibility that the whole thing is nothing other than a mistake of *rather* large magnitude, and that it never *was* supposed to work out .... Well, look at your divorce rate. Look at the incidence of homosexuality ... the number of violent, sex-connected crimes ... all the anti-social behavior that chooses sex as its form of expression, eh? ... physical and mental mutilations we perpetrate on each other, day in, day out ... trying to fit ourselves to a pattern we can neither *understand* (although we pretend to) nor truly afford to *investigate* (although we pretend to).... It's a dirty joke ... the whole godforsaken business. (scene 20, pp. 37–38)

Joan's sentiments are explored further in a short play Mamet wrote in 1977 entitled *All Men Are Whores: An Inquiry;* the female character in that play muses:

... What if this undignified and headlong thrusting toward each other's sex is nothing but an oversight or physical malformity? *(Pause.)* Should we not, perhaps, retrain ourselves to revel in the sexual act not as the consummation of pre-destined and regenerate desire, but rather as a two-part affirmation of our need for solace in extremis.... In a world where nothing works. (scene 17, p. 199)

Exactly how seriously we are meant to take all this is left deliberately unclear. Certainly in Joan's case, Mamet has her spout her ideas as she and Deborah have lunch; Joan frequently undercuts the sobriety of the situation by casual interruptions such as "Are you going to eat your roll? ... This roll is excellent" (scene 20, p. 38) and so on. Deborah responds only intermittently and monosyllabically, twice announcing "I disagree with you" and stating that she is "moving in with Danny." Mamet therefore makes Joan's grave sentiments psychologically questionable; could not there be a suggestion that she is, in fact, jealous of her friend's success with Danny and that her denigration of heterosexuality is little more than resentment? Deborah's disagreement with her friend's ideas is also based on rather ambiguous premises; she has just decided to live with Danny, and so Joan's criticism of the basis of sexual relationships between men and women could be seen as a threat. Her friend's castigation undermines Deborah's security and the reasons for her decision to move in with her lover. It is not, therefore, altogether surprising that she should repeat that she disagrees with Joan—in her present situation, she cannot really afford to do otherwise. There remains the possibility that she secretly agrees with Joan; her silence as her friend rambles on could indicate either concurrence or disapproval. Mamet deliberately leaves the sexual psychology of his female characters ambiguous—and somewhat ambivalent.

In *Sexual Perversity in Chicago*, the characters can conceive of themselves only as sexual beings; the world in which they live forces them to do so. Theirs is a much harsher world than that portrayed in Edward Zwick's cinematic version of the play, *About Last Night* (1986). In the film the director chose to concentrate almost exclusively upon the "romantic" aspects of Danny and Deborah's affair, which completely distorted the meaning and altered the balance of the work. Bernie and Joan were reduced to wise-cracking cyphers who existed on the sidelines of the protagonists' lives. What is intended by Mamet to be a bitterly perceptive satire on contemporary sexual mores became, in the film, little more than a routine Hollywood teenage romance, albeit with a slightly harder edge and a rather more brittle script.

In Mamet's play, the characters' sexual experimentation and hard-edged aggression function as their principal means of expressing their urban neuroses. There is little time for romance or sweet words. Moments of self-perception, or a brief, fleeting acknowledgment of life outside of sex, are undercut by the relentless pragmatics of everyday life. An earlier bout of Joan's lamentations is interrupted by that unavoidable aspect of modern life, the telephone:

> *Joan:*   It's a puzzle. Our efforts at coming to grips with ourselves ... in an attempt to become "more human" (which, in itself is an interesting concept). It has to do with an increased ability to recognize *clues* ... and the control of energy in the form of *lust* ... and *desire* ... (And also in the form of hope). But a *finite* puzzle. Whose true solution lies, perhaps, in transcending the rules themselves ... and pounding of the fucking pieces into place where they DO NOT FIT AT ALL.... Some things persist. "Loss" is always possible ... (*Pause. Phone rings.*)
>
> *Deb:*   I'll take it in the other room. (scene 13, pp. 29–30)

When Mamet's characters indulge in philosophical theory, their language inevitably takes on a heightened, linguistically more sophisticated tone. It is as though they have moved beyond their usual limited range of discourse into another sphere of understanding; there is a "textbook" literalness in what they have to say. Joan speaks as she seldom does at such times—her streetwise banter is suddenly replaced by careful phrasing and elevated terminology—and only once does a familiar obscenity intrude. But this speech is unnatural; it is contrived, pretentious, and didactic. Joan tries to sound authoritative, impressive, and in command of what she avers but there remains a sense that Mamet is also satirizing this level of awareness. Like the rest of his characters' conversation, Joan's is artificial—although in a more educated way. That Mamet constantly undercuts high-flown sentiments with crass banalities or ringing telephones is perhaps his way of suggesting that *nothing* these people can say is truly authentic; it is all the manufacture of a false society.

Joan and Deborah share an apartment and are, apparently, close friends. Whether their relationship is of a platonic or a sexual nature is unclear, but Mamet does drop the occasional hint that their friendship may be at least partly lesbian. For example, when Deborah first meets Danny, she announces that she is "a Lesbian" (scene 5, p. 18), although later she refutes this claim, choosing to imply that although she has had "some Lesbianic experiences. ... and ... enjoyed them" (scene 7, pp. 20–21) she is, in fact, happily heterosexual. In any case, the friendship between Joan and Deborah seems to be warm and genuine, if a little overpossessive on Joan's part. What is noticeable, both about Joan in her reaction to Danny, and Bernie in his opinion of Deborah is that both parties are jealous of any outside involvement. As Christopher Bigsby notes, they "value only the apparently simple, undemanding and essentially adolescent camaraderie of the same sex,"[24] viewing members of the opposite sex as an intrusion upon their privacy. On both sides, each appears to possess an element of protective concern for his or her friend's welfare; each sees sexual involvement leading inevitably to pain and unhappiness and as something to be avoided on anything other than the most casual basis. The following exchange takes place between Deborah and Joan when the former has been seeing rather a lot of her new boyfriend:

Joan: So what's he like?
Deb: Who?
Joan: Whoever you haven't been home, I haven't seen you in two days that you've been seeing.
Deb: Did you miss me?
Joan: No. Your plants died. *(Pause.)* I'm kidding. What's his name?
Deb: Danny.
Joan: What's he do?
Deb: He works in the Loop.
Joan: How wonderful for him.
Deb: He's an assistant Office Manager.
Joan: That's nice, a job with a little upward mobility.
Deb: Don't be like that, Joan.
Joan: I'm sorry. I don't know what got into me.
Deb: How are things at school?
Joan: Swell. Life in the Primary Grades is a real picnic. (scene 8, pp. 21–22)

From her opening question, it is clear that Joan will in no way be persuaded that the intrusive Danny could possibly be a worthy lover for her friend. In that initial query is an aggressive hard-boiled bitterness, which is not concealed by the question's commonplaceness. The tone of the question is one that invites a response of denigration rather than approval and Joan's edginess and barely suppressed sarcasm establish her mood for the rest of the scene. An actress playing Joan's part could interpret her mood in several ways: she could be hurt, bitter, resentful, aggressive, chiding, or even playful. As always with Mamet's work, great sensitivity to the text is required if all the nuances and subtleties are to be exploited. It would be only too easy to portray Joan as an unsympathetic harpy who is intent upon destroying her friend's relationships. This would, indeed, be a great shame since Mamet has written the part with sensitivity and understanding for the character's emotional position. Although Joan *does* resent Danny's involvement with Deborah, it is important to be aware of her vulnerability and the reasons for her resentment. Joan has found a good and kind friend in Deborah and is understandably loath to lose her to someone who might be a harmful influence.

Joan's convoluted but brilliantly authentic sentence: "Whoever you haven't been home, I haven't seen you in two days that you've been seeing" has been described by Ross Wetzsteon as "the utter clarity of total grammatical chaos."[25] Such language owes something to that heard in Woody Allen films, particularly those that chronicle the increasing incidence of urban neurosis such as *Play it Again, Sam, Annie Hall,* and *Manhattan.* The idiom is purely American, with no concessions made toward "good" English. As Jack Shepherd has observed, Mamet "is so in touch with the way American people talk that he often doesn't use any discernible English grammar."[26] Thus, sentences are relentlessly broken up midway, tenses are confused, and grammatical accuracy is the least priority. It is all ostensibly very naturalistic but, as Shepherd has also observed, "in [Mamet's] text ... everything that is written is *intended* ... it is never just there for the sake of it."[27]

Through Joan's convolutions and inconsistencies, Mamet suggests so much about her state of mind. His inspired use of anarchic rhythms is another way in which he extracts every ounce of humor from a situation. Joan's defensive sarcasm—"Your plants died" immediately followed by "I'm kidding"—serves to illustrate her adopted veneer of urban toughness, which can be so easily shattered when she finds herself cornered and in a vulnerable position. Despite her assertion that she is "kidding," she goes on to denigrate Danny's job as a pathetic one for a man to hold and, finally, having failed to elicit any criticism from Deborah, seems to blame her for the fact that "Life in the Primary Grades is a real picnic." It is clear from the tone that it is anything *but!* Joan suggests that her life is tormented and fraught with problems enough as a kindergarten teacher, without Deborah adding to her misery by keeping away from home. Cleverly and insidiously, Joan manages to make Deborah feel guilty for her actions. In Joan's eyes, the selfishness is not her own but that of her gadabout friend.

Bernie is as wounded as Joan by his friend's love affair. As he tells imaginary "buddies" at the gym all about Danny's relationship (about which, presumably, Danny had told him in confidence), Bernie takes on once again the role of seasoned mentor and advisor:

> *Bernie:* So the kid asks me "Bernie, Blah, blah, blah, blah, blah, blah, blah, blah, blah. The broad *this*, the broad *that*, blah, blah, blah." Right? So I tell him, "Dan, Dan, you think I don't know what you're feeling, I don't know what you're going through? You think about the broad, you *this*, you *that*, you think I don't know that?" So he tells me, "Bernie," he says, "I think I love her." *(Pause.)* Twenty eight years old. So I tell him, "Dan, Dan, I can *advise*, I can *counsel*, I can speak to you out of my *experience* ... but in the final analysis, you are on your own. *(Pause.)* If you want my *opinion*, however, you are pussy-whipped." (I call 'em like I see 'em. I wouldn't say it if it wasn't so.) So what does he know at that age, huh? Sell his soul for a little eating pussy, and who can blame him: But mark my words. One, two more weeks, he'll do the right thing by the broad *(Pause.)* And drop her like a fucking hot potato. (scene 19, p. 37)

Bernie establishes the avuncular tone that he will use to denigrate Danny's relationship with Deborah in the opening words of this speech: he calls Danny "the kid" and suggests that Danny's reliance upon his advice is far from unusual. Bernie's dismissal of the seriousness of Danny's affair moves from his claim that he, too, has felt exactly the same way to his contention that Danny is "pussy-whipped." En route, he has condescendingly sneered that a mere boy (of twenty-eight!) could entertain such feelings and has wasted no time in repeating, over and over, that Deborah is nothing more than a broad. There is something pathetic in Bernie's assumption that Danny could not know he was in love "at that age"; after all, twenty-eight is an age by which many men are already married with a family. Bernie tries to make Danny sound like a lovelorn child—"Bernie ... I think I love her"—and negates Danny's sentimental outburst by once again reducing the relationship to the crudest level. He implies that Danny is ready to "sell his soul for a little eating pussy," rushing his words and abbreviating his sentence in an effort to emphasize the absurdity of Danny being "in love." He immediately follows this coarse statement with a phrase that accurately sums up his phony "macho" bonhomie: "and who can blame him". With studied, casual conceit, Bernie implies that he has, himself, been similarly misguided; the folly of youth is rejected in knowing maturity. The underlinings emphasize those words that Bernie feels are most relevant and important to his argument. For him, they are the essence of friendship but, as he pointedly remarks, "in the final analysis"—a sly dig by Mamet at a dreadful Yuppie-type cliché—Danny must make his own decisions. The false effort Bernie makes to sound fair and reasonable and, above all, *sympathetic* to his friend's plight, is both appalling and irresistibly funny.

At the end of his speech, Bernie suddenly changes tack. He announces that Danny will "do the right thing by the broad" by dropping her like "a fucking hot potato." In his mind, this is precisely what Danny will do; all he needs is some careful prodding and manipulation. Subtlety is not one of Bernie's strong points. After he has rid his and Danny's relationship of the offensive Deborah, things can be the same again between the two friends. There has been no mention that Deborah is being somehow exploited or used by Danny—quite the opposite. However, in order to give his story a well-rounded and equitable conclusion, Bernie chooses to imply that she would, in fact, be far better off without Danny, who will soon see the error of his ways.

It is significant that Bernie should begin his destruction of his friend's affair with a string of nonsense words. Again and again, Mamet's frightened characters lapse into nonsense language when under pressure, and Bernie is no exception. He chooses to forsake normal speech on more than one occasion in the play and each time he does so he undermines the seriousness of his subject. His reductive chant, already quoted elsewhere, takes its rhythms from nonsense words: "Blah de Bloo. Blah de Bloo. Blah de Bloo. Blah de Bloo" (scene 30, p. 47). The "Tits and Ass," which makes up the rest of the litany is, therefore, reduced to similar meaninglessness. In *Glengarry Glen Ross*, Richard Roma refers to the couple to whom Levene has just sold $82,000 worth of land as "Harriett and blah blah Nyborg" (act 2, p. 38) and in *American Buffalo*, Teach pretends that he is not angry with Grace and Ruthie because he has lost a large sum of money at cards, choosing to affect a world-weary tone of selfless resignation:

> *Teach:*   These things happen, I'm not saying that they don't ...
>   and yeah, yeah, yeah, I know I lost a bundle at the game
>   and blah blah blah. (act 1, p. 15)

In *The Squirrels*, Arthur responds to Edmond's question about the sense of a particular passage in one of the plays they are writing with a stream of repetition, making gibberish of the words he speaks:

Edmond:	What does this mean?
Arthur:	Meaning? Meaning?
Edmond:	Yes.
Arthur:	Ah, meaning! Meaning meaning meaning meaning meaning. Meaning meaning meaning. You ask me about meaning and I respond with gibberish ... (episode 1, p. 23)

Roma's description of Mr. Nyborg as "blah blah" suggests his contempt for and sheer disinterest in the unfortunate man; as far as the ruthless salesman is concerned, Mr. Nyborg is now completely irrelevant. Teach's concluding "blah blah blah" takes up the rhythm he sets up in the preceding "yeah yeah yeah" and is intended to convey his detached emotional stance in the matter. It fails miserably. Arthur's repetition of "meaning" is a desperate attempt at ironic humor; both men are supposedly creative writers but are struggling with a banal story. To conceal his very real sense of impotence, Arthur chooses to joke about it, masking his loss of control in self-deprecating irony in an effort to appear self-effacing and sardonic. It is clear from these random examples that gibberish can be utilized in a most versatile manner; in Mamet's drama, even nonsense can speak volumes.

A number of scenes in *Sexual Perversity in Chicago* are set in night clubs and bars; the one-night stand and casual barroom encounter are obviously familiar occurrences for the individuals dramatized here. In particular, the frequenting of singles bars—those peculiarly horrible inventions of the fake friendly American culture of excess—has become a way of life. In a book that among other things, outlines the contemporary sexual mores of New Yorkers, Stephen Brook recalls a visit to "Rascals," a singles bar on First Avenue:

> This is real singles territory, and lone wolves scour this stretch of the East Side for prey. ... Opposite the crowded bar, a ... gutsy-voiced female lead belted out old Stones and Motown numbers. I bought a drink and stood about feeling foolish, then left.[28]

Early in *Sexual Perversity in Chicago*, Mamet satirizes the kind of encounter that can take place in such establishments. Bernie tries to pick up Joan as she sits alone in the bar, and he becomes very hostile indeed when she makes it clear to him that she is not interested:

> *Bernie:* How would you like some company. *(Pause.)* What if I was to sit down here? What would that do for you, huh?
> *Joan:* No, I don't think so, no....
> *Bernie:* ... So here I am. I'm just in town for a one-day layover, and I happen to find myself in this bar. So, so far so good. What am I going to do? I could lounge alone and lonely and stare into my drink, or I could take the bull by the horn and make an effort to enjoy myself ...
> *Joan:* Are you making this up?
> *Bernie:* So hold on. So I see you seated at this table and I say to myself, "Doug McKenzie, there is a young woman," I say to myself, "What is she doing here?", and I think she is here for the same reasons as I. To enjoy herself, and, perhaps to meet provocative people. *(Pause.)* I'm a meteorologist for T.W.A. ... (scene 3, pp. 14–15)

Bernie carries on in this vein for some time, lying about his name and his job, trying to make his life sound romantic and thrilling until, finally, Joan has heard enough:

> *Joan:* Can I tell you something?
> *Bernie:* You bet.
> *Joan:* Forgive me if I'm being too personal ... but I do not find you sexually attractive. *(Pause.)*
> *Bernie:* What is that, some new kind of line? Huh, I mean, not that I mind what you think, if that's what you think ... but ... that's a fucking rotten thing to say.
> *Joan:* I'll live.
> *Bernie:* All kidding aside ... lookit, I'm a fucking professional, huh? My life is a bunch of having to make split-second decisions. ... You think I don't have better things to do. ... nowhere cunt... You're a grown woman, behave like it for chrissakes. ... I mean what the fuck do you think society is, just a bunch of rules strung together for your personal pleasure? Cockteaser. ... You got a lot of fuckin' nerve. (scene 3, pp. 16–17)

Bernie completely ignores Joan's assertion that she would not, in fact, be interested in his company, preferring to launch into his elaborate, supposedly sexy routine. His line is an extraordinary amalgam of lies, patronage, and soap-opera bravado. It is interesting to note that he uses a typical WASP name, rather than admit to his own very ethnic name, Bernie Litko. In his fantasy projection of himself, Bernie not only takes on another man's job but also another man's name—one that may be more acceptable to a woman who might, just possibly, be class conscious or even anti-Semitic. He also emphasizes the temporariness of his "fling" by stating that he is "just in town for a one-day layover." Mamet's use of the term "layover" rather than "stopover" adds a suggestive subtext to Bernie's opening gambit, as does his statement that he acted on impulse when he saw her, taking the "bull by the horn." The use of the word "horn" in the singular, rather than in the more familiar plural, is surely intended as a phallic quip.

Bernie cannot allow even the smallest detail of his story to slip; even when Joan wounds his ego with the news that she doesn't find him "sexually attractive," he stubbornly hangs on to his fantasy about being a high-flying meteorologist. This, like the rest of his spiel, is an integral part of the act. Cut to the quick by her remark, his rhetoric becomes more and more vicious. He alternates obscenities with biting sarcasm until, finally, he resorts to something that Mamet's characters often rely upon when under pressure: he cites civic rules of conduct. Bernie appears to be under the impression that the "bunch of rules" that apply to his own "personal pleasure" should in no way extend to Joan.

Just as the salesmen in *Glengarry Glen Ross* see themselves only in terms of their jobs, so Bernie views himself purely in terms of a sexual athlete, no matter how absurd this may seem. He has built up for himself a fantasy world that is quite as powerful as that invented by George and Martha in Edward Albee's *Who's Afraid of Virginia Woolf?* or by Susan in Alan Ayckbourn's *Woman in Mind.* Joan's remark that Bernie is not sexually inviting to her is more than a mere insult to such a man; it is tantamount to negating his existence. She has punctured his dream and devastated his self-image. Bernie's violent reaction and frightening aggression is, therefore, understandable. His predicament is reminiscent of that of the Vicomte de Valmont in Christopher Hampton's adaptation of de Laclos's *Les Liaisons Dangereuses;* when the Vicomte's sexual reputation and vanity are threatened, he crumbles. He has become so much a part of his assumed persona that the real man beneath the sophisticated exterior hardly exists. Rather than risk exposure of his essential vulnerability, he decides to give up the love of his life and to accept death. So it is with Bernie, although his dilemma is dramatized

in considerably less romantic and expansive terms. As the abuse tumbles out
and his grammar collapses, Bernie's agony is almost tangible; he does all he can
to crush the woman who has, in a sense, murdered him with words.

After his singular lack of success with Joan, Bernie's first reaction is to
advise Danny to behave in exactly the same way! His manner of speaking is
infused with the nonchalance of one who has just enjoyed runaway success
with his quarry:

> *Bernie:* The main thing, Dan.... The main thing about *broads*....
> Is two things: One: The Way to Get Laid is to Treat 'Em
> Like Shit.... and Two: Nothing ... *nothing* makes you so
> attractive to the opposite sex as getting your rocks off on
> a regular basis. (scene 4, pp. 17–18)

Bernie's linguistic slip in the first two lines suggests his haste to communicate
his great knowledge to Danny. At first, it is enough to suggest the "main
thing" but then he recalls that there are, in fact, "two things." Bernie has
clearly learned little from his encounter with Joan—in fact, the whole
incident seems to have receded to the back of his mind or been hastily
reconstituted into a success story of which he can be proud. His dictum for
success with women is echoed in *Lakeboat*. In that play, too, the men are
lonely and ignorant, spending most of their time talking about encounters
that have probably never taken place. In a moment of pedagogic fervour,
Fred tells Dale how to succeed sexually with women, and exactly reproduces
Bernie's advice:

> *Fred:* ... my uncle, who is over, is conversing with me one night
> and as men will do, we start talking about sex. He tells a
> story. I tell *My* story. This takes him aback. "What?" he
> says, "The way to get laid is to treat them like shit." Now
> you just stop for a moment and think on that. You've
> heard it before and you'll hear it again but there is more
> to it than meets the eye. Listen: THE WAY TO GET
> LAID IS TO TREAT THEM LIKE SHIT. Truer
> words have never been spoken. And this has been tested
> by better men than you or me. (scene 10, pp. 54–55)

Fred's recipe for success is lamentable. To give it further weight, he imbues
his speech with a number of well-worn, risible clichés and platitudes, which
he fondly believes will consolidate its truth. *Lakeboat* is a play without a single

female character; there is certainly more than a suggestion that all the fantasizing and bragging is little more than a means of disguising latent homosexuality—or, at least, the kind of homosexuality that can develop in an all-male environment. In a short work written by Mamet to be performed as a companion piece to the 1979 revival of *Sexual Perversity in Chicago*, the following, very telling, line is included: "Our most cherished illusions—what are they but hastily constructed cofferdams restraining homosexual panic?" (*Sermon*, p. 157).

A number of critics have commented upon the distinct possibility that Bernie could be homosexual. Certainly, his insistent and overemphatic displays of masculinity seem to suggest this. When questioned on the topic, he reacts in a rather panicky way, at first stating that an early childhood experience with a pervert in a cinema could have ruined him for life and, moments later, countering this with, "A kid laughs these things off. You forget, you go on living" (scene 17, p. 36). The level of hatred he displays toward such men also has a touch too much hysteria about it; he viciously decries a homosexual sales assistant as "a fucking fruit" (scene 17, p. 33) and the man in the cinema as a "faggot queer" (ibid., p. 35).

Underneath their sardonic acceptance of the world as it is, and their rare insights into the cause of their anxiety, Mamet's characters are achingly lonely. Without exception, they seek affection but are unable to sustain relationships based upon emotion. Deborah and Danny enjoy some moments of tenderness but outside pressures eventually force them to declare their love affair null and void, and to negate the experience as a waste. Neither of them has a good word for the other once the relationship has been dissolved; perhaps to acknowledge that genuine feelings were ever present is somehow to admit weakness. However, the need for love and the expression of love persist.

A character in *All Men Are Whores: An Inquiry* sums up the overwhelming feeling of powerlessness and abandonment felt by so many of Mamet's individuals:

> Our concept of time is predicated upon our understanding of death.
> Time pases solely because death ends time. Our understanding of death is arrived at, in the main, because of the nature of sexual reproduction.
> Organisms which reproduce through fission do not "die."
> The stream of life, the continuation of the germ plasm, is unbroken.

Clearly.
Just as it is in the case of man.
But much less apparently so in our case. For we are sentient.
We are conscious of ourselves, and conscious of the schism in our
    sexuality.
And so we perceive time. *(Pause.)* And so we will do anything for
    some affection. (scene 1, p. 185)

Later in the play, the same character laments the lack of true affection in the
world:

Where are our mothers, now? Where are they?
.... In cities where we kill for comfort—for a moment of reprieve
    from our adulterated lives—for fellow-feeling *(Pause.)* (I have
    eyelashes, too ...)
.... One moment of release.
.... We have no connection.
.... Our life is garbage.

We take comfort in our work and cruelty. We love the manicurist
    and the nurse for they hold hands with us. Where is our
    mother now? We woo with condoms and a ferry ride; the
    world around us crumples into chemicals, we stand intractable,
    and wait for someone competent to take us 'cross the street.
    (scene 16, p. 197)

The need for affection is sensitively spelled out in *Sexual Perversity in Chicago*
when Danny, unsure of his position with Deborah in the latter stages of their
relationship, presses for a response to his questions in the middle of the
night:

Danny: Deborah. Deb? Deb? You up? *(Pause.)* You sleeping?
    (Pause.) I can't sleep. *(Pause.)* You asleep? *(Pause.)* Huh?
    (Pause.) You sleeping, Deb? *(Pause.)* What are you
    thinking about? *(Pause.)* Deb? *(Pause.)* Did I wake you
    up? (scene 26, p. 43)

Although it is plain that Deborah is sleeping, Danny childishly insists upon
awakening her. The short, simple sentences are indicative of the insecurity
he feels; their brevity and repetition bring some form of comfort to one who

craves assurance. Merely by hearing the words spoken aloud, Danny is afforded some solace; Deborah's stillness must, at all costs, be broken.

A little earlier in the play, Danny defends Bernie to "an imaginary co-worker" who has presumably criticized his friend. Aware that his love affair may soon be over, Danny holds on steadfastly to the reality of his friendship with Bernie:

> *Danny:* ... I know what you're saying, and I'm telling you I don't like you badmouthing the guy, who happens to be a friend of mine. So just let me tell my story, okay? So the other day we're up on six and it's past five and I'm late, and I'm having some troubles with my chick ... and I push the button and the elevator doesn't come, and it doesn't come, and it doesn't come, so I lean back and I kick the shit out of it three or four times.... And *he*, he puts his arm around my shoulder and he calms me down and he says, "Dan, Dan ... don't go looking for affection from inanimate objects." *(Pause.)* Huh? So I don't want to hear you badmouthing Bernie Litko. (scene 25, p. 43)

Mamet manages to incorporate a great deal of urban despair into this one, short speech. Danny's defense of Bernie is quite ludicrous, given the set of circumstances he describes. At first glance, it is difficult to understand why Bernie's advice should have inspired such loyalty—especially to the extent that it is cited as a shining example of friendship—but if the language is analyzed, various aspects emerge. In the loveless world he inhabits, *any* constant, unswerving, *steady* manifestation of kindness is lifeblood to Danny; it is immaterial how this kindness presents itself. As he viciously attacks the elevator door (probably fantasizing that it is, in fact, Deborah) Bernie calms him down by suggesting that he should not seek affection from "inanimate objects." This is a strange statement, but one that nevertheless communicates affection to the wretched Danny. There are two ways of looking at Bernie's advice. The first—and less interesting—is that one must not expect elevators to work upon command. The society in which Bernie and Danny live is a mechanized and complex one, and mechanical objects often malfunction. It is, therefore, futile to expect "affection" (or cooperation) from such objects. The second—and most likely—possibility is that Bernie somehow regards Deborah as just such an "inanimate object" and suspects that deep down, Danny probably agrees with him. She doesn't "function" properly; she has caused great difficulties for both men; she has interrupted the natural, easy flow of their lives and is, therefore, less than human. As a good, caring friend, Bernie endeavors to convince Danny that he, alone, is worthy of Danny's love and trust; Deborah is a very poor substitute indeed. This information appears to be subliminally communicated to Danny because his defense of Bernie exceeds any other display of affection that can be found in the work.

As Danny and Deborah's affair crumbles, each vies for the last word during their many arguments. It is their growing impatience with and lack of tolerance for their partner's position that prompts them into endless verbal sparring. They both use black, sardonic humor and cruel remarks to upstage one another and their quickfire dialogue temporarily disguises the emptiness that lies just beyond their words:

> *Danny:* ... You know very well if there's any shampoo or not. You're making me be ridiculous about this. *(Pause.)* You wash yourself too much anyway. If you really *used* all that shit they tell you in *Cosmopolitan* (And you *do*) you'd be washing yourself from morning til night. Pouring derivatives on yourself all day long.
> *Deb:* Will you love me when I'm old?
> *Danny:* If you can manage to look eighteen, yes.
> *Deb:* Now, that's very telling. (scene 23, p. 41)

The sheer pettiness of this is a well-observed and painfully accurate reflection of the absurdity of many arguments between the sexes. Danny blames Deborah for making him "be ridiculous" about the existence of shampoo; in a neat jump, he shifts the responsibility. His sarcasm is meant to chasten, but its only effect is to further enrage Deborah, who responds with cynical and platitudinous remarks. Danny ridicules her need to keep up with all the beauty hints in *Cosmopolitan*, at the same time requiring her to "look eighteen" even when she's old. Since this is both unrealistic and absurd, it compounds the superficiality of their love and underlines the all-embracing obsession with physical attractiveness to the exclusion of all else.

The couple's linguistic battle for supremacy continues in a similar vein:

> *Danny:* I love your breasts.
> *Deb:* "Thank you" *(Pause.)* Is that right?
> *Danny:* Fuck you. (scene 23, p. 42)

Deborah's parody of the stereotyped response expected from a docile woman prompts Danny to lash back with a coarse expletive. When the pair eventually does break up, the verbal recriminations reach an almost frightening level of intensity:

Danny:	Cunt.
Deb:	That's very good. "Cunt", good. Get it out. Let it all out.
Danny:	You cunt.
Deb:	We've established that.
Danny:	I try.
Deb:	You try and try.... You're trying to understand women and I'm confusing you with information. "Cunt" won't do it. "Fuck" won't do it. No more magic. (scene 28, p. 46)

A desperate sarcasm pervades these lines. Deborah's assertion that Danny is trying to understand feminine psychology by way of means that in no way *involve* him is at once brilliantly funny and painfully true. As Colin Stinton remarks, "Mamet captures so accurately the tension which builds up in situations like this; Danny pretends that he wants to understand Deborah but, deep inside, he can't really be bothered. He wants to learn painlessly, by a kind of osmosis, not by having to make any effort!"[29] Danny now seems to be as insensitive as his influential friend; although he must be aware that Deborah is deeply hurt by their arguments, the only way he can respond to her self-defense is to call her a "cunt." Communication between them having reached such a nadir, it is little wonder that Deborah should reflect that there is simply "no more magic." Nothing either of them can say could inject life into what is now moribund and wretched. Whatever romance once existed has dissolved, and the sexual attraction that once passed for true love has been reconstituted into something fetid and obscene.

Throughout the play, Bernie and Danny reduce the women they encounter to purely physical dimensions, but this activity reaches its apotheosis in the final scene when they lie on the beach, admiring or deriding the women who pass by them. This episode, more forcefully than any other, underscores their sheer inability to perceive women as people. It is vulgar, tragic, and very funny. Bernie draws Danny's attention to what is presumably a well-endowed woman:

Bernie:	Hey! Don't look behind you.
Danny:	Yeah?
Bernie:	Whatever you do, don't look behind you.
Danny:	Where?
Bernie:	Right behind you, about ten feet behind you to your right.

Danny: Yeah?
Bernie: I'm telling you.
Danny: *(Looks.)* Get the fuck *outta* here!
Bernie: Can I pick 'em?
Danny: Bernie ...
Bernie: Is the radar in fine shape?
Danny: ... I gotta say ...
Bernie: ... *Oh* yeah ...
Danny: ... that you can *pick* 'em. (scene 34, p. 51)

This echoes the rhythms of the opening scene, in which Bernie and Danny feed on each other's enthusiasm, but there has been a definite change. Danny is less the eager pupil to Bernie's teacher than a wised-up accomplice in lechery. Bernie may still be the man with "the radar," but Danny is rapidly catching up to him. Mamet utilizes the mock-irony of remarks like, "Whatever you do, don't look behind you," to suggest the renewed camaraderie between the two men. As the words are uttered, it is clear that Bernie wants Danny to do exactly the opposite! It is *essential* for Danny to "look behind" to see the object of Bernie's disbelief. He even issues exact directions. Both men use humor as a means of boosting morale and confirming their macho bravado—thoroughly enjoying their "game." This idyllic pastime is suddenly shattered, however, when Bernie's behavior takes a strange and unnerving turn. As they criticize the women around them, he notices one whom he denounces as "something of a pig" (scene 34, p. 54). The presence of this woman on the beach seems to spark something in Bernie and he begins to blame her and the rest of the women for flaunting their assets, beautiful or ugly:

> *Bernie:* ... I mean who the fuck do they think they are ... coming out here and just flaunting their bodies all over? ... I come to the beach with a friend to get some sun and watch the action and ... I mean a fellow comes to the beach to sit out in the fucking sun, am I wrong? ... I mean we're talking about recreational fucking space, huh? (scene 34, p. 54)

As Bernie castigates and villifies the women in his midst, his words take on a rather hysterical note. His sentiments are reminiscent of those who would defend an act of rape by suggesting that the victim, after all, "asked for it" by the clothes she wore or by her provocative behavior. Bernie's (low) opinion of women arises, he suggests, through their cheapness and brazenness. He repeats that the only reason for his and Danny's presence on the beach is "to get some sun." This is so blatantly untrue that it becomes a pathetic plea for understanding. That he should refer to the beach as "recreational fucking space" is also deeply telling; Bernie presumably uses the obscenity as an expletive but there is, surely, a sense that he wishes it were a verb instead!

Eventually, Bernie realizes that he has said too much for his own good—and for the good of his image as a suave womanizer. Danny's perplexed question prompts Bernie into defensive action:

> *Danny:* Are you feeling alright?
> *Bernie:* Well, how do I look, do I look alright?
> *Danny:* Sure.
> *Bernie:* Well, than let's assume that I feel alright, okay.... I mean, how could you feel anything *but* alright, for chrissakes. Will you look at that body? *(Pause.)* What a pair of tits. *(Pause.)* With tits like that, who needs ... anything. (scene 34, pp. 54–55)

Within seconds, Bernie has reverted back to his old routine. He simply cannot afford to let down his "front" in this uncharacteristic way, and his aggression in the phrase, "how do I look, do I look alright?" is a warning to Danny not to probe any further. It is, however, clear that all this bluster and bravado is no more than that; we have briefly seen beneath the surface brittleness into a morass of insecurity and fear.

Bernie's final words, ignorant as they are, manage to speak volumes about the tragic state of his sexuality: "With tits like that, who needs ... anything." By once again diminishing the importance of women to their sexual anatomy, Bernie demonstrates his supreme lack of imagination and his need for fantasy. He plainly requires much more than "tits," but it is highly unlikely that he will ever attain it. Behind the arrogant façade lies a fearful naïveté. Both men hatch plans and exchange ideas about the best ways in which to bed the women they ogle, but their potential success is questionable, to say the least. On a beach full of people, Bernie and Danny remain isolated, solitary. Perhaps more so now than ever, they are on the outside looking in. More bruised by life experience than they had been at the beginning of the play, they appear overwhelmed by a deep-seated bitterness. This is borne out by the final words in the work, which manage to combine arrogance, cruelty, and sarcasm. When a woman passes them, she ignores their greetings:

> *Bernie:* Hi.
> *Danny:* Hello there. *(Pause. She walks by.)*
> *Bernie:* She's probably deaf.
> *Danny:* She did *look* deaf, didn't she?
> *Bernie:* Yeah. *(Pause.)*
> *Danny:* Deaf *bitch*. (scene 34, p. 55)

Bernie's misogyny has apparently influenced Danny to a fatal degree; perhaps he has become a more dangerous type of sexist than his friend. The absurdity of his observation that the girl "did *look* deaf" and his need for corroboration from Bernie—"didn't she?"—suggest that the veil of ignorance and insecurity has, at least partially, been transferred from Bernie to Danny. Until now, Danny has been portrayed as a fairly normal, if unimaginative young man, but one who was largely without real malice. For him to utter the final, brutal words in a brutal play is Mamet's way of dramatising how fatally Danny has come under Bernie's spell and how he has absorbed the deadening influence of an artificial and sterile society.

Sexual Perversity in Chicago is a very fast—and very black—comedy. The sheer exuberance of the dialogue is compelling, although its vitality is essentially illusory. The characters end the play as they began—confused and vulnerable, and perhaps even more lonely. Friedrich Hebbel once wrote, "Drama shouldn't present new stories but new relationships."[30] In this work, Mamet certainly seems to have fulfilled this requirement. With an accurate ear for the cadences of supposedly sophisticated urban speech and with an acute observation of contemporary sexual mores, he has produced a work that is wholly original and that dramatizes the emptiness of relationships in an empty society. Mamet has devised a play that is absolutely contemporary in its verbal style; the text is a bubbling amalgam of slang, clichés, and what the characters take to be wit, and he invents a linguistic personality for each character that is totally believable. Bernie's false shield of confidence is superbly exposed in the subtext to his aggressive linguistic forays, which have been described as "a combination of whiplash and theatrical swoops"[31] and Danny's ingenuousness and growing dependence on his friend reveals itself in his employment of certain phrases favored by his mentor. Deborah's speech has about it a vitality and innocence that is squashed as the play progresses; she finds only disappointment and frustration in a relationship she believed to be truly loving. Joan is a woman who longs for love but is afraid of it; her language may be cynical and hard but Mamet is able to suggest that under Joan's brittle, sassy linguistic bravado, a subtext of vulnerability and fear remains.

A sharp satire on contemporary sexual mores in the urban America of the 1970s, *Sexual Perversity in Chicago* is also an exposé of what a media-dominated, capitalist-structured society can produce. But finally, Mamet's greatest strength lies not in his persuasiveness as a social critic, nor even in his sensitivity to the plight of human relations: it resides in his superb timing and peerless control over language.

NOTES

1. Mamet, *Writing in Restaurants*, p. 30.
2. Karl Marx cited in Erich Fromm, *Beyond the Chains of Illusion: My Encounter with Marx & Freud* (London: Abacus, Sphere Books, 1980), pp. 46–47.
3. Bigsby, *Contemporary Writers*, p. 50.
4. Eder, "David Mamet's New Realism," p. 40.
5. Fraser, "Mamet's Plays," p. L7.
6. Ibid.
7. Tom Wolfe, *The Kandy-Kolored Tangerine-Flake Streamline Baby* (London: Jonathan Cape, 1981), p. 46.
8. Fraser, "Mamet's Plays," p. L7.
9. Ibid.
10. Peter Stothard, *Plays & Players* 25, no. 5 (February 1978): pp. 30–31.
11. Marshall Walker, *The Literature of the U.S.A.* (London: Macmillan, 1983), p. 194.
12. John Elsom, *The Listener*, 8 December 1977, p. 774.
13. Jules Feiffer, *Carnal Knowledge* (London: Penguin, 1972), pp. 10–12.
14. Ibid., pp. 18–19.
15. Stinton, interview with author, 22 March 1986, National Theatre, London.
16. Ibid.
17. Connie Booth, interview with author, 2 December 1986, Hampstead, London.
18. Stinton, interview with author, 22 March 1986, National Theatre, London.
19. Richardson, interview with author, 8 December 1986, National Theatre, London.
20. Fraser, "Mamet's Plays," p. L7.
21. Ibid.
22. Ibid.
23. Ibid.
24. Bigsby, *Contemporary Writers*, p. 48.
25. Wetzsteon, "New York Letter," (September 1976): pp. 37–39.
26. *The South Bank Show*, London Weekend Television, 20 March 1985.
27. Shepherd, interview with author, 13 March 1986, National Theatre, London.

28. Stephen Brook, *New York Days, New York Nights* (London: Picador, 1985), p. 47.

29. Stinton, interview with author, 22 March 1986, National Theatre, London.

30. Friedrich Hebbel cited in *Playwrights on Playwriting*, ed. Toby Cole (New York: Hill & Wang, 1982), p. 286.

31. Nicholas de Jongh, *The Guardian* 19 March 1984 p. 11.

DOUGLAS BRUSTER

David Mamet and Ben Jonson: City Comedy Past and Present

American critics often react chauvinistically to David Mamet's work, a response prompted, perhaps, by a perceived lack of a premier national playwright. More than one critic has revelled in Mamet's sense for Americana, echoing Jack Kroll's assessment of the dramatist as "a language playwright" whose "ear is tuned to an American frequency."[1] And while the frequently guttural dialogue of plays like *American Buffalo* and *Glengarry Glen Ross* has drawn its share of critical censure, more often than not Mamet has been lauded for situations, characters, and speech patterns that his champions are quick to label as quintessentially American. Praise of this kind, however, tends to institutionalize his work, removing the sting from Mamet's satire as it simultaneously promotes the cultural aspect of his aesthetic achievement and disassociates itself from the brutal reality of his dramatic world. An additional act of omission is made when we fail to recognize Mamet's connection with the long tradition of western drama satirizing urban venality, for the best of his work deals directly with capitalism and an ethical system perverted by greed. Although Mamet's drama shares definite affinities with that of more contemporary playwrights—Chekhov, Beckett, Pinter, and Albee come immediately to mind—perhaps it possesses even stronger ideological, linguistic, and dramaturgical connections with the style and work of a more distant

From *Modern Drama* 33, no. 3 (September 1990). © 1990 by the University of Toronto.

predecessor, to the city comedy and genius of Ben Jonson.[2] While a recent critic noted that Mamet's *The Shawl* comes in the tradition of *The Alchemist* and later dramatic satires, he went on to dub it "a significant *postmodern* attack on the place illusion occupies in our inner and external reality" (emphasis mine).[3] Certainly twentieth-century Chicago and Jacobean London are separated by an enormous gulf of distance: temporal, spatial, and cultural. To their respective dramatists, however, both represent the abstract City. Indeed, a comparison of the two playwrights' drama reveals significant similarities. By forgoing our insistence upon his national identity and waiving the extra-temporal status too often accorded contemporary dramatists, we may see more clearly David Mamet's place within the dramatic tradition. Further, we may comprehend as well the basic form of a genre arising in response to the relationship between money and sin—one which, Mamet suggests, currently dominates American culture.

I

Certain typed characters, bearing different names and occupations, appear again and again throughout the whole of Mamet's dramatic works. One such character, the smoothly persuasive, sometimes belligerent charlatan figure materializing in *American Buffalo* as Teach, as three characters in *Glengarry Glen Ross*, and one in the slightly abbreviated *The Shawl*, seems to have captured Mamet's attention early on. We find him represented by several individuals in the 1970 play *Lakeboat*; two aging aspirants to the type in *The Duck Variations* (1972); and as Bernie Litko in his 1974 *Sexual Perversity in Chicago*.[4] In Mamet's recent film, *House of Games*, the charlatan, Mike, is an actual con man. Yet only with one of his most recent and, perhaps not incidentally, most successful plays has Mamet specifically located his charlatan figure within the identifiable boundaries of capitalism.

By dramatic definition no less than by financial necessity, every charlatan must have a gull. What was true for Renaissance city comedy remains valid for Mamet's handling of comedy in a contemporary urban setting. In *Sexual Perversity*, Bernie's credulous other is an amazingly trusting Dan Shapiro, whom Mamet describes in the list of characters as "An *urban* male in his late twenties" (emphasis mine). As in Jonsonian city comedy, we find the archetypical myth of the ignorant country bumpkin reversed: it is *because*, and not in spite of, the fact that a character has spent all his life in the city that he is susceptible to the charlatan's incredible tales. In *The Alchemist*, Face and Subtle convince a host of credulous city dwellers of the possibility—rather, the certainty—of the philosopher's stone, the Queen of Fairies, and many other fantastic, supernatural exoticisms. Though their gulls are greedy, it is mainly from the persuasiveness of their rhetoric that Jonson's two tricksters are able to transform tales of the most outrageous order into believable stories. Indeed, they sell themselves, rather than any actual object. Jonson provided a neat definition of his charlatan figure in the introductory description of Fastidious Brisk in *Every Man out of His Humour*:

> He will borrow another man's horse to praise, and backs him as his own. Or, for a need, on foot can post himself into credit with his merchant only with the jingle of his spur and the jerk of his wand.[5]

In verbal persuasiveness Brisk, forerunner of the Restoration rake, anticipates as well the self-suffiency of the twentieth-century salesman, a character surviving on a smile and shoeshine. Brisk, like Willy Loman, fails "when they start not smiling back." While they are able to convince, however, rhetoric paves their way. With Mamet's charlatan, story becomes a commodity in its own right.

Dan Shapiro of Mamet's *Sexual Perversity* is gulled by the almost unbelievable rhetoric of Bernie Litko, the play's charlatan. Bernie's relation of what one has to perceive as an entirely fictional sexual encounter—his vivacious partner, having donned an army flak jacket and doused the walls with gasoline from a "five-gallon jerrycan," eventually sets the room on fire and begins singing "Off we go into the Wild Blue Yonder" before Bernie is able to evacuate the flaming hotel—is remarkable not only for its patent outrageousness, but for the fact that Dan believes it completely. "Nobody does it normally anymore," he solemnly intones to close Mamet's piece. Later in the play, with Dan eagerly soliciting his tale, Bernie waxes sentimental about some rather dubious military service in Korea in 1967 and spins a wild story about King Farouk's sexual adventures in Illinois. Throughout, Dan is entirely credulous. Jonson's gulls express the same willingness to believe in the unbelievable. Dapper so wants to come in contact with the mythical Queen of Fairy that he abandons all hold on rational process; likewise the otherwise sceptical Puritans, Ananias and Tribulation Wholesome, let credulity triumph over discrimination. Sir Epicure Mammon's overwhelming endorsement of Face and Subtle's alchemical abilities stands equivalent to the faith with which Dan Shapiro accepts Bernie's fantastic tales. Both characters are possessed by a desperate need to believe. The absence of spirituality creates a vacuum which credulity quickly fills. Where Jonson indicts his gulls for failing to accept traditional morality, Mamet suggests that, for his characters, no other possibilities exist.

The Alchemist sees rapid changing of disguise and character. Whenever a new gull arrives on stage, Face, Subtle, and Dol Common metamorphose into a new group of tricksters. With Dapper they are one thing, with Mammon another. The announcement of the arrival of a gull is sounded, plans are discussed in a hurried manner, and the house quickly becomes a different place, full of new devices and deceptions. In a recent study, Robert Watson points out the "correspondence between Lovewit's house and the theaters of Elizabethan London."[6] Playhouse becomes place of business becomes playhouse. When Lovewit finally restores some sense of order to the stage with his unexpected return, the façade which the trio has constructed suddenly, and—as though in a theater—almost magically disappears. While Tribulation Wholesome and Ananias, angry at the "chemical cozener" for having taken advantage of their gullibility, search for the wily tricksters, Lovewit scans the interior of his house (until only recently a busy establishment), remarking:

> Here, I find
> The empty walls, worse than I left 'em, smoked,
> A few cracked pots, and glasses, and a furnace (5.5.38–40)

At this moment the myths of enchanted wealth constructed by desire fade into the dreary realm of the actual—a place which, in the world of Jonson's dramatic imagination, relentlessly insists upon its proper due.

Like Face, Subtle, and Dol Common, the charlatans of *Glengarry Glen Ross* disguise themselves when profit is a factor. Seeing a repentant customer named James Lingk approaching from outside the real estate office Richard Roma quickly turns to Levene and says:

> You're a client. I just sold you five waterfront Glengarry Farms. I
> rub my head, throw me the cue "Kenilworth." (p. 78)

Levene, employing the vocabulary—"cue"—as well as the methodology of the theater, duplicates the profit-oriented theatricality of the Alchemist's shop. Lingk enters, and Roma attempts to overcome his hesitations concerning real estate investment with a flurry of talk about Shelly, whom Roma now introduces as "D. Ray Morton," director of "all European sales and services" for American Express (p. 79). The embellishment of the story creates an attractive picture of a successful salesman and his client—

ostensibly a wealthy and powerful corporate executive. This verbal art is even more impressive when taken in context: the business has been robbed the previous night, as Mamet's stage description indicates: "*The real estate office. Ransacked. A broken plate-glass window boarded up, glass all over the floor*" (p. 52). Not until late in the action, however, does Lingk notice anything amiss with the firm. Significantly, almost from the very moment that Lingk is able to procure an admission from Roma that "We had a slight burglary last night" (p. 94), the Chicago alchemist's shop begins to lose its magical aura. Lingk at last catches Roma in a contradiction, and, shortly thereafter, Levene is snared tightly in his own verbal web: Williamson realizes that Levene himself robbed the office. At this point the audience begins to perceive, along with Lingk, the "cracked pots and glasses" of the business office, the symbols of an illusionary enterprise and, no less than Williamson, the ephemeral vapors of an aging salesman's rhetoric. Baylen, the police officer who ends this masque of deception, stands as the dramatic equivalent of the householder Lovewit. That Baylen is a representative of bureaucracy, rather than a private citizen (as in Jonson's comedy), testifies to the institutionalization of modern society frequently portrayed in Mamet's drama.

Jonson's characters seldom seem as incomplete as Mamet's. This emptiness is what makes Mamet's individuals such eager buyers of stories and false friendship. While the Jonsonian gull is fraught with antisocial dreams of possession, the idea of community remains Jonson's measure of things: with Mamet, it has become an almost unknown entity. Often English city comedy perceived the threat of venality as emanating from the New Man, a seemingly novel creature whose conversion, recognizance, or punishment might rejuvenate the community. Of course, there was nothing very new about the New Man—there were simply more of him—but this did not prevent the dramatists from making him a scapegoat, regardless. Thus many city comedies end on a festive note. The return of Lovewit at the frenzied crescendo of *The Alchemist* appears to restore a healthier moral order to the world of the play, and Justice Overdo, by inviting the cast of *Bartholomew Fair* home to dinner, seems to set things aright through his financial and culinary provisions. Even thus does the obviously ritualized comeuppance of a highly venal Falstaff in Shakespeare's much neglected city comedy, *The Merry Wives of Windsor*, re-establish the *status quo* at Windsor. Nearly always, however, there exists a strong attraction about the charlatan: for much of the play, he is the cast's most intelligent and resourceful character. Therefore there is often a noticeable reluctance or regret connected with his expulsion. The cony-catching pamphlets of the 1590s, after all, are more a celebration of gulling and trickery than any kind of preventative guide or moral condemnation.

By the time capitalism reaches Mamet, greed seems to have infected the community *in toto*, pervading the thoughts, actions and rhetoric of its citizens. Cony-catching has been institutionalized. There is no indication that the expulsion of any particular character will result in a beneficial outcome for the community. On the contrary, the Dan Shapiros of Mamet's world would be equally directionless without the Bernie Litkos; Shelly Levene's impending retirement from the real estate company in *Glengarry Glen Ross* promises no real change: he has already passed on the subtleties of his verbal art to his younger apprentice, Richard Roma. The comedy ends not with a celebration of things won, but with an acknowledgement of the vicious circle in which business ethics—or lack thereof—lead behavior.

Jonson's trickster strings his victims along with the promise of great things to come. To the greedy Puritans he offers the elusive philosopher's stone; to Dapper the clerk, a chance to be with the Queen of Fairies. While these characters are controlled to varying extents by their humours, they are rarely powerless in regard to decisions. And, indeed, often they are purged of their humours. Where Jonson places a certain amount of emphasis on individual choice and moral responsibility, that is, upon the role of individual avarice in the venal ills of his society, Mamet depicts his characters as lacking the free will to make such decisions. Each person is lost within the system. When Charles Lang invents an engine which can run on water in the "American Fable" of *The Water Engine*, his approach to the leaders of big business is the first step toward ruin. He is cheated and killed, his engine destroyed. The machinations of society grind him up like the gears of his smooth-running invention. *American Buffalo*, closing almost exactly as it has begun with a soft conversation between Don and Bobby, portrays effort as utterly meaningless. A very violent interlude—one, in fact, which has taken place over nothing—has briefly punctuated their existence, yet the weary order of their lives will continue its monotonous crawl into the future. Nothing lies beneath their humours which might be reformed.

Audience and players alike can leave the world of Jonson's *Bartholomew Fair*: the journey into it has been a progress toward saturnalia and festivity. It is not the world which one inhabits from day to day. The closing of Face and Subtle's alchemical shop is testament to this celebratory aspect of Jonson's comedy: a seemingly short hiatus in the normal order has occurred. By contrast, Mamet's charlatans are the rotten pillars of American society. Where he differs from Jonson, then, lies in the extension—and not the nature—of his vision. Mamet sees Face and Subtle as having assumed positions of permanent, institutional, importance in America's business-oriented culture.

II

Clearly the satire of venality and its embodiment in character form a thematic link between Mamet and Jonson. Yet there are other clear connections between their work. Their dramatic language, separated by time, culture, and geography, is one area of surprising similarity. Jonson's dramatic diction, as described by Jonas Barish, contains a certain "explosiveness," is "abrupt, staccato, sharp."[7] Another critic has said of the characters of *The Alchemist*:

> All these people use language to impress and bewilder others. Language does not unite them; it divides them. It is a vehicle not so much of sense as nonsense.[8]

We should remember that Jonson enjoys the first recorded use of the word "nonsense" itself, and take into account the fact that his characters are the city comedy forerunners of Mamet's guttural salesmen—whose speech, full of the stressed but empty abstract noun, is nothing if not nonsense. Mamet's dramatic language, like Jonson's, is explosive, abrupt, staccato, and sharp. His characters also speak in short, choppy phrases indicative of their unstable mental process.

Jonson worked in a literary environment dominated to a certain extent by its predilection for balanced rhetorical patterns. Shakespeare's dramatic language, for example, often functions within the bonds of symmetry, along lines of balance and antithesis. Even in prose passages, his characters' thoughts frequently find themselves flowing into balanced rhetorical molds. Jonson, more often than not, tends toward the opposite. His city comedy appropriately begs the colloquial. The opening lines of *The Alchemist*—"FACE Believe't, I will./ SUBTLE Thy worst. I fart at thee."—with their unpatterned, cacophonous resonance, stand fairly representative of Jonson's comic dialogue. *Epicoene* begins with a simple question—"Ha' you got the song yet perfect I ga' you, boy?"—so extremely casual in tone as to rival the highly realistic dialogue of Middleton.

Tucca, a comic character in Jonson's *Poetaster*, habitually violates the rules of stylistic decorum. From a passage in Dekker's *Satiromastix* we know that the language of Jonson's blowhard was most probably an imitation of the speech of an actual Elizabethan, one Captain Hannam. The resemblance between Tucca's speech patterns and those of Mamet's charlatans is informative. One scholar, commenting on the wide range of Tucca's rhetorical register, described his speech as a "linguistic St. Vitus' Dance."[9]

Like Mamet's charlatans, Tucca is addicted to the use of his own brand of language, frequently employing the vulgar "whoreson" where his modern counterparts in Mamet use four-letter expletives. His style, like that of a Teach or Levene, is highly repetitive. Epanalepsis, in which the same word or clause is repeated after a brief interruption, is one of his favorite rhetorical figures. Tucca will say "thou knowest it (my noble Lucullus) thou knowest it" (1.2.159–160) and Teach will echo him "No it's not, Don. It is not" (p. 98). Tucca uses the same construction for the imperative, "Pass on, my good scoundrel, pass on" (3.4.88), followed by Teach in the same manner: "don't get smart with me, Bob, don't get smart with me" (p. 98). Here the epanalepsis reveals psychology: by unnecessary repetition, characters express their desire to change reality through language as well as their frustration at their inability to do so. What we see as enjoyable humours comedy in Jonson—filtered, perhaps, through our acquaintance with Dickens's characters and their speech patterns—reveals itself in Mamet as angry impotence. Though some of Teach's language is only too representative of modern speech, we overlook the complexity of Mamet's verbal craftsmanship when we deny his tricksters a special grammar all their own. Teach and his kindred charlatans—including Mike in *House of Games*—use and misuse contemporary language like Tucca and fraternal characters did Jonson's. Language, in their possession, becomes a reflection of a mingled and confused psyche.

Where Shakespeare places heavy emphasis on logical connections and on harmony of language and situation, Jonson often finds himself unable to harmonize speech in a world he sees as chaotic. Barish suggests that

> just as a writer who repeatedly uses causal connectives is thinking in terms of cause and effect, so a writer who shuns them is thinking in other terms, perhaps of a world so bewildering and disintegrated that nothing in it seems causally related to anything else, a world in which the atoms of impulse, act, and even collide haphazardly in a void.[10]

This pertains directly to Mamet's dramatic world as well, where sense and nonsense seem to be one. Characters like Teach are able to convince themselves and others that, by keeping friendship and business separate, "maybe we can deal with each other like some human beings" (p. 15). The world bewilders, and irrational rhetoric is utilized in hopeless attempts to make order where none can exist. Indeed, the number of verbal non-sequiturs in Mamet is astounding: one could say, in fact, that his dramatic world is built on them. Language is no longer communal, but a frightening reflection of the self. Once more Barish:

> In Jonson, the avoidance of logical particles and the preference for the exploded period reflect the discontinuous plot structure; society is conceived as a collection of disconnected atoms, in which each character speaks a private language of his own, pursues ends of his own, collides from time to time with other characters, and then rebounds into isolation.[11]

The language of Jonson's London, so different from the courtly register of blank verse, anticipates the demotic dialect of twentieth-century America as evidenced in Mamet's city comedies. The unstable, rapidly changing carnival world of *Bartholomew Fair*, in which each character pursues his own ends and speaks his own language, is mirrored by Mamet's autistic modern City and its denizens. When Mamet's charlatan says *"business"* or *"loyalty"* or even "senny-*nine*," he knows less of his subject than of his desire. Words and concepts are a means to an end. Like the gull, even the audience falls prey to the charlatan's smooth banter. One finds oneself entranced by Roma's line of philosophy, yet there is no sense there. The form of his rhetoric, the force of his argument and the strength of his self-confidence are the real elements of attraction. Like the Jonsonian speaker, he communicates in a language all his own. The sound of the strange words—words once believed to be general property—holds us and, like his gulls, we listen.

At first glance there appears to be a frightening realism to the common language of Mamet and Jonson's plays. Early critics used this extreme realism of the language as a basis for negative appraisal. John Simon noted Mamet's ability "to reproduce quirky or mindless demotic speech" and, in a characteristically caustic sentence, wished that Mamet "had more insight into heads and hearts instead of merely gluing his ears in arrested development to people's mouths."[12] Admittedly, Mamet's characters speak less than formal English. Frequently they elide syllables, dropping out letters, such as in Levene's "senny-nine." More often they will omit prepositions. Don tells Bob that "You don't have *friends* this life ... " (p. 8). Teach enters the junk shop some minutes later and informs them of an incident earlier in the day:

> I come into the Riverside to get a cup of *coffee*, right? I sit down at the table Grace and Ruthie. (p. 10)

Shelly Levene promises Williamson that "I get back the hotel, I'll bring it in tomorrow" (p. 25). Mamet's ear for language, tuned as it is "to an American frequency," captures the slovenly nature of contemporary diction, amplifying its idiosyncratic texture.

Ben Jonson's ear seems to have been no less tuned to the speech of his own day, and like Mamet he elaborates typed singularities of speech. One is struck by his emphasis on slang and cant. His characters are full of the street language of Jacobean London. Indeed, his dramatic speech seemed so mimetic to his contemporaries that it drew the following piece of criticism in the War-of-the-Theaters satire, *The Return From Parnassus II*:

> [Jonson is] A mere empiric, one that gets what he hath by observation, and makes only nature privy to what he endites.[13]

The parallel between this charge against Jonson's imitative craftsmanship and recent comments concerning Mamet's ear for dialogue is illuminating. Both playwrights are scorned for imitating reality. Yet neither Mamet nor Jonson seems obsessively concerned in his drama with naturalistic reproduction for its own sake: perhaps "surrealistic" better describes their achievements. Nor must one mistake Face and Subtle's alchemist shop only for an actual place of business, or Bartholomew Fair only for an actual fair. Their inhabitants are members of a larger universe as well. Similarly, Don's Resale Shop in *American Buffalo* represents not so much a single store, but all businesses. Its characters are ones we have met before in Mamet, and ones that we will meet again. Their language is the spontaneous overflow of confused emotions and ideas. Seeing it as merely a strict reproduction of actual conversation detracts from the broad level of significance the drama can convey.

Barish points out that the social-climbing characters in Jonsonian comedy "clothe themselves in the jargon and gestures of a superior class in order to be accepted by it."[14] One thinks of Fastidious Brisk, Fitzdottrel, Lady Politic Would-be, and Diaphanous Silkworm: all characters desperately, if politely, attempting to progress in social standing. Indeed, in many ways Jonson's City is a Darwinian locale, where character types and raging humours utilize deception and fraud to advance themselves on the social ladder. Very often the trickery manifests itself as self-deception. Whatever the means, and whoever the gull, his characters aspire to endure through advancing themselves upwards in society.

Mamet's characters are bent more on sheer survival. Significantly, much of the playwright's ideology seems to assume the principle of natural selection.[15] Struggling in society, his characters attempt to carve niches for themselves through language. Often they try to adopt what they believe to be the formal, ordered rhetoric of a more successful class. Teach tries in vain to convince himself of the justness of his morality, stating that "Someone is *against* me, that's their problem," before profoundly concluding, in a weighty piece of judgement: "the only way to teach these people is to kill them" (p. 11). To Teach, this is wisdom of lasting significance. That he states his belief so judiciously—as though someone who has spent long hours in philosophic contemplation of the matter—indicates a desire to have his proverb accepted as sincere. His sentence, if disturbing, is for once complete. Yet his maxim makes little impression upon his companions in the shop; Don merely proceeds to ask Teach if he would like any coffee. The significance of such a line rests not only in its ironic black humor, but also in the fact that Teach, like Richard Roma when he philosophizes eloquently—but obtusely—upon human existence, frames his remarks in the mock formal rhetoric of a higher class. In Mamet's world, to survive is to *seem* to succeed.

III

From Mamet's early plays to his most recent, a somewhat distinct progression manifests itself in an advancement from the personal tenor of *The Duck Variations* to the conscious didacticism of works dealing specifically with the city and urban venality: plays such as *American Buffalo, Glengarry Glen Ross, The Shawl,* and, more recently, *House of Games.* It would be a mistake, however, to see the whole of his work as anything but urban. Even a Mamet play entitled *The Woods* concerns itself with the language and relationships of the city: how its characters, a pair of young lovers lacking almost all acquaintance with each other's true feelings, are unable—and in a placid, rural setting—to shrug off the burden of urban values and attain any kind of communicative relationship. In three of his most recent plays, Mamet's dramatic imagination has been focused upon a subject which remained only partially explored throughout the course of his earlier drama, the American business ethic. In many ways *Glengarry Glen Ross* seems merely a more obvious version of *American Buffalo*: Mamet holds the opinion that "There's really no difference between the *lumpenproletariat* and stockbrokers or corporate lawyers who are the lackey of business."[16] Reactions to *American Buffalo* were mixed, and Mamet showed some disappointment that its message was not widely understood. Businessmen walked from the theater without realizing it is about *them.* No less than *Glengarry Glen Ross* it is a play about the whole of American business. Yet its reception necessitated a revision. By garbing his charlatan in the dress of the socially respected— hence making his point very obvious indeed—Mamet succeeded at communicating his dissatisfaction with what he perceives as the infectious venality of contemporary American business.

Jonson's insistence on the evils of avarice and venality rings through his work. The following passage from his *Discoveries* is perhaps representative:

> *What* petty things they are wee wonder at? like children, that esteem every trifle; and prefer a *Fairing* before their Fathers: what difference is between us, and them? but that we are dearer Fooles, Cockscombes, at a higher rate? They are pleas'd with Cockleshels, Whistles, Hobby-horses, and such like: wee with Statues, marble Pillars, Pictures, guilded Roofes, where under- neath is Lath, and Lyme; perhaps Lome. Yet wee take pleasure in the lye, and are glad we can cousen our selves. Nor is it onely in our wals, and seelings; but all that we call happinesse, is mere painting, and guilt: and all for money:[17]

In one of Jonson's last plays, *The Magnetic Lady*, Sir Interest Moth, a usurer, sets up money as the rightfully ruling property of the commonwealth. He argues that

>   'tis natural to all good subjects
> To set a price on money; ... every piece
> Fro' the penny to the twelvepence being the hieroglyphic,
> And sacred sculpture of the sovereign. (2.6.71–75)

Along these lines Mamet's *American Buffalo*, revolving as it does around the purchase and planned theft of a buffalo-head nickel, contains a pun in its title. Where Moth's sovereign-headed coin is described as the proper ruler of society, the coin Teach dwells upon calls to mind a significant connotation: in American slang "buffalo" means "to pressure" or "intimidate." Usually this meaning carries with it some sense of tricking or fooling the person "buffaloed."[18] Thus the sovereign of America's business culture is indeed the buffalo, the mascot of the charlatan's trade. When we notice Jonson's distaste for the behaviour which accompanies avarice—an attitude which can be seen in any one of a number of plays, from *The Alchemist* to *Volpone* and *Bartholomew Fair*—and compare his "Statues, marble Pillars, Pictures" to the Cadillacs, Hawaiian vacations, and Floridan real estate of Mamet's *Glengarry*

Glen Ross, the strong similarity suggests a moral kinship between the dramatists.

The gulf between Jonson and Mamet is almost four centuries wide, and includes Marx, Brecht, and Thorstein Veblen, the Chicago economist whose theories on culture, commerce and society have heavily influenced Mamet's ideology. Where Jonson will halt his discussion of venality and will-to-consume at a dichotomy comparing adult materialism with childish fascination—a cockleshell being no more or less than a marble pillar—Mamet examines the difference, or rather lack of difference, between the contemporary criminal and businessman:

> As Thorstein Veblen says, the behaviour on this level, in the lumpenproletariat, the delinquent class, and the behaviour on the highest levels of society, in the most rarefied atmospheres of the leisure class, is exactly identical.[19]

The sickness at the heart of the American business ethic expounded here by Mamet is the twentieth-century version of a complaint once voiced in a different register by Jonson.

Influenced by Stanislavsky's linguistic theory, Mamet feels that language often precedes and prompts both action and thought: "Rhythm and action are the same ... words are reduced to the sound and rhythm much more than to the verbal content."[20] Mamet also expends a great amount of creative effort in the genesis of his dialogue, stating that "a line's got to scan" and confessing that "I've been known to be caught counting the beats on my fingers."[21] The nature of his characters' language, however, originates in society. Reflected in dramatic speech, this society is chaotic and valueless, with no coherency or community. Those who would see only the language of the vulgar class in *American Buffalo* miss the larger social—sometimes metaphysical—intentions and implications of the play. It appears that Mamet means Teach, Don, and Bobby to represent the breadth of our society: certainly, he feels, their ethical structure does. Perhaps we need to rediscover ways to understand the morality play, for like Jonson's, Mamet's city comedies borrow from its methods and meaning.

Jonson held similar views regarding language and society. In his *Discoveries* he remarks:

> *There* cannot be one colour of the mind; an other of the wit. If the mind be staid, grave, and compos'd, the wit is so; that vitiated, the other is blowne, and deflowr'd. Do wee not see, if the mind

languish, the members are dull? Looke upon an effeminate
person: his very gate confesseth him. If a man be fiery, his motion
is so: if angry, 'tis troubled, and violent. So that wee may
conclude: *Wheresoever, manners, and fashions are corrupted,
Language is. It imitates the publicke riot. The excesse of Feasts, and
apparell, are the notes of a sick State; and the wantonesse of language,
of a sick mind* (emphasis mine).[22]

For Jonson, language was still mainly a private commodity: it "imitates" but
does not necessarily derive from the "public riot." Ostentation and public
behavior could bring down Jonson's harsh judgement on the state of a
society, but speech revealed primarily the private self. "*Language* most shewes
a man," Jonson remarks later in the *Discoveries*, "speake that I may see thee."[23]
Characters like Tucca, then, are flawed as private individuals, not as
immediate representatives of the *status quo*. The dichotomy between public
and private, at this point becoming less distinct, by Mamet's time erodes
almost completely.

   While we are not ready to label Don, Teach, and Bob the actual
representatives of The World, The Flesh, and The Devil—as we are with
Face, Subtle and Dol Common—we should realize that they trace their
ancestry to this parodic trinity. Character, thought, and language: the list of
similarities between these two writers of city comedy is telling. Each is highly
distressed in the face of greed, something which surfaces in a similar,
desperate moral tone in their plays. And both playwrights illustrate the
dependence of business upon theatrical methodology and dramatic illusion.

   But the great number of parallels between the two playwrights implies
that Mamet shares connections with his predecessor which extend beyond
the generic demands of city comedy. I suggest that such parallels are not
merely products of formal demands, but owe their existence to similarities
in ideological convictions and the historical position of their respective
societies. In many ways Mamet's America shares with Jacobean London the
same creeping pessimism, the same lack of confidence in a state so obviously
having progressed from confidence to doubt and from grandeur to error in
such a brief period of time, and the same intense self-scrutinizing tendencies
which lead inevitably to dissatisfaction. The uncertainty often—and
myopically—claimed as the property of modern or post-modern literature
and society is not without its precedent in the malaise of Jacobean England.
Sanburg's wicked and brutal "City of the Big Shoulders" is what London
was, and Mamet's work echoes Jonson's. Such a parallel pictures David
Mamet playing a role in the drama of decadence which he himself

delineated at the annual Spencer Lecture in Cambridge, Massachusetts in 1986:

> Our civilization is convulsed and dying, and it has not yet gotten the message. It is sinking, but it has not sunk into complete barbarity ... [24]

However implicitly a message of equal weight may seem, to the modern reader, to inhabit the plays themselves, such overt pessimism was not part of the critical vocabulary of the playwright of Jacobean city comedy.

NOTES

1. "The Muzak Man," *Newsweek*, 28 February 1977, p. 79.

2. City comedy means different things with different critics. I use the term to mean, very generally, drama set in a city or place—shop, store, tavern—dedicated to matters of finance and / or commodity exchange: legal and illegal alike. For an insightful discussion of the genre see Harry Levin's "Notes on City Comedy" in *Playboys & Killjoys* (New York, 1987), pp. 155–174. Brian Gibbon's *Jacobean City Comedy* (Cambridge, MA, 1968; revised, New York, 1981) and Alexander Leggatt's *Citizen Comedy in the Age of Shakespeare* (Toronto, 1973) are the more recent major studies. L.C. Knights's famous *Drama and Society in the Age of Jonson* (London, 1937) referred to "social drama." Also useful is Arthur Brown's "Citizen Comedy and Domestic Drama" in *Jacobean Shakespeare* (London, 1960). pp. 63–84.

3. Philip C. Kolin, "Revealing Illusions in David Mamet's *The Shawl*," *Notes on Contemporary Literature*, 16, 2 (1986), 9–10.

4. Quotations from Mamet's drama are taken from the following editions: *American Buffalo* (New York, 1977); *Sexual Perversity in Chicago* and *Duck Variations* (New York, 1978); *Glengarry Glen Ross* (New York, 1984). All page references are given parenthetically following the quotation.

5. G.A. Wilkes, ed., *The Complete Plays of Ben Jonson*, 4 vols. (Oxford, 1981–1982). All citations to Jonson's plays are from this text.

6. *Ben Jonson's Parodic Strategy* (Cambridge, MA, 1987), pp. 113 ff.

7. *Ben Jonson and the Language of Prose Comedy* (Cambridge, MA, 1960), pp. 79, 55.

8. Ian Donaldson, "Language, Noise, and Nonsense: *The Alchemist*," *Seventeenth-Century Imagery* ed. Earl Miner (Berkeley, 1971), p. 76.

9. Arthur H. King, *The Language of Satirized Characters in Poetaster* (Lund, 1941), p. 109.

10. *Prose Comedy*, p. 77.

11. *Prose Comedy*, p. 83.

12. "Queasy Quartet," *New York Magazine*, 5 November 1979, p. 87.

13. O. Smeaton, ed. (London, 1905), 1.2.183–4.

14. *Prose Comedy*, p. 89.

15. See the essays in *Writing in Restaurants* (New York, 1986), especially "Decay."

16. Quoted in "The 'Engine' That Drives Playwright David Mamet," *The New York Times*, 15 January 1978. Section 2, p. 4.

17. C.H. Herford, P. and E. Simpson, eds., *Ben Jonson*, 11 vols. (Oxford, 1925–52); vol. 8, p. 607.

18. The Supplement to the *OED* cites the verb "buffalo" as "North American slang" meaning "To overpower, overawe, or constrain by superior force or influence; to outwit, perplex."

19. Quoted in C.W. Bigsby, *David Mamet*, (New York, 1985), p. 78.

20. Ibid., p. 28.

21. Ibid., p. 124.

22. Herford and Simpson, loc. cit., pp. 592–3.

23. Ibid., p. 625.

24. Typescript copy, courtesy of the American Repertory Theatre. This speech appears under the title of "Decay" in *Writing in Restaurants*, pp. 110–117.

TOBY SILVERMAN ZINMAN

Jewish Aporia: The Rhythm of Talking in Mamet

When David Mamet came to Philadelphia in January of 1990 for the opening night of a new production of his little-known play, *Squirrels*, first performed fifteen years before in Chicago, he sat in the audience and decided the play was lacking a last line. On the spot he made one up and it was included in the rest of the production's run, although it has not appeared in the Samuel French Acting Edition.[1] This tag line, "Or words to that effect," sums up both the play and the argument of this essay.

In the play, a writer, suffering from writer's block, hires a younger man, also suffering from writer's block, to assist him; they spend their days in an office trying to write a story or a novel or a script or a something about a man and a squirrel. The third character, the Cleaning Lady, comes in from time to time to kibitz and to dust and to work on her own story. The clichés whiz around, the characters take turns hindering each other, and nothing much gets done. It is a one-joke play played for all it is worth. For instance:

> Arthur: Well, toss it out then. We'll not be hidebound by convention, eh? We start afresh. We search for guts. A simple man (which is to say a man not heretofore invested with qualities) goes to the park to feed a squirrel. Wait. A man goes to the park to feed the squirrels. (*Pause*) A man

From *Theatre Journal* 44, no. 2 (May 1992). © 1992 by The Johns Hopkins University Press.

accustomed to feeding squirrels finds himself one day in the park. (*Pause*) Into a park usually inhabited by squirrels there came one day a man. (*Pause*) The park! Scene of human violence and animal hunger![2]

This goes on for about an hour, until the Cleaning Lady enters the now-empty office, and reads what she has written on her pad:

Squirrels. (Squirrels.)
Gatherers of nuts.
Harbingers of autumn.
Clucking and strangling.
Strangling and being strangled.
Rushing to your logical conclusion.
Searching to be free.

She crumples up the paper, tosses it in the wastebasket, and delivers the inspired tag line to the audience: "Or words to that effect."

That line is crucial to the way I read Mamet. Content is never at issue; *what* Mamet has to say has been said before (American society is corrupt, Hollywood is more corrupt, life is lonely, loveless sex is empty, men treat women badly), but it is the *way* he says it that is so appealing. Perhaps the best illustration of this comes from the epigraph to *Squirrels*, a poem by Mamet:

The reason I like
Edna St. Vincent Millay
Is that her name
Sounds like a basketball
Falling downstairs.
The reason I like
Walt Whitman
Is that his name
Sounds like
Edna St. Vincent Millay
Falling downstairs.

Rhetoric has never been so destitute nor rhythm so triumphant.

In *Lakeboat*, Fred tells us that "everyone says 'fuck' all the time.... in direct proportion to how bored they are."[3] But Mamet's "fucks" are not boring—he can inflect the word in more ways than anyone could have imagined. Every critic, every reviewer, every writer of book-cover blurbs tells us how Mamet's ear is so finely attuned to American speech; he is the magician of macho, the wizard of obscenity. This seems to be so obvious that it has even become an already old joke: a panhandler asks a man for money. The man pompously replies, "'Neither a borrower nor a lender be.' William Shakespeare." The panhandler replies, "'Fuck you.' David Mamet." Every interview, every personal essay tells us about Mamet's early family life where "we liked to while away the evenings by making ourselves miserable, solely based on our ability to speak the language viciously."[4] So it is not what the words say that is Mamet's typical achievement, but the effect they create: "words to that effect." We can discover how Mamet creates those remarkable, essentially rhythmic effects by attempting to identify the rhetorical device crucial to his style.

Mamet's dialogue is full of questions.[5] These questions are not exactly examples of *erotesis*, the device usually called the "rhetorical question," in that they are answered, sometimes by another character, sometimes by the asker himself. The device seems, rather, to be a variation on *aporia*, the trope of doubt, the real or pretended inability to know what the subject under discussion is.

Just about every play has a passage in it that frames the question-filled play with a question; the marriage of form and content aporetically creates a play that seems to withhold from us the very fact/word/truth its characters *seem* not to know, but which we leave the theatre knowing, and which we— and they—suspect they have known all along. When in *Speed-the-Plow*, Fox says, "experiences like this, *films* like this ... these are the films ...," Gould replies, "... Yes ...," and Fox continues, "*These* are the films, that whaddayacallit ... [*long pause*] that make it all worthwhile."[6] This "whaddayacallit" syndrome pervades the play, as language—especially the language of value, of what is worthwhile—fails them. Consider the spectacular catechism which concludes this play:

> *Fox*:   Well, so we learn a lesson. But we aren't here to "pine," Bob, we aren't put here to *mope*. What are we to do (pause) Bob? After everything is said and done. What are we put on earth to do?
>
> *Gould*:   We're here to make a movie.
>
> *Fox*:   Whose name goes above the title?
>
> *Gould*:   Fox and Gould.
>
> *Fox*:   Then how bad can life be?

The play ends with a question which the play has, in horrifying effect, already answered.

The elusiveness of a center, the lack of a clear subject, the loss of specific nouns, control play after play. For instance, in *American Buffalo*, Don says, "We have a deal with the man."

> *Teach*:   With Fletcher.
> *Don*:   Yes.
> *Teach*:   We had a deal with Bobby.
> *Don*:   What does that mean?
> *Teach*:   Nothing.
> *Don*:   It don't?
> *Teach*:   No.
> *Don*:   What did you mean by that?
> *Teach*:   I didn't mean a thing.
> *Don*:   You didn't.
> *Teach*:   No.[7]

This exchange turns on the word "Nothing" which is both an evasion of and an answer to the question, "What does that mean?" "Nothing" here is both noun and elliptical clause (that is, Teach's shorthand way of saying, "I didn't mean anything"); either way, the center of the conversation eludes them, just as the moral obligation of a honorable "deal" does. "Nothing" as an abstract noun becomes a concrete noun (as it is in Beckett, as it is in Hemingway) where the absence of meaning *is* the meaning.

A variation on this aporetic conversation takes place in the third of the *Duck Variations*, when Emil declares that "The law of the universe is a law until itself," and George replies, "You can't get away with *nothing*":

> *Emil*:   And if you could it would have a purpose.
> *George*: Nobody knows that better than me.
> *Emil*:   ... Well put.[8]

The human problem, of course, is that one cannot get away with nothing. The grammatical problem is whether "nothing" here constitutes a double negative, or whether it is the baffling subject of the discussion. Either it is "well put" or it is badly put, and Mamet withholds resolution of that ambiguity just as he withholds the subject. Consider the similar assault on the audience's expectations in scene nineteen of *Lakeboat*:

Stan:	There are many things in this world, Joe, the true meaning of which we will never know. (Pause) I knew a man was a Mason ...
Joe:	Uh huh ...
Stan:	You know what he told me?
Joe:	No.
	(Pause)
Stan:	Would you like to know?
Joe:	Yes.

They walk offstage before we can hear Stan's explanation of one of the "many things" we will never know the "true meaning" of, creating what might be termed aporetic blocking.

In a monologue called "A Sermon," written in 1978 as a companion piece for the Chicago revival of *Sexual Perversity*, Mamet meditates on the same difficulty. The monologue begins with a clergyman acknowledging the perplexing state of universal affairs:

> In September, 1939 a dentist in Viceroy, Louisiana placed a human tooth into a jar of Coca Cola and let it stand overnight. The next morning Hitler invaded Poland. A man has a deaf yak. The yak cannot hear. It grew up deaf. And this man speaks to it: "How are you today, King?" "Bow wow," says the yak one day.... And the next day the yak goes "moo." (Pause) The animal has no *idea* of its responsibilities. It knows that something is required of it; it knows that it should make a sound, but it has no idea what that sound is supposed to be. Life is like that. I feel. If it were not one thing it would surely be another. It *is*, however, one thing. Though it is by no means the *same* thing. Although it's always something of that nature.[9]

That man is a deaf yak somehow comes as no surprise. The yak suffers from aporia, and we, like the yak, have no real idea what it is we are talking about, nor can we locate the right words.

It is one thing to read Mamet's drama as social critique; after all, he himself has said that *American Buffalo* is about "how we excuse all sorts of great and small betrayals and ethical compromises called business";[10] the play is, as C. W. E. Bigsby calls it, "a savage satire on the collapse of American values, on the process whereby American liberal principles have been accommodated to a rapacious self-interest. It enacts the disintegration of community and the failure equally of language and morality."[11] But, although this description is unarguable, and *Glengarry Glen Ross* and *Speed-the-Plow* obviously continue this inspection of the ruins, I would suggest that the malady Bigsby identifies as American aphasia[12] is compounded by Jewish aporia; the sociopsychological is informed by the metaphysical, and bent by irony.

Aporia is not usually an interrogative mode, but in Jewish hands, or mouths, it becomes one. Consider here another old joke which sounds much like a bit of Mamet dialogue cleaned up:

> Goldberg and Levine were sitting on the porch after supper.
> "Did you hear about the accident Stein had in his new car?" asked Levine.
> "How could I not?" answered Goldberg. "It was in front of my house, wasn't it? I've got eyes, haven't I?"
> Levine continued, "Were you sitting right there when it happened?"
> "What then?" answered Goldberg. "I was maybe lying here? Have I got a bed here?"
> Levine was exasperated. "Goldberg, why do Jews answer a question with another question?"
> Goldberg answered, "And why not?"[13]

In a recent essay, Howard Stein suggests that "the Jewish sensibility that ... flourished from the 1930s to the beginning of the 1960s, culminating with Arthur Miller, a sensibility which was appropriate and valuable for articulating the pain, the problems, and the hardship of a society suffering economic depression and its second world war in twenty years" has been replaced by a new lapsed Catholic sensibility, which, although it started with O'Neill, flourished in the 1970s in such playwrights as David Rabe, John Guare, Christopher Durang, and Albert Innaurato. Stein feels this "new" sensibility is marked by the permanently wounding loss of faith.[14]

It seems to me that Mamet is second-generation Jewish sensibility; he is without the entitlement to either the angst of Miller or the enraged grief of Rabe. Mamet has carved out for himself new psychocultural territory: he flies in the face of every stereotype of the Jewish intellectual, the Jewish artist, the nice Jewish boy. Mamet has invented Jewish tough, and he did it with language. Consider Mamet's enormous admiration for his sister's breathtakingly tough talk; in *Writing in Restaurants* he tells the story of one evening when they were out "drowning [their] sorrows at a delicatessen, and [he] said of [his] pastrami sandwich,"

"How can we eat this food? This is *heart*-attack food ... how can we eat this?"

"Listen," she remonstrated, "it gave six million Jews the strength to resist Hitler."
["True Stories of Bitches"][15]

Mamet has raised Jewish allusions to the level of universal shorthand that Roman Catholic allusions have always enjoyed, although I would be curious to know how the hilarious line of Charlie Fox's in *Speed-the-Plow*— "I know you, Bob. I know you from the *back*. I know what you're staying for .... You're staying to Hide the Afikomen" (34)—plays to audiences outside big American cities. The resonance here, although I may be overreading the text considerably, is fascinating. The Afikomen is the piece of matzoh, wrapped and hidden, which the children search for during the seder, the elaborately ritualized meal of the Passover celebration. The seder itself depends on questions—"Why is this night different from all other nights?"—which the children ask the parents, as set forth in Exodus 12. But the word *afiqimon* or *afiqomon* has been much debated by Talmudic scholars; "most agree it refers to some type of banquet custom.... the term denotes after-dinner revelry commonly found at banquets or symposia."[16] The point of the afiqomen or Afikomen seems to be to prohibit the drunken singing and house-hopping partying usual after banquets. The ironic implications of the line become more pointed considering the infidel carryings-on which subsequently take place between Bobby Gould and Karen. Even more tempting to interpretive overreading is this advice about conduct during and after the seder from the Mishnah: "In general, we must eliminate every such base sight or sound—in a word, everything immodest that strikes the senses (for this is an abuse of the sense)—if we would avoid pleasures that merely fascinate the eye or ear, and emasculate."[17] (It's the perfect halakic indictment of Hollywood movies.)

The rhythm of Jewish speech turns out to be crucial; as Hersh Zeifman has pointed out,[18] in *American Buffalo* the following lines of Don's are altered considerably depending on the delivery:

There's lotsa people on this street, Bob, they want this and they want that. Do anything to get it. You don't have *friends* in this life .... You want some breakfast?

[8]

If that third sentence is read as a declarative statement, it becomes an utterly cynical refusal to believe in the possibility of friendship. If, alternatively, it is read interrogatively, with the voice trailing off during the ellipses, and if the beginning of the sentence is an implied "If," if the delivery is rhythmically given a Jewish inflection, then the meaning changes to something like, "if you don't have *friends* in this life, life is intolerable." This second, far more affirming modulation of the line, makes much more sense in the play. Don is talking to Bob, his young and devoted friend, and the whole play turns on the betrayal of friendships, the belated reassertion of friendship's claims, and the collision between the cynical amorality of Teach and the feeble humanity of Don. If the actor playing Don mistakes the rhythm of this speech, he may derail the play. Don must believe, at some level, in the importance of having *friends* in this life, and we must know he does, or the central conflict of the play is lost.

Mamet has been very conscious of being a Jew in America, and that consciousness is the core of his *Three Jewish Plays—The Disappearance of the Jews* (1982, 1987), *Goldberg Street* (1985), and *The Luftmensch*, (1984, 1987). It is the first of these which introduces Bobby Gould, a character we come to know all too well in Mamet's two most recent plays, *Speed-the-Plow* and *Bobby Gould in Hell*. The second of these three plays, *Goldberg Street*, is only a few pages long and nearly cryptic, and *because* it is utterly aporetic (*what* are they talking about?), it is, finally, heartbreakingly moving. It begins with a meditation on antisemitism and its disenfranchising, alienating effects:

> *Man*:   Goldberg Street. Because they didn't *have* it. They
>   had *Smith* Street—they had *Rybka* Street.
>   There was no Goldberg Street.
>   You can keep your distance and it's fine.
>   If a man is secluded then he feels superior. Or rage.
>   But where's the good in that?
> *Daughter*: There is no good in it.
> *Man*:   I'm not sure.... [19]

In a recent newspaper interview, Mamet talked about his newest film, *Homicide* which is about a New York detective who is a Jew: "I mean, 'Homicide' is one of the first movies in which you hear the word 'Jew' rather than 'Jewish.' ... And as a Jew it kind of burns me that the only way that the Jewish experience is ever treated in American films is through the Nazi murder of European Jews." Echoing his own play, Mamet told the interviewer, "Have you ever noticed that in spite of the fact that there were authentic Jewish heroes during World War II, there are no streets named Goldberg Street in America? The very idea sounds funny to our ears."[20] And

Joe Mantegna (who plays the detective) added, "It's like the obscenity in David's plays, which has always been controversial. David doesn't dabble in anything. If he's going to lay something on you, well, here's 10 tons of it. He's handling the Jewish aspect of this script in the same way."[21]

Even when his characters are not Jewish, even when they seem to be goyishe hoodlums (like Teach in *American Buffalo*), they *sound* Jewish. For instance, in *Squirrels*, the Cleaning Lady is working on a cowboy script about The Kid and Black Bart. "So the Kid says, 'Slap leather, Bart' and Bart says, 'Kid the man can beat me to the draw ain't been born yet, and the man don't live who ain't been born yet.' Kid says, 'Enough fucking rhetoric, huh, go for your gun you're getting old.' Bart says, 'Who isn't?'" (15).

It is telling that of all Mamet's characters, the most conspicuously *not* Jewish character is John Williamson. The office manager in *Glengarry Glen Ross* is distinguished from the rest of the men in that office (both the Jews and the Italians) by the rhythms of his speech. And, as in *American Buffalo*, those rhythms speak the meaning of the play. Consider this vivid, decisive exchange as the plot's crisis approaches, an exchange about *ways* and *kinds* of talking:

Roma:	You want to learn the first rule you'd know if you ever spent a day in your life ... you never open your mouth till you know what the shot is. (*Pause.*) You fucking *child* ...
Levene:	You *are* a shithead, Williamson ...
Williamson:	Mmm.
Levene:	You can't think on your feet you should keep your mouth closed. (*Pause.*) You hear me? I'm *talking* to you. Do you hear me ... ?
Williamson:	Yes. (*Pause.*) I hear you ...
Levene:	You can't learn that in an office. Eh? He's right. You have to learn it on the streets. You can't *buy* that. You have to *live* it.
Williamson:	Mmm.
Levene:	*Yes.* Mmm. *Yes. Precisely. Precisely.* 'Cause your partner *depends* on it. (*Pause.*) I'm *talking* to you, I'm trying to tell you something.
Williamson:	You are?
Levene:	Yes, I am.
Williamson:	What are you trying to tell me?
Levene:	What Roma's trying to tell you. What I told you yesterday. Why you don't belong in this business.

Williamson:	Why I don't ...
Levene:	You listen to me, someday you might say, "Hey ... " No, fuck that, you just listen what I'm going to say: your partner *depends* on you. Your partner ... a man who's your "partner" *depends* on you ... you have to go *with* him and *for* him ... or you're shit, you're *shit*, you can't exist alone ...
Williamson:	*(Brushing past him.)* Excuse me ...
Levene:	... excuse you, *nothing*, you be as cold as you want, but you just fucked a good man out of six thousand dollars, and his goddamn bonus 'cause you didn't know the *shot*.... you're scum, you're fucking white bread....

[96-98]

"White bread" asks only the kinds of questions which require direct answers, and has only one kind of "talk"; unlike the other characters, his lines are tame, colorless, and although he may be the only character in the office not a con man, his lack of rhythm makes him *seem* the play's villain. Of course, Mamet can always get us to root for the bad guys because the bad guys talk so good.

In his book of essays, *Some Freaks*, Mamet writes about American Jews' sense of inferiority, and cites Mel Brooks's movie, *The History of the World, Part I*, in which Cloris Leachman, as Mme. Defarge, says "in a wonderfully dreadful French accent, ... 'We have no home, we have no bread, we don't even have a *language*—all we have is ziz lousy *accent*.'" For Mamet, the second-generation Jews—his generation—had no language: "Our parents eschewed Yiddish as the slave language of poverty, and Hebrew as the dead language of meaningless ritual."[22] And the second generation doesn't even have the lousy accent; all we have is plenty of Nothing—and Mamet's aporetic dialogue reveals that void.

In *Squirrels*, Mamet uses his character as the paradigmatic dramatic author and the plotless play as the paradigmatic dramatic vehicle:

Arthur:	Man meets squirrel. Squirrel bites man. Man kills squirrel. From nothing, *to* nothing. Watch now. "Nothing," rising action. Climax. Falling action. "Nothing." Eh?....
Edmond:	May I ask a question?
Arthur:	That's what you're here for.
Edmond:	What does this mean?
Arthur:	Meaning? Meaning?

Edmond: Yes.
Arthur: Ah, meaning!

[23]

Jewish aporia demonstrates the loss, not only of the subject and its meaning, but the loss of a language with which to articulate that loss, and even the loss of an accent to deliver it in. All that is left for Mamet is a rhythm of speech to give Nothing shape and sound. So what more do you need?

NOTES

1. William B. Collins, "Mamet's tag for his play on words," *The Philadelphia Inquirer*, 29 January 1990: D-3.

2. David Mamet, *Squirrels* (New York: Samuel French, 1974), 11. All subsequent page references are to this edition.

3. David Mamet, *Lakeboat* (New York: Grove, 1981), 52.

4. Samuel G. Freedman, "The Gritty Eloquence of David Mamet," *The New York Times Magazine*, 21 April 1985, 46.

5. Mimi Kramer comes closest to identifying the problem in a throwaway line in a review of *Bobby Gould in Hell*, "that slow, ponderous pattern of rhetorical question and Talmudic answer we have come to think of as Mamet's style." See "Heavenly City," *The New Yorker*, 25 December 1989, 80.

6. David Mamet, *Speed-the-Plow* (New York: Grove, 1988), 33. All subsequent page references are to this edition.

7. David Mamet, *American Buffalo* (New York: Grove, 1977), 75. All subsequent page references are to this edition.

8. David Mamet, *Duck Variations* in *Sexual Perversity in Chicago and Duck Variations* (New York: Grove, 1978), 87. All subsequent references are to this edition.

9. David Mamet, "A Sermon" in *Short Plays and Monologues* (New York: Dramatists Play Service, 1981), 43.

10. C.W.E. Bigsby quotes Mamet from Richard Gottlieb, "The 'Engine' that Drives Playwright David Mamet," *New York Times*, 15 January 1978, D-4.

11. C.W.E. Bigsby, *A Critical Introduction to Twentieth-Century American Drama*, Vol. 3 (Cambridge: Cambridge University Press, 1985), 262.

12. "American aphasia" is my phrase, summarizing Bigsby's account of Mamet's use of language:

The power of naturalistic language lies in what it reveals; the force of the language that Mamet's characters speak lies in what it attempts to conceal.

Teach's aggressive language is designed to cover his paranoid fears, but on either level it proves inoperative and this aphasia suggests something of his inability to shape experience into meaning.

See Bigsby, *A Critical Introduction*, 3:266.

13. Simon R. Pollack, *Jewish Wit for All Occasions* (New York: A&W Visual Library, 1979), 134.

14. Howard Stein, "The Lost People in David Rabe's Plays", in *David Rabe: A Casebook*, ed. Toby Zinman (New York: Garland, 1991), 25.

15. David Mamet, *Writing in Restaurants* (New York: Penguin, 1987), 43.

16. Baruch M. Bokser, *The Origins of the Seder* (Berkeley: University of California Press, 1984), 65.

17. Bokser, *The Origins of the Seder*, 66.

18. When I presented a shorter version of this paper at the Modern Language Association convention in Chicago in December, 1990, Hersh Zeifman, also on the panel, added this example during the question-and-answer period at the end of the session.

19. David Mamet, *Goldberg Street* in *Three Jewish Plays* (New York: Samuel French, 1987), 31.

20. Peter Brunette, "Mamet Views Cops Through a New Lens," *New York Times*, 10 Feb. 1991: 2, 13:3.

21. Brunette, "Mamet Views Cops," 13:3.

22. David Mamet, "The Decoration of Jewish Houses" in *Some Freaks* (New York: Viking, 1989), 9.

DAVID RADAVICH

Man among Men: David Mamet's Homosocial Order

Apart from C.W.E. Bigsby's booklength study (1985), curiously little scholarly attention has been paid to the insistent masculinity of David Mamet's plays. Published in editions frequently bedecked by the author's tauntingly phallic photo-portrait with cigar, the major plays either totally exclude or marginalize women, concentrating instead on myriad variations of homosocial male order. Mamet's dramatic world is both self-consciously and half-consciously male, with references to homosexuality, fear of violation by other men, insistent desire for male friendship, and pursuit of domination and acceptance operating at the core of the dramatic conflict. In one interview, Mamet admitted, "I don't know anything about women.... I'm more around men; I listen to more men being candid than women being candid" (Fraser 1976). Only two of his more successful plays, *Sexual Perversity in Chicago* (1978) and *Speed-the-Plow* (1987), include female characters at all, who, in both instances, are experienced by the male characters and by the audience as essential disturbers of the natural male order. The central body of Mamet's work concentrates on a single-minded quest for lasting, fulfilling male friendship protected from the threats of women and masculine vulnerability on the one hand and the destabilizing pursuit of power and domination on the other.

From *Fictions of Masculinity: Crossing Cultures, Crossing Sexualities*, edited by Peter F. Murphy. © 1994 by New York University.

Mamet's concerns about masculinity take on a particularly intense resonance in the latter part of the twentieth century, as the traditional bastions of male companionship have increasingly been called into question. Eve Kosofsky Sedgwick (1985) has described homosocial desire in a "pattern of male friendship, mentorship, entitlement, rivalry, and hetero- and homosexuality ... in an intimate and shifting relation to class" (1). This reference to class may be expanded to include age, rank, and other social factors creating a functional inequality. Chapter 1 of her pathbreaking *Between Men: English Literature and Male Homosocial Desire* details "male homosocial desire within the structural context of triangular, heterosexual desire" (16). Mamet's *Sexual Perversity* and *Speed-the-Plow* highlight this triangular configuration, whereas other of his plays deal with the struggle to form and define exclusively male bonds. A desire for dominance, usually between men of unequal rank or age, battles with an equally strong desire for loyalty and acceptance, resulting in a hard-won, intense, fundamentally unstable intimacy established in the absence of women.

From the outset, Mamet's plays have asserted the primacy of male friendship: "A man needs a friend in this life.... Without a friend, life is not .... It's lonely.... It's good to have a friend.... To help a friend in need is the most that any man can want to do" (97–98). This excerpt from the Seventh Variation of *The Duck Variations* (1978) represents a paean to such friendship, as two men in their sixties engage in "Spectator Sports" together, in this case observing ducks (not "chicks"), as a means of solidifying their bond. The men of Mamet's later plays bond through frequenting bars (*Sexual Perversity*, 1978), performing together (*A Life in the Theater*, 1977), or driving business deals (*Glengarry Glen Ross*, 1983; and *Speed-the-Plow*, 1987), but in each case the primacy of close male friendship is asserted in the face of intruders, either rival men or, more seriously, women.

Sexual Perversity presents the challenge in the form of Deborah, erstwhile lesbian, who becomes involved with Dan, the steady buddy of Bernie. In the course of the play, many sexual perversions are trotted out for verbal display, as the title suggests, but most involve the degradation of women: "The Way to Get Laid Is to Treat 'Em [Women] Like Shit"(22). In an early extended narrative, Bernie describes his encounter with a "chick" who dresses for sex in a Flak Suit, asks him to make war noises, then douses them both with gasoline and sets all on fire. A later narrative centers on King Farouk, who arranges to have "his men run a locomotive right through the broad's bedroom" and later "whacks her on the forehead with a ballpeen hammer" (34–35). Bernie acts as spokesman for most of these "perversities," though Deborah and Joan act out some of the vicissitudes of lesbian affections and jealousy. The one "perversion" omitted in the play—probably the most common variation from heterosexuality in our culture—is adult male homosexuality. Its absence appears all the more striking as Bernie successfully undermines and fights off the challenge Deborah presents to his relationship to Dan, so that at the end the two men reunite in a friendship that, although nominally situated in a heterosexual context of "casing chicks," nonetheless posits a male bond of superior endurance.

Although lacking some of the intellectual trappings of traditional comedy, Mamet's plays embody many of its major elements, including the disruptive intrusion by an outsider followed by chaos and the final reunion of the happy couple (in this case male). In *Sexual Perversity*, Dan's sexual interest in Deborah threatens to shatter the male bond, forcing Bernie to counterattack with measures that one usually associates with heterosexual dating: outings to the movie house, evenings in Bernie's apartment, and sojourns to the beach. After this concerted effort on Bernie's part, Dan succumbs to his eventual partner's way of thinking, explaining to another co-worker, "And *he* [Bernie], he puts his arm around my shoulder and he calms me down and he says, 'Dan, Dan ... don't go looking for affection from inanimate objects'" (53). The subtextual reference to women as "inanimate objects" brings the supremacy of male bonding full circle by play's end.

In the absence of a clear cause for Dan's break-up with Deborah, the bonding activities with Bernie that negate or exclude women serve to reassert the primacy of their same-sex friendship. Both men find it difficult to appreciate the otherness of female experience, which they consider either frivolous or irrelevant. While in bed with Deborah, Dan cannot imagine "having tits": "That is the stupidest question I ever heard. What man in his right mind would want tits?" (40). When Deborah confesses to having fantasized about other women the last time they made love, Danny responds, "The last time I masturbated I kept thinking about my left hand" (40). The solipsistic impulse, albeit in a comic context, serves to isolate both men from a deeper experience of the feminine. The fear of the female, and of female sexuality in particular, dominates Mamet's early plays, as males jostle for position and affection among themselves apart from women.

American Buffalo ([1975], 1981), one of Mamet's most successful plays, features an all-male cast in a Chicago pawnshop where homosocial desire finds its decadent arena. Unlike *Duck Variations*, with its placid contemplations, this play foregrounds homosocial pursuit and defense and introduces the cuckolding and rape imagery important to Mamet's portrayal of American capitalism. In an interview Mamet reiterates the important link: "Look at Delorean. He completely raped everybody in Northern Ireland with that scheme" (Roudané 1986, 74–75). Although in *Sexual Perversity* Bernie and Dan work together in a faceless contemporary office, the underworld of second-rate business functions in *American Buffalo* as a more symbolic setting for Mamet's portrait of capitalism gone awry.

At the outset of *Buffalo*, Dan chastises Bob for incompetence, exerting his dominance in a pattern that clearly establishes Mamet's concern with the man "above" and the man "below." In *Sexual Perversity*, Bernie functions as Dan's superior in experience, offering fatuous advice and controlling much of the subsequent action. Don maintains supremacy in *American Buffalo* more clearly through financial control of Bob, and through his rôle as teacher/mentor and status male. The allusion to education embodied in Joan is transferred here to both Teach and Don, who continually moralize, philosophize, and pontificate about the nature of life, people, and business. The "knowledge" actually taught, however, is both corrupt and clumsy, so that by the end, the traditional mentoring of males in the world of business has collapsed into mutual incompetence.

American Buffalo differs from other Mamet works in the intense triangular relationship among the men, where Teach clearly poses a threat to the central if unequal bond between Don and Bob. Their friendship is only haltingly acknowledged—at the end, after injuries and humiliation/threat bring them together—but Teach recognizes it and hopes to establish his own relationship with Don by replacing Bob and ousting Fletcher. The men jockey for one-on-one friendship within whose boundaries emotional loyalty can be assumed and women can be regarded with mutual distrust. Denigrations of women abound: "Only ... from the mouth of a Southern bulldyke asshole ingrate of a vicious nowhere cunt can this trash come" (803–4). And whenever Teach seeks to vent frustration with himself or his fellows, he resorts to homosexual slander ("you fruit") or images of impotence/emasculation ("dick on the chopping block") (884, 893). Clearly, insults that homosexualize or womanize men negate their potency, thereby diminishing their status and value.

Anxiety about manhood pervades these plays, at least partly the result of "improperly construed [masculine] initiations" (Raphael 1989, 144). "Makeshift" males struggle with "the deep-seated fear that [they] might never become 'men'" (145, 190). In *American Buffalo*, Teach responds to Don in anger, "I am not your wife.... I am not your nigger," where, presumably, the secondary status of both doubles the rhetorical effect of his outburst (888). Later, feeling rejected, he laments, "There is no friendship," and "I look like a sissy" (895). The threat of being emasculated, either by women (Grace and Ruthie, a lesbian couple) or by men, is everpresent, only to be allayed through a strong male bond that empowers each male in it. Hence the "honor among thieves" element in *American Buffalo* maximizes potency through a supposed pooling of expertise (in this case, a shared incompetence). (Roudané 1986, 76). At the end of the play, Don, through a clever Mametesque pun, tacitly acknowledges the intimate connection between sex and business: "It's all fucked up ... You fucked my shop up" (894). The twisted initiation ritual embodied in their struggle results in closer male bonds but leaves in its wake both physical wounds and the destruction of the locus of their enterprise.

Supplementing the central, all-male triangle in *American Buffalo* is a recurring motif of cuckoldry, whereby coins function as the battleground for sexual revenge on the successful man ("fucking fruit") as well as on the wife("dyke cocksucker"): "Guys like that, I like to fuck their wives" (847, 820). For the first time, Mamet ties business practices to the sexual/power act of rape in a singularly evocative metaphor of masculine revenge for perceived inadequacy. Indeed, rape and prostitution, primarily of men by men, becomes the central metaphor for American capitalism in Mamet's later plays. The desire for an enduring male bond is inextricably linked to a mutually conceived crime for the dual purpose of perpetration and profit. Beneath the comic surface, the dramatic structure reveals the swirling, conflicted emotions of men for and against other men.

A Life in the Theater (1977) contains the most penetrating stage metaphor of homosexual interconnection in all of Mamet's work. The older actor, Robert, discovers that his zipper is broken and reluctantly agrees to allow his younger colleague, John, to pin his fly for him. As Robert stands up on the chair, he urges John in the endeavor:

> *Robert*: Come on, come on. *[JOHN puts his face up against ROBERT's crotch.]* Put it in.... Come on, for God's sake.... Will you stick it in?
> *John*: Hold still. There. *[Pins fly awkwardly.]*
> *Robert*: Thanks a lot. (144–45)

This arresting metaphor captures the latent homosexual desires and fears implicit in the playwright's characterization of male friendship. Robert, symbolically emasculated by a broken zipper, stands physically above John on the chair and metaphorically above him by age and experience, while the young man attempts to "pin" him—a clever pun on sexual penetration and domination. At no point in the entire scene, clearly intended as a stage ruse for the audience's titillation, do the two males acknowledge either the humor or the sexual implications of their actions; subsequent interactions reflect no awareness of this sequence of events. The symbolic failure of the pinning suggests a taunting almost-consummation that results instead in collapse and lack of connection.

The sexual triangle implicit in several Mamet plays receives up-front treatment in *A Life in the Theater*, although the shared woman never appears. John accuses Robert of impregnating his wife, Gillian, but in a consummately comic scene, does not seem overwhelmingly shattered by the revelation: "What are we going to do about this?" (31). Elsewhere, the two men assert the primacy of their bond as Robert denigrates his female co-star, "When we're on stage she isn't there for me," and John responds by acknowledging his desire for substitution: "I wanted to be up there with you" (14–15). Later, John wipes the makeup off Robert's face, and they go out to dinner together, an occasion reported subsequently by John in a telephone conversation as "going out with ... an Actor" (24). At the end of the play, Robert cries, complaining that John makes him "feel small" (49). The transaction becomes complete when the older man gives the younger one money, solidifying the reversal in power and the insistent connection between (unconsummated) sex and lucre.

In contrast to *A Life in the Theater*, *Glengarry Glen Ross* (1983) showcases the sexopolitical battle of the male "pack," with one-on-one friendships relegated to somewhat lesser status. In yet another all-male play of characters now middle-aged, the focus shifts to male rape ("fucking up the ass") and enslavement (18). And the "screwing" is not merely verbal. The audience watches Moss "screw" Aaronow by forcing him into a criminal plot, one of many attempts by the men to emasculate other men, either psychologically or financially. In a moment of frustration, Roma declares, "We're all queers," and Levene accuses Williamson of "not having balls," establishing a figurative equivalence between homosexuality and castration (27,49). As Leverenz (1989) has pointed out, such cut-throat sexual dueling among males "has to do with manhood: a way of empowering oneself through someone else's humiliation" (245).

The sexual images in this play therefore turn correspondingly negative. Moss insults the police investigator by referring to him as a "cop without a dick" (41). Roma turns later to Williamson: "You stupid fucking cunt ... I don't care ... whose dick you're sucking on" (65). Here, the eunuch, the homosexual, and the female become equally debased versions of the male, as gender slurs are used to harass, insult, and blackmail other males. Such language of bravado, domination, and humiliation is immediately understood and never questioned by any of the characters. When Levene thinks he has made a legitimate blockbuster sale, he announces his triumph in genital terms: "And now ... I got my balls back" (70). The phallus thus valuates the currency not only in business but also in society at large. In the ethos of Mamet's plays, a man symbolically deprived of his penis through personal insecurity or deprecation by other males becomes, by definition, a faggot or a cunt, debased both sexually and professionally.

What's curious about *Glengarry*, and about most of Mamet's better-known works, is the marginalizing of any real sex. Gould and Karen spend a night together (on a male wager) in *Speed-the-Plow* but say virtually nothing about the love-making itself afterward. In *Sexual Perversity*, Dan and Deborah lounge together in bed, discussing the apartment, Deborah's lesbian experiences, and the virtues of "come" and penises. The noticeably tentative affection disappears altogether later in the play, for reasons unknown. In *Glengarry Glen Ross*, Roma declares sex essentially meaningless: "The great fucks that you may have had. What do you remember about them?" (28). In the masculine world of Mamet's early plays, men primarily pursue not sex but position ("above" or "below"), power, and male loyalty.

Somewhat later, in *The Woods* and *Edmond* (1987), what Sedgwick (1985) calls "homosexual panic" emerges as a central theme (89). In the latter play, Edmond and Glenna discuss their hatred of "faggots":

> *Edmond*: Yes. I hate them, too. And you know why?.... They suck
>   cock. (Pause.) And that's the truest thing you'll ever hear.
>   (266)

The context here, decidedly tongue-in-cheek, provides a stark contrast with Nick's confessions to Ruth in *The Woods*. Having invited Ruth to share a vacation by the lake, Rick makes clear his disinterest in making love: "Why don't you leave me alone?" (86). Finally, Nick confesses to a homosexual past:

> *Nick*: I have to tell you something.... I have to tell you we
>   would come up here as children. *[Pause.]* Although some
>   things would happen.... Although we were frightened....
>   And many times we'd come up with a friend. With
>   friends. We'd ask them here. *[Pause.]* Because we wanted
>   to be with them. *[Pause.]* Because.... *[Pause.]* Wait.
>   Because we loved them.
> *Ruth*: I know.
> *Nick*: Oh, my God, *[Pause. He starts to cry.]* I love you, Ruth.
>   (115–16)

Ruth's knowledge and acceptance in this passage provide the essential absolution, allowing Nick to break down and purge his anxieties. If the play ends inconclusively, Nick nonetheless moves tentatively beyond what Ruth calls "this manly stuff" he has "made up" (102).

Speed-the-Plow (1987) seems to move beyond the homophobia articulated in Mamet's earlier plays. Here, the homosexual imagery is noticeably positive and comic, accepted without reservation by the two main characters. Rather than hurling gay-bashing insults at each other, as in earlier plays, Fox and Gould refer to themselves as "two Old Whores" and the "*Fair*-haired boys" (23, 31–32). References to "*your* boy" and "*my* boy" turn males into commodities, and other gay references flow freely in the assumedly more tolerant atmosphere of the Hollywood movie set. Fox proposes filming a "*Buddy* picture" featuring black guys who "want to get him [the protagonist].... going to rape his ass" (12). The intimate link between rape and business is reiterated: "It's 'up the ass with gun and camera'" (27). As studiously as Mamet's earlier male characters refused to acknowledge homosexual elements in their behavior, Gould and Fox trade gay one-liners with a new-found freedom of expression: "They'll *french* that jolly jolly hem"; "Just let me turn one more trick"(33).

Like *Sexual Perversity* and *American Buffalo*, *Speed-the-Plow* again features a tight male bond threatened by an intruder and eventually reestablished after a threat of dissolution. Karen's rôle emerges more fully than in *Sexual Perversity*, partly because Joan and Deborah have become fused into one voice, offering a direct frontal attack on the bastion of male unity. Again, the relationship between Gould and Fox is noticeably unequal (Gould has been "bumped up" above Fox), and sexual references link directly to business:

> *Gould*: You put as much energy in your job as you put into kissing my ass ...
> *Fox*:   My job is kissing your ass. (39)

Their relationship dates back some eleven years, with Gould, in his new position, functioning as Fox's protector. As archetypal woman, however, Karen represents a severe threat to this male harmony, advocating the "moral high ground" that both Gould and Fox have abdicated in their pursuit of success in the world of men.

Karen is a secretary, symbolically temporary both professionally and sexually, with no surname, rendering her several stages inferior to either man, so that Fox, with obvious impunity, can threaten to have her killed if she does not leave. Unlike Gould, Karen exhibits a complete awareness of the sexual implications of their appointment to discuss the merits of the radiation screenplay, offering to palliate their mutual loneliness in a night together. Gould, the same man Fox wagered could not bed Karen, seems caught off guard by the straightforwardness of her proposition. Karen's probing dialogue reduces Gould to monosyllabic questions: "You came to? ... I asked you here to sleep with me? ... *I'm* frightened.... Why did you say you would come here anyway ... " (76–77; final ellipsis in original).

Fox counterattacks by calling Gould a "wimp," a "coward," a "whore," and a "ballerina" (92–94). In one of his most extreme insults, Fox claims, "You squat to pee" (92). The womanizing deprecations, noticeably lacking homosexual equivalents in this play, finally collapse as Fox utters his two quintessential claims on Gould's attention: "I love this guy, too" and, more poignantly, "Bob: I need you" (102,104). In all of Mamet, this is the baldest statement of homosocial desire for intense male friendship, forceful enough to overrule any female objection. When Karen later admits that she probably would not have slept with Gould had he not favored the "radiation script," their night together crumbles into a sham of (self-) deception and strategy, with whatever affection they might have exchanged evaporating into silence. Gould decides in favor of the "*Buddy* play," and the work ends suitably with the male "couple" reunited, albeit without any overt sexual interaction.

In *Speed-the Plow*, the perception of women as sexual "weakeners" or "corruptors" of men receives its most direct expression. Karen's influence on Gould diverts his attention and attitudes from what works in the male world (the "*Buddy* play") to what works in the world of higher, more humane values traditionally associated with women (the "radiation play"). More cogent than Deborah's in *Sexual Perversity*, her point of view nearly persuades Gould to take the "high road" he has abdicated in a long climb up the professional ladder. But Fox's claim proves the stronger, and Gould succumbs to the pressures of male bonding implicit in the world of business. Once again in Mamet, male friendship emerges as more powerful, more significant, and, ultimately, more enduring. As Roland Barthes (1978) described the potential threat of women in another context, "A man is not feminized because he is inverted but because he is in love" (14).

The male characters in Mamet's plays inhabit a homosocial milieu where male bonds offer the primary reality, where women threaten the tightly stretched, fragile if enduring fabric, and where sexuality is largely expressed in words and distorted transactions rather than in mutually satisfying love-making. The Mamet males, with the possible exception of Fox and Gould, fear the sexual intimacy their bond implies, turning that fear outward instead into a denigration of females and of other males as homosexuals and *castrati*. Sedgwick (1985) sees this "homosexual panic" as a central motivating force in the maintenance of the capitalist patriarchy (89). Not surprisingly, Mamet's plays wed male bonding to the often corrupt practices of business. The instability of the bonding, the fierce competitiveness with which his characters struggle to escape the dichotomy of their announced desires for women and their more enduring preference for the company of other men, suggests both the decay of the relatively comfortable old professional order and the panic of being forced to acknowledge the needs such relationships imply.

As Leslie Fiedler so provocatively pointed out in his *Love and Death in the American Novel* (1966), the masculine desire for an innocent, intimate bond transcending sex and operating outside the perceived strictures of female society has remained an enduring theme in American literature: "In our native mythology, the tie between male and male is not only considered innocent, it is taken for the very symbol of innocence itself; for it is imagined as the only institutional bond in a paradisal world in which there are no (heterosexual) marriages or giving in marriage (350)." Mamet's characterizations of male friendship establish him firmly within this tradition, evoking images of latter-day Huck and Jim attempting to negotiate the shoals of modern life on a raft. But the contemporary playwright's interpretation of this theme differs considerably from earlier manifestations by foregrounding the tensions inherent in such relationships and by deconstructing their self-willed innocence. The agitated "casing" of Dan and Bernie, the hard-won, unstable intimacy of Don and Bob or Gould and Fox, ranges far from the stylized boyhood innocence of Twain's Huck and Tom. More than any other American playwright, Mamet enacts a searching, multivalent drama of homosocial desire questioning and assessing itself.

As strategist, Mamet is essentially a comic satirist, with an underlying sense of anxiety and pain. On the one hand, his plays can be savagely funny in attacking the predatory instincts of Western enterprise capitalism. And his exploitation of sexual taboos for ridiculous effect places him squarely in the comic mainstream of verbal dexterity and social "tweaking". On the other hand, the central quest for satisfying male friendship underlies all his works, adding a more serious element that encourages audience sympathy for men seeking to find loyalty and acceptance in a world disturbingly competitive, hostile, and transitory. The duality of this conception results in a darkly comic artistic vision suited to a society in transition, moving from the comfortable economies of empire to the new, less stable realities of shared power and enterprise.

The structure of Mamet's major plays typically revolves around fortifying and defending besieged male friendships that nonetheless cannot be fully acknowledged or relied on. This sets up an inherently ironic perspective. Although most of Mamet's work results in a united male "couple," the dénouement cannot assure much equilibrium, given the professed heterosexual imperatives and inherent competitiveness of males as the playwright portrays them. Male friendships in Mamet are also destabilized by inequalities of age, rank, or experience, as well as by the men's inability to weave male friendships into their relations with women. The men in the later plays seem more comfortable with the terms of their bond, but without successful integration into the larger world of dual-gender interactions, such friendships must remain fragile, isolated, and defensive.

Yet the troubling, contradictory elements of Mamet's view of masculine reality provide much of the taut intensity of his dramatic view of decadent, wounded patriarchy. The old loyalties have broken down or become corrupt, and the formerly comfortable structures of male interactions have given way to confusion and dissatisfied longing (Robert Bly's, 1990, "grief for the absent father"). Pervading the major plays is a spirit of melancholy for something lost, a kind of lamentation for male friendship that seems ever-volatile and subject to unpredictable dissolution. Mamet's contribution has been to articulate the intimate connection between sexual and business practices and to underscore the homosocial desire driving relations among men. His characters seem caught in a shifting social pattern they do not comprehend, locked into what Rich (1984) calls "archaic sexual attitudes" (B4). Yet whatever faults they may have, whatever incompetence, stupidity, or dishonesty, they are driven by the extremity of their situations to admit a need and affection for each other that hitherto remained unvoiced. Mamet's searching, half-articulated stage vision of contemporary masculinity dramatizes the struggle of American males to accept and affirm one another in a shifting climate of gender expectations and identities.

BIBLIOGRAPHY

Barthes, Roland. *A Lover's Discourse: Fragments*. Trans. Richard Howard. New York: Hill and Wang, 1978.

Bigsby, C. W. E. *David Mamet*. Contemporary Writers Series. New York: Methuen, 1985.

Bly, Robert. *A Gathering of Men with Bill Moyers*. PBS Interview. WILL-TV, Champaign-Urbana. January 8, 1990.

Fiedler, Leslie. *Love and Death in the American Novel*. New York: Stein and Day, 1966.

Fraser, C. Gerald. "Mamet Plays Shed Masculinity Myth." *New York Times*, 5 July 1976, A7.

Leverenz, David. *Manhood and the American Renaissance*. Ithaca, NY: Cornell University Press, 1989.

Mamet, David. *American Buffalo*. 1975. In *Nine Plays of the Modern Theater*. Ed. Harold Clurman. New York: Grove, 1981.

———. *The Duck Variations*. In *Sexual Perversity in Chicago and The Duck Variations*. New York: Grove, 1978.

———. *Glengarry Glen Ross*. New York: Grove, 1983.

———. *A Life in the Theater*. New York: Samuel French, 1977.

———. *Sexual Perversity in Chicago and The Duck Variations*. New York: Grove, 1978.

———. *Speed-the-Plow*. New York: Grove, 1987.

———. *The Woods; Lakeboat; and Edmond*. New York: Grove, 1987.

Raphael, Ray. *The Men from the Boys: Rites of Passage in Male America*. Lincoln: University of Nebraska Press, 1989.

Rich, Frank. "Theater's Gender Gap Is a Chasm." *New York Times*, 30 September 1984, B1, 4.

Roudané, Matthew C. "An Interview with David Mamet." *Studies in American Drama, 1945–Present* 1 (1986): 72–81.

Sedgwick, Eve Kosofsky. *Between Men: English Literature and Male Homosocial Desire*. New York: Columbia University Press, 1985.

EDWARD J. ESCHE

David Mamet

T his chapter attempts to move away from a critical perspective that necessitates making absolute decisions about an entire play and towards an approach that is more open to the moment of audience response in the theatre. It follows Jocelyn Trigg's suggestions for further research on David Mamet by describing the playwright's own dramatic theory, and then discussing the technique of audience participation in Shakespeare's problem plays as a possible influence on Mamet's ideas.[1] The chapter concludes by applying the theoretical approach developed to two particular moments in *American Buffalo* and *Reunion*.

I

A considerable amount of criticism on drama addresses its material as if it were a static piece of writing. No doubt, for written texts or scripts of plays this is a perfectly legitimate methodology, time-honoured with such phrases as 'words on the page', but when speaking of a 'play', the fact of the live performance continually moving through time is often considered only slightly or even ignored. Thus, we often find plays read as bearing 'messages', or they have a 'final effect': *American Buffalo* shows the

From *American Drama*, edited by Clive Bloom. © 1995 by Lumiere Co-operative Press Ltd.

'possibilities for communion between men destroyed by "business"
pressures' and 'we are left in ... *American Buffalo* ... with a pessimistic sense
of the possibilities of human relationships'.[2] Perhaps so, but this kind of
criticism, which is by far in the majority of writing on Mamet, does not
address itself to what happens to an audience through the lineal time event
of spectating. It also places a heavy emphasis upon the didactic element in the
'final response', and does not consider the sometimes ambiguous element of
immediate response to moments in the plays.

The experience of a performed play is not static, even when we know
the entire script or 'what happens at the end'. Take, for example, a
production of *Measure for Measure*, a script I happen to have almost by
memory. Each time I see it in the theatre I am always 'caught' in the
performance in such a way as to have to make choices involving decisions
about character or situation. The choices are always open because there are
always alternatives. Let me cite just one example. At the point where Isabella
is requested by Marianna to beg Duke Vincentio to spare the life of Angelo,
Isabella's attempted rapist, I am always moved to choose for myself what
should be done: I always want to see Angelo executed for his crime. In some
productions I have even heard an inner voice chant directions to the Duke:
'Kill him, kill him, kill him ... '. But then, of course, I do not get my wish:
Isabella succeeds in her appeal and, as the Duke rescinds the order of
execution, Angelo is dragged kicking and screaming into the necessary
responsibilities of life. There are at least two points of interest here: first, the
character's choice to beg for her attempted rapist's life, and secondly, my
response *at that moment* as part of an audience. The second point of interest
is the one that most fascinates me, particularly in relation to David Mamet's
drama, because he often uses similar points of open choice to take us through
a process of participatory discovery, and further understanding through
reflection.

Mamet is extremely forthright about his art. He has written well and
clearly on dramatic theory, which will help us not only with his own plays but
also with the example of *Measure* mentioned above. He returns to three
specific areas in his writing on drama: the actor, the subject and the audience.
He says that the successful actor's 'performance will be compared not to *art*,
but to *life*; and when we leave the theatre after his performance we will speak
of *our life* rather than *his technique*'.[3] So, if *Measure* is acted well (and for the
sake of argument let us say that it has been), then the response to which I
referred above is really related to my life and not to false or cheap 'tricks' of
the acting. Mamet is very concerned with skill in acting learned through
practice and study:

This is what can and must be passed from one generation to the next. Technique—a knowledge of how to translate inchoate desire into clean action–into action capable of communicating itself to the audience. This technique, this care, this love of precision, of cleanliness, this love of theatre, is the best way, for it is love of the *audience*—of that which *unites* the actor and the house: a desire to share something which they know to be true.[4]

Here is one of the cornerstones of Mamet's dramatic theory: theatre is the unity of actor and audience in search of truth. Notice how the stress is, refreshingly and unusually, upon the act of communication to us as an audience. But what is that truth and what does it tell us?

Mamet clearly knows what it is not, and he indicts a great deal of contemporary American drama for presenting that which is not true:

To the greatest extent we, in an evil time, which is to say a time in which we do not wish to examine ourselves and our unhappiness; we, in the body of the artistic community, elect dream material (plays) which cater to a very low level of fantasy. We cast ourselves (for in the writing and the production and the patronage of plays we cannot but identify with the protagonist) in dreams of wish fulfilment.[5]

Such subject matter has no salutary effect; it merely gives us what we want, and we learn nothing. 'We leave the theatre after such plays as smug as after a satisfying daydream. Our prejudices have been assuaged, and we have been reassured that nothing is wrong, but we are, finally, no happier.'[6] So plays must not be purely wish fulfilment; they must be more, and for a very specific reason: because wish fulfilment will not make us truly happy. Again, the emphasis is on the effects created on an audience.

In an extremely useful piece entitled 'Radio Drama', Mamet articulates other essential elements of his theory.

To be effective, the drama must induce us to suspend our rational judgement, and to follow the *internal* logic of the piece, so that our *pleasure* (our 'cure') is the release at the end of the story. We enjoy the happiness of being a participant in the process of *solution*, rather than the intellectual achievement of having observed the process of construction.[7]

Although Mamet is writing about the experience of a play as a whole here, 'process' is one of the key words: it insists on the fact of a time continuum and it involves the audience directly in that continuum as a participant. 'He has said that the theatre is a place in which intent and will can be celebrated, and that no subject is a fit subject for drama which does not involve a possible choice.'[8] Choice is thus an absolute necessity, both from the point of view of character and, by extrapolation, from the point of view of the audience. But the experience of the choice is a fleeting one because the 'magic moments, the beautiful moments in the theatre always come from a desire on the part of artist *and* audience to live in the moment—to *commit* themselves to time'.[9] Again, Mamet is articulating a theory based upon audience participation in the temporal experience of drama, but this is not to say that a commitment to time necessitates the impossibility of analysing that moment we live in, as Mamet himself fully realises: 'the theatrical experience must be an *adoration* of the *evanescent*, a celebration of the transient nature of individual life (and, perhaps, through this, a glimpse at some less-transient realities)'.[10] Those 'less-transient realities' are nothing less than the truths he claims as the object of the commitment of actor and audience. Even though the moment is evanescent, the critic can keep faith with Mamet by freezing that moment in time through memory, which is one way of demonstrating how we leave the theatre reflecting upon our world.

So, to take the simple Shakespearean example above, my wish to see Angelo dead tells me nothing about the character; rather, it tells me a great deal about myself when faced with the possibility of the implementation of forgiveness or even grace in the face of what I find most appalling. When my choice is 'wrong'—when the logic of the play dictates that Angelo must live, rather than die as I wish—the experience of the moment forces me into a recognition or a remembrance of my morality in my world, which is exactly the opposite of wish fulfilment. In Mamet's terms, drama fulfils its proper function: 'The theatre is not a place where one should go to forget, but rather a place where one should go to remember.'[11] The participant who reflects is then led on to questions of further exploration. Who am I to decide issues of life and death, particularly when the 'victim' herself disagrees with me, or on what basis do I make my choices at the moment I make them? Every participating member of the audience undergoes a similar experience. In short, we leave the theatre talking about ourselves and our relation to the moral world in which we live. The point is that the 'play' is not posing an abstract question about mercy or justice; it is putting us in the position where we must *make* choices in a particular moment, if, that is, we are active participants in the drama. The moment is open for us in the sense that more than one option exists at the time of compulsory choice, but the moment is so constructed that only one alternative carries the logical weight of the play. A write who has confidence in an audience pays us all a compliment by having faith in us, faith that we will have enough intelligence to try to understand our participation, particularly when it is wrong, and to reflect upon it. Shakespeare is such a writer, and so is David Mamet.

I did not choose *Measure for Measure* gratuitously: it employs exactly the same techniques of audience participation that Mamet uses in *American Buffalo* and *Reunion*. In other words, David Mamet is working in a form that could be described as the contemporary problem play along Shakespearean lines: a problem play focuses on 'a concern with a central moral problem, which will inevitably take the form of an act of choice confronting the protagonist, and in relation to which we are in doubt of our moral bearings'.[12] I would like to isolate two moments of participatory choice in Mamet's plays, similar to the one described above in *Measure for Measure*, which force us into positions where we may be unsure of our moral bearings, but which also force us to reflect upon truths about ourselves and our world.

II

The first moment that I would like to examine is one in the climax of the play *American Buffalo* where Teach and Don believe that Bobby has treacherously betrayed them, so they turn on him and Teach beats him. The process of active audience participation in this moment is almost exactly the same as in Shakespeare's *Measure for Measure*: we are led in one direction only and to one choice, but with, I think, much more chilling results. The script is as follows:

Teach:	I want for you to tell us here and now (and for your own protection) what is going on, what is set up ... where *Fletcher* is ... and everything you know.
Don	[*sotto voce*]: (I can't believe this.)
Bob:	I don't know anything.
Teach:	You don't, huh?
Bob	No.
Don:	Tell him what you know, Bob.
Bob:	I don't know it, Donny. Grace and Ruthie ... [TEACH *grabs a nearby object and hits* BOB *viciously on the side of the head*]

> *Teach*:   Grace and Ruthie up your ass, you shithead; you don't
> fuck with us, *I'll* kick your fucking head in. (I don't give
> a shit ...)
> [*Pause*][13]

We are near the end of the play, and the scene has been contrived to take us
into a moment of choice concerning Bob. We are forced to judge him, as we
were forced to judge Angelo, and, as in *Measure*, we make our decision based
upon a considerable amount of background knowledge informing the
situation of the moment.

Don and Teach are waiting in 'Don's Resale Shop' for Fletcher; all
three are going to rob a vacant apartment. Much earlier in the play Bob said
that he had spotted a man leaving the apartment with a suitcase as if going
on a weekend holiday. The man recently bought a buffalo-head nickel from
Don for a very high price, $90, but Don believes that he has been 'swindled'
because the coin could be worth considerably more money.[14] The planned
robbery is to steal whatever coins are available in the apartment and sell them
to a coin dealer. The participants were originally to be Don and Bob, but
Teach has forced Bob out and Don has brought Fletcher in. As Don and
Teach wait on the night, Bob appears twice: once to sell Don a buffalo head
nickel, and then to bring the news that Fletcher has been mugged and taken
to hospital with a broken jaw. Both appearances have a direct bearing on the
above moment of the scene.

Bob is a drug addict that Don has befriended, and something has been
made of the surrogate father–son relationship between them,[15] but for our
purposes the addiction is much more important because the addict is a highly
charged sign in our society, one which reads in several ways: the sign has
connotations possibly of evil, but certainly of untrustworthiness. And we
know that Bob is indeed incapable of performing even the simplest of tasks,
because earlier in the play he was sent to buy breakfast but did not bring back
a coffee for Don and forgot to buy something for himself. A good actor will
keep the fact of the addiction firmly in the audience's consciousness: Bruce
Macvittie, for instance, constantly sniffed throughout the 1984 London
revival of the play.[16] Finally, the addict is also a sign of cunning: s/he will do
anything to feed the habit. So when Bob enters earlier in the scene under
discussion with the buffalo-head nickel and requests $50 for it, one
explanation that could be chosen by the audience might well be that he wants
the money for his habit. But a short time later, at Bob's second appearance
in the scene, when he conveys the information of Fletcher's mugging and
thus his inability to take part in the robbery with Don and Teach, we are led

to suspect with Teach that Bob and Fletcher have indeed carried out the robbery themselves.

The suspicion deepens when Bob says that Fletcher has been taken to Masonic Hospital and Don's telephone call to the hospital proves that no one by the name of Fletcher Post has been admitted. I think that simply to agree with Teach would be impossible even at this point, because he is not closely attached to the audience anywhere in the play, but Don's siding with him in the interrogation is, I think, the deciding factor in our choice as to whom to believe and as to which scenario of off-stage action we choose to construct for our own reading. Thus, the buffalo-head nickel that Bob earlier sold to Don is obviously a spoil of the Bob–Fletcher theft of the apartment, and Don has been fooled into buying it back when he had wanted to steal it himself. Bob's behaviour, as we, I think, must judge it up to the moment of the blow, is dishonourable, even among these petty thieves.

I am arguing nothing less than that, although we may not like it, our judgement at the point immediately before Teach's attack on Bob is clouded by the choices forced on us by Mamet, or rather the choice of judgement that Mamet leads us into making, which is that Bob has transgressed. The moment of enlightenment, of reversal, of recognition that we are wrong begins at the moment that the 'object' cracks Bob's skull. But the point is that in the theatre the dramatic effect of the scene is such that we are 'caught out'. We may well know that Teach is also extremely dishonourable, or we may think that Bob's punishment does not fit his crime, but as we are following the logic of this story, at the moment of the scene I have quoted, if Bob has done what I am certain we think that he has done, then our choice of judgement is against him and in favour of the line of argument advanced by Teach and, most importantly, by Don.

Of course we are wrong. Bob is obviously an addict, and as such he operates as a sign, not of evil or menace, but of confusion. His untrustworthiness is a result of his confusion. Instead of saying 'Columbus' when asked about the hospital Teach was in, he confused it with 'Masonic'. Instead of the individual *par excellence* who founded the country he lives in, Bob thought of an organisation pledged to a collective position of help within the society (a popular reading of the Masonic hospital activity in Mid-Western America). And his confusion is throughout the play. Instead of actually seeing the man leave his apartment, he lied to redeem himself in Don's eyes after Don had lectured him for neglecting to keep a constant watch. I suppose one might say that he confusedly tried to be part of a mini-society, that which revolves around Don's shop, into which he was incapable of fitting. He was simply in pursuit of that which we all 'desire most, which is love and a sense of belonging'.[17] But we have drifted very far away from the stated critical position now: an analysis of the effect of *our* choice to believe, with Don and Teach, that Bob had 'crossed' them and carried out the robbery with Fletcher.

We must admit that we were wrong in our choice, in much the same way that we had to admit we were wrong in *Measure*; but, more importantly, here we are wrong without cause. We judge in the way we do because Bob is an addict and, therefore, flawed, not because he (unlike Angelo) has done anything wrong. Quite the contrary, he has tried to do what he thinks is right throughout the play, and his actions have always been motivated by a friendliness to others, not by an obsession with himself. Examples of this include his asking Ruthie if she is mad at Teach, of buying a new buffalo-head nickel for Don, and even of lying to Don about the man leaving his apartment. In fact, he is the only character of the three in the play to have consistent contact with figures outside the junkshop. Upon reflection, he is an immensely sympathetic, although pathetic, creation, but why not just before he is attacked? Mamet has made us choose our judgement, exactly as Shakespeare does, which places us upon unsure moral ground: we judge the way we do because we have within us a desire to victimise, a desire to define ourself as not like whatever 'other' we care to identify, and there are few more 'other' than a shifty, scheming junkie, or so the inner voice might tell us. The platitudes are familiar. And immediately after the attack, Don says, 'You brought it on yourself.' He, like us, mistakenly believes that Bob has misbehaved and deserves what he gets, but the terrible irony of the line is that Bob did in fact bring it on himself by trying to behave with some degree of integrity of friendship in a predatory world. Here is the moral issue at the centre of the moment, that a real need of friendship can be so rewarded in this (our) world, a world described by Teach:

> [*Teach picks up a dead-pig sticker and starts trashing the junkshop*]
> The Whole Entire World.
> There Is No Law.
> There Is No Right And Wrong.
> The World Is Lies.
> There Is No Friendship.
> Every Fucking Thing. (p. 107)

Here is the sound of despair. But we would be wrong to listen to it, and what attracts me to Mamet's drama is that he gives us credit for the intelligent honesty to recognise that we would be wrong, however seductive such a position may be at the time. He has said that 'Every reiteration of the idea that *nothing matters* debases the human spirit',[18] and by recognising not only that our choice just before Bob is struck was wrong, but also why it was wrong, we can gain an insight into one of those 'less transient realities' which constitutes moral truth in our world.

III

Reunion is a play composed entirely of conversations which weave into one long exchange between a father, Bernie, aged 53, and a daughter, Carol, aged 24. He is a reformed alcoholic who abandoned her and her mother 20 years ago. The meeting we witness as the play is their first for 20 years and Carol has initiated it. Although Bernie speaks about three-quarters of the scripted lines, Carol's words carry most of the weight of the drama. In the penultimate scene of the play, Carol confesses, 'I feel cheated. / And, do you know what? I never had a father.'[19] She follows this with a more detailed articulation of her needs, and why she has chosen the present moment to address them:

> *Carol*: And I don't want to be pals and buddies; I want you to be
> my father.
> [*Pause*]
> And to hear your goddamn war stories and the whole
> thing.
> And that's why now because that's how I feel.
> [*Pause*]
> I'm entitled to it.
> Am I?
> Am I? (pp. 38–9)

Here is a point in the play where an active audience must make a choice as we share in the character's experience. We are, presumably, at the heart of the matter—she came to claim Bernie as her father. First, do we accept the question Carol asks: is she entitled to 'it', that is, a father? After what we have seen and heard, particularly about the misery which the absence of the father has caused, we, like Bernie, have no choice but to reply, 'Yes'; however, that assent is forced upon us by the obvious nature of the question. We might even say that we reveal our desire for wish fulfilment in our answer. But the affirmative answer poses a further complication: can someone who 'never had a father' (in the sense of lived experience) get one? Now the answer to that question lies at the heart of our response to the play, and, I think, at the heart of our response to our world.

Bernie goes on to say that 'there's no reason ... / I can't make it up to you' (p. 39), but, again, we must judge the statement. From what we have seen and what we have heard, this cliché, like so many others Bernie has mouthed, sounds hollow and weak; again, the precise characteristics of wish fulfilment. What does 'make it up to you' mean? Carol, who is so clearly the central character of the play, earlier responded to another of Bernie's clichés, 'Life goes on'. She said, '... Oh, yeah, life goes on. And no matter how much of an asshole you may be, or may have been, life goes on' (p. 29). In other words, the cliché levels the meaning of its object, here life, to basic banalities, but Carol's response is questioning that levelling process and subtly shifting the ground of our criteria of decision-making to a wider assessment of behaviour—either you are or are not an asshole. Bernie, by almost anyone's judgement, must fit that role to a T, but the judgement of character is not of prime concern here. What is of concern is the simple and easy recourse to cliché as a way of sliding off the issue of responsibility. But an active audience cannot so easily slide with Bernie, because to endorse his position is to judge that Carol's plight is acceptable. It is to say, quite simply, that she is not entitled to a father.

This brings us back to the penultimate scene of the play, where Bernie uses another cliché, which is not only banal but has no meaning at all. The assertion that he will 'make it up' must refer to the losses that Carol has suffered through Bernie's 20-year absence. That absence has occurred through time, the same dimension through which we watch the play, but unlike our experience, the 20-year 'past' contains no memory of shared experience, so there is no possibility of reclamation. Bernie is actually suggesting that he can recreate time;[20] he is pathetically absurd, but, again, his wish is not the point. A sympathetic spectator may also wish to see a 'happy Reunion', and may even jump at the cliché offering, as have several critics,[21] but such a sentimental reaction is only to support an impossibility: time cannot be reclaimed. Or to put it another way, because lost time is irretrievable (such is the crushingly terrifying truth of our world), our desire to wish it not so only points to the enormous importance of time, which, in this case, can be noted as a stable and constant father–daughter relationship.

The real strength of *Reunion* as a play lies in its forcing us into recognising the dilemma where comfortable wish fulfilment passes for truth. Mamet takes a very large risk by giving us the credit to think and reflect on the choice that he has forced us into within the context of drama. The point of our answer to Carol's question is that it focuses on the large moral question of proper paternal behaviour in our world, a world in which a cliché such as 'I'll make it up to you' passes for an acceptable response to loss. Paternal responsibility, once dodged, creates irreversible damage. This is a moral point of almost extreme simplicity, and, I think, it is irrefutable, given the 'fact' of the misery Carol continually voices throughout the play. As she stands in front of us claiming her right to have a father, and as we agree with her, we know, by the very depth of our desire, that she is simultaneously demonstrating the impossibility of reclaiming her father in that lost past. The play then presents a dilemma of profound moral dimensions; and our unsureness, the problem of the paly, lies in the final irreconcilability of desire with fact.

NOTES

1. Jocelyn Trigg says that 'studies need to devote more time to Mamet's indebtedness to classical and Renaissance plays [and] his own views of theatre (as expressed most characteristically in *Writing in Restaurants*)' (Jocelyn Trigg, 'David Mamet', in Philip C. Kolin (ed.), *American Playwrights since 1945: A Guide to Scholarship, Criticism and Performance* (New York: Greenwood Press, 1989) pp. 282–3). To date (early 1991) only one study has been made of Renaissance influences on Mamet: see Douglas Bruster, 'David Mamet and Ben Jonson: City Comedy Past and Present', *Modern Drama*, vol. 33 (September 1990) pp. 333–46.

2. Dennis Carroll, *David Mamet* (London: Macmillan, 1987) pp. 51, 50.

3. David Mamet, *Writing in Restaurants* (New York: Viking Penguin, 1986) p. 127. All quotations from Mamet's essays are from this easily available reprint edition rather than the sometimes less accessible originals.

4. Ibid., pp. 20–1.

5. Ibid., p. 10.

6. Ibid.

7. Ibid., pp. 13–14.

8. Caroll, *Mamet*, p. 20, citing David Mamet, 'Decadence' (typescript), pp. 1–2.

9. Mamet, *Writing*, p. 30.

10. Ibid.

11. Ibid., p. 29.

12. Ernest Schanzer, *The Problem Plays of Shakespeare: A Study of 'Julius Caesar', 'Measure for Measure', 'Antony and Cleopatra'* (London: Routledge & Kegan Paul, 1963) p. 5. I cite Schanzer's definition even though he locates the moral dilemma at a different point than I do in *Measure for Measure*. Mamet, of course, labels *American Buffalo* a tragedy: see Henry I. Schvey, David Mamet Interview, 'Celebrating the Capacity for Self-knowledge', *New Theatre Quarterly*, vol. 13

(February 1988) p. 94, for the playwright's most cogent statement on the play's genre to date.

13. David Mamet, *American Buffalo* (London: Methuen, 1984) p. 97. All subsequent page references are to this edition.

14. For discussions of the play as attacking the American business ethic, see Jack V. Barbera, 'Ethical Perversity in America: Some Observations on David Mamet's *American Buffalo*', *Modern Drama*, vol. 24 (September 1981) pp. 270–5; June Schlueter and Elizabeth Forsyth, 'America as Junkshop: the Business Ethic in David Mamet's *American Buffalo*', *Modern Drama*, vol. 26 (December 1983) pp. 492–500; C.W.E. Bigsby, *David Mamet* (London: Methuen, 1985) pp. 63–85; Caroll, *Mamet*, pp. 31–40; and William W. Demastes, 'David Mamet's Dis-integrating Drama', in *Beyond Naturalism: A New Realism in American Theatre* (New York: Greenwood Press, 1988), among others.

15. See, for instance, Bigsby, *Mamet*, p. 84.

16. Long Wharf Theater Company, Duke of York's Theatre, London, 24 July 1984 (directed by Arvin Brown; with J. J. Johnston as Donny, Bruce Macvittie as Bobby, and Al Pacino as Teach).

17. Mamet, *Writing*, p. 36; see also p. 73 for comments on Mamet's own position as outsider.

18. Ibid., p. 21.

19. David Mamet, *Reunion & Dark Pony* (New York: Grove Press, 1979) p. 38. All subsequent page references are to this edition.

20. I am convinced that Bernie's view of the past has a literary precedent in Jay Gatsby: "'Can't repeat the past?' he cried incredulously. "Why of course you can!"' (F. Scott Fitzgerald, *The Great Gatsby*, in *The Bodley Head Scott Fitzgerald*, vol. 1 (London: Bodley Head, 1958) p. 106).

21. See extracts from reviews by Richard Christiansen, Richard Eder and Harold Clurman in Nesta Jones (ed.), *File on Mamet* (London: Methuen, 1991) pp. 29–31; Ruby Cohn, *New American Dramatists, 1960–1980* (London: Macmillan, 1982) pp. 44–5; and Carroll, *Mamet*, pp. 111–12, But for an opposing view, see Bigsby, *Mamet*, pp. 38–9.

MICHAEL L. QUINN

Anti-Theatricality and American Ideology: Mamet's Performative Realism

Davidᴰ Mamet's dramatic writing, for all its apparent seriousness, and the artistic enthusiasm its effects have aroused, has not been very thoroughly explained.[1] That it seems conventionally realistic helps to make it seem familiar, and some of the best criticism of Mamet has been an attempt to recuperate the value of an artistically fluent and culturally sensitive realism.[2] But from the standpoint of meaning, Mamet's apparent lack of a representational strategy—that is, his realism—tends to make his work seem even more opaque. Simple representational realistic explanations of Mamet are too easy, if the vividness of the dramatic effect and the intensity of the intellectual controversies that the plays have aroused are also to be taken seriously by poststructuralist critics. I argue that Mamet's plays use a specific realistic rhetoric to strike a deep but somewhat inaccessible chord in American intellectuals—inaccessible because the critics themselves often participate in the same ideological processes that form the matrix of Mamet's work.[3] Realism is not in this case representational but expressive, focusing on performed actions rather than mimesis, and making judgments of truth a matter of active construction rather than of comparison with an *a priori* reality. As Mamet notes in his own essay on the subject, "In discarding the armor of realism, he or she [the artist] accepts the responsibility of making

From *Realism and the American Dramatic Tradition*, edited by William W. Demastes. © 1996 by the University of Alabama Press.

every choice in light of specific meaning, of making every choice assertive rather than protective."[4]

Mamet's self-proclaimed iconoclasm is a kind of doctrine informed by a system of ritualized liberal dissent in which membership in the national tradition depends upon a declared rejection of the current state of cultural affairs. The principal theorist of this perspective is Sacvan Bercovitch, who points out not only how this pattern manifests itself in a set of texts from the Puritans through the foundational documents of American government to the New England Renaissance, but also how this narrative of American Puritan culture is a deliberate creation of twentieth-century literary historians like Perry Miller and F.O. Matthiessen.[5] Perhaps the crucial figure in this tradition is Emerson, who "had decided, on reconsidering the attacks on individualism, that the remedy was not to abandon it, but to draw out its potential,"[6] that is, the link between individual self-creation and the collective creation of American community. Bercovitch points out that such a closure is virtually impossible, but in working through its visionary demands, American artists have used this political paradox as a basis for constantly renewed visions of authentic American creativity. Bercovitch's thesis also points out how Dennis Caroll's reading of Mamet as an artist of "dichotomy" and "paradox", cohering "in the personality he projects" can be joined with C. W. E. Bigsby's attempts to locate Mamet within an American cultural landscape.[7]

In theatrical history, this pattern of community formation through dissent—the rejection of American culture in the name of American values— is very common. (Consider, for example, the Group Theatre.) Such a cultural pattern, applied in an analysis of Mamet's favorite ideas and artistic techniques, can help to establish a critical context for understanding Mamet's work while also explaining something about his embattled but enthusiastic reception. Americans, like anyone working in the context of a naturalized ideology, often find it very difficult to undertake a culturally based analysis of their own literature; what passes for such criticism usually tends to participate in the politics of empowering denunciation, not theorizing its own implication in the pattern. In Mamet's case, the ideologically effective aspects of dramatic construction are often simply taken for something bold, hardheaded, and realistic, rather than as gestures in a standard romantic ritual of American intellectual culture.

Only a few steps are necessary for a writer like Mamet to position himself in the role of a dissenting, revolutionary artist with a unique perspective. One of the first steps is to identify some orthodoxy that can be decried as ruinous, or perhaps un-American. In Mamet's case, this orthodoxy tends to follow the pattern outlined by his intellectual hero, Thorstein

Veblen, of excoriating a greedy bourgeoisie—the class that requires conformity to a way of doing business and administering justice that serves those in power, and ruins the life of the ordinary man.[8] In theatre history, this kind of dissent usually finds its object in Broadway.[9] The decadent commercial theatre is then indicted in a vituperative jeremiad—laden with the rhetoric of the pulpit—which also often outlines a visionary path to redemption through the restoration of neglected moral values: truth, authenticity, selfless commitment to art, reason, etc.[10] In Mamet's case, such public comments are easy to find, especially in his essays and speeches. In "Decadence," for example, he decries the corruption of what he sees as the current dominance of a "theater of good intentions":

> We are in the midst of a vogue for the truly decadent in art— for that which is destructive rather than regenerative, self-referential rather than outward-looking, elitist rather than popular. This decadent art is elitist because it cannot stand on its merits as a work of personal creation. Instead it appeals to a prejudice or predilection held mutually with the audience.
>
> This appeal is political, and stems from the political urge, which is the urge to control the actions of others. It is in direct opposition to the artistic urge, which is to express oneself regardless of the consequences. I cite "performance art," "women's writing" ... badges proclaiming a position.
>
> Plays which deal with the unassailable investigate nothing and express nothing save the desire to investigate nothing.
>
> It is incontrovertible that deaf people are people, too; that homosexuals are people, too; that it is unfortunate to be deprived of a full and happy life by illness or accident; that it is sobering to grow old.
>
> These events ... equally befall the Good and the Bad individual. They are not the result of conscious choice and so do not bear on the character of the individual. They are not the fit subject of drama, as they do not deal with the human capacity for choice. Rather than uniting the audience in a universal experience, they are invidious. They split the audience into two camps; those who like the play and those who hate homosexuals (deaf people, old people, paraplegics, etc.).[11]

Mamet's grouping of banal social realists and the formalist avant-garde may have seemed in 1986 like an unlikely orthodoxy, though it has been repeated often in recent years in denunciations of the "politically correct."[12] What matters for ritual purposes, though, is merely Mamet's ability to construct the current scene as moribund, in a kind of statement that is not argued but rather performed. J.L. Austin would call such a ritualized statement an "illocutionary speech act," a kind of "performative" speech that constitutes some state of affairs through linguistic action; other examples would be things like promises, oaths, and declarations, including the political documents that form the bases of governments.[13] Despite Mamet's often acute consciousness of ritual behaviors, especially within the American contexts of holidays and masculine activities, he does not seem particularly sensitive to his own use of the jeremiad as a tool for his political empowerment.

The second requirement for Bercovitch's ritual of dissent is the construction of a unique individuality, a narrative of genesis and personal growth. Mamet's exceptionalist character is again constructed most clearly in his essays: in personal reflections, descriptions of his unhappy childhood at home, the idealizing influence of Old Chicago, his part-time jobs, his Slavic-Jewish heritage, and comments on the unique progress of his career. In one of the notes from *The Cabin* on Chicago radio, Mamet shows considerable cultural awareness about constructing his personality in this creative political context: "The idea in the air was that culture was what we, the people, did. The idea was—and is—that we were *surrounded* by culture. It was not alien to us. It was what the people did and thought and sang and wrote about. The idea was the particularly Chicagoan admixture of the populist and the intellectual. The model, the Hutchins model, the Chicago model of the European freethinker, was an autodidact: a man or woman who so loved the world around him or her that he or she was moved to investigate it further—either by creating works of art or by appreciating those works."[14]

Many of the exceptional characteristics that Mamet claims for himself, which have found expression in his plays, are tied to one aspect or another of what seem to be perfectly ordinary experiences. Yet the conviction remains in Mamet that the unique combination of experiences—the history of choices and conditions that produces his artistic consciousness—is solely his own, as fully individual as are his inherent human talents. This approach to identity is not representational but expressive; people constitute themselves not by thinking of themselves as copies but rather by thinking of themselves as constituted through actions based in their innate desires and qualities. These actions can then take on a pronounced cultural charge. For example, Mamet often seems so fully identified with the Chicago of the past that his nostalgia strains credibility; though born in 1947, he writes with an acute consciousness of his own "aging", and as if he were himself present at crucial cultural moments like the 1934 Century of Progress Exhibition. Mamet, then, claims exceptional status primarily because he thinks of himself as though he has come from an earlier time: the grittier, more inventive, and more communal Chicago before 1968, the time between Al Capone and Richard Daley (when Chicago writers like Carl Sandburg routinely claimed to represent America, too, by embodying its energy or its history of bootstrap immigrant prosperity). The absurdity of Mamet's wish for this subjectivity only emphasizes its constructed quality, which is even more evident when he folds into it—sometimes even in messianic terms—the ideal of the autodidact and the romantic writer. The title of his second book of essays, *Some Freaks*, is Mamet's way of identifying those individuals, like himself, who are leaders because they "do not fit the norm."[15] Mamet's Chicago is as fully laden with American ideology as was the New England of Henry David Thoreau, whom Mamet imitates in his Vermont cabin.

Typically the American narrative of dissent ushers in a new vision of community, often a political ideal retrieved through personal struggle or travel to a strange place. Mamet treats his ordinary experiences, in French Canada, in a neighborhood pool hall, or at a part-time job, as if they were such such struggles or journeys; in any case, they supposedly offered life lessons. In Mamet's life today this ideal community might be Cabot, Vermont, the village where he sometimes lives and writes, or the neighborhood of his Boston row house, before the area was ruined by division into rental units. In Mamet's version of theatre history, such an ideal scene might be something like the Group Theatre's retreat, or the long day in the Slavyansky Bazaar when the Moscow Art Theatre was conceived. But Mamet's broader political vision is never quite so concretely stated; it seems to be conventionally Jeffersonian, though perhaps even more nearly Rousseauian: an American community where politicians tell the truth, friendship is sacred, simple customs are cherished, and men can be men.[16] This sort of sustaining vision underlies many of the plays like an ideological subtext, a wish tacitly shared among sympathetic characters. Yet Mamet's America is rarely dramatized as a place that might actually exist; rather, Mamet's realism is a coming to terms with the difficulty—even the impossibility—of living such ideals.[17]

If the artist and the American individual are free to constitute themselves, to create their visions through the simple action of declaring or performing them, of acting them out, then the negative aspect of Mamet's realism, its paradoxical ideological unveiling, is the dramatic debunking of such constitutive gestures as mistakes of confidence, as willful illusions that the current state of the world cannot sustain. Realism in this context is not a scientific avant-garde, nor even, as Mamet himself notes, is it quite a "scenic truth" in the same way as it was for Stanislavsky; rather, the realistic attitude becomes a skeptical, often physical control on dreams of a better life.[18] This is not exactly the same kind of realism that Jonas Barish would call an "anti-theatrical prejudice," though Mamet often indicts the theatrical when it is abused as a rhetoric of deception in everyday life.[19] Mamet's constant concern in his writings on the theatre, and in his explanations of his style, is with *action*, which he theorizes as a constitutive, authentic movement of the mind and body, as opposed to a less vital, static or mimetic way of living and showing life. In this regard the Method actor is even, for Mamet, an emblem of virtuous life: "When, once again, actors are cherished and rewarded who bring to the stage or the screen generosity, desire, *organic life*, actions performed freely—without desire for reward or fear of either censure or misunderstanding—that will be one of the first signs that the tide of our introverted, unhappy time has turned and that we are once again eager and prepared to look at ourselves."[20] To the extent that Mamet's theatre of action is an attempt not merely to *represent* but actually to *constitute* his vision of a better life, the theatre has special powers. Theatre in such a view does not consciously imitate poetry, but the enactment of vital dialogue might attempt to perform the poetry of life. Theatricality exists in this case in a strange double bind; it can express the truth of things and events, but it can also be used to hide that truth through fantasies or lies. Such an emphasis on action may explain Mamet's preference for a small group of loyal performers, which keeps offstage dramatic intrigue at a minimum.

Consequently the theatrical act within Mamet's work is also, most often, an act of everyday deception, a risky move to create an illusive advantage. Mamet's theatre constitutes an orthodox, illusively realistic world of the play, full of lies, and then these must eventually come undone in an even "more real" scene of social debunking, physical constraint and/or theatrical undercutting. There are a few basic kinds of theatrical scenes in Mamet's work, and these are usually central to what is at stake in the drama. Once these are outlined, I think the anti-theatrical, ideological flow of Mamet's realistic writing will be fairly clear—a dissenting American anti-theatricality, designed to affirm his characters' self-constitutive, performative actions but also to reveal the destructiveness of lies.

THE BUSINESS SCAM

Probably the most famous kind of theatricality within Mamet's dramas, continuing through the filmscript for *Hoffa*, concerns the intrigues of businessmen, whether their purposes are within or, most often, outside of the laws of commerce.[21] In the former case, Mamet seems to criticize the conventional structure of capitalism from the top down; those with the most power and money tend to be able to create situations in which those with the least must scheme for an advantage. When these same ordinary people choose to live outside the law, Mamet's implied criticism falls more directly on the illusions they produce to dupe their victims. In *American Buffalo*, Donny Dubrow is poised on the brink of such a choice. He begins his scheme with Bobby to steal the coin collection as a kind of fantasy, a way of working together with his protégé on an imaginary project that seems to promise more than the poor prospects of his own junk store. Teach forces the scenario, taking the play of theft seriously, and consequently obliging Donny to betray his friend for the sake of the plan.

Glengarry Glen Ross similarly makes financial desperation over into a problem of identity, but it carries the deception two steps further. Shelly "The Machine" Levene built his good name on his ability to close real estate deals, but by the time the action of the play begins, he has failed to maintain the sales record that his self-esteem and his livelihood require. In the first scene Levene asks the office manager, Williamson, to accept a bribe so that he can get better client lists and begin to make more actual sales. Williamson refuses. The second scene does not include Levene, but in it Moss proposes to Aaronow the robbery scam that Levene will eventually enact. The third scene, the shortest of the first act, is an exemplary performance by the most successful agent, Roma, showing how the ordinary business of Levene's firm, the sale of swampland in Florida to gullible investors, requires a rhetorically intense and emotionally exhausting confidence game. In the second act Levene has already robbed the office of its client list and in the meantime believes he has convinced an unsuspecting buyer into signing for "eight units of Mountain View"; he thinks he has reclaimed his identity, but he must sustain himself by performing his own innocence as the break-in is being investigated. In a crucial play-within-a-play scene with Roma, Levene shows the audience that he can still pitch a scam, the two managing to improvise a scene that is designed to put a client off until his check has cleared the bank. As Roma tells Levene, "That shit you were slinging on my guy today was so good ... it ... it was, and, excuse me, 'cause it isn't even my place to say it. It was admirable ... it was the old stuff."[22] It is after playing the old game with

Roma, and defending the game itself, that Levene eventually lets slip his crucial knowledge of the contract he saw during the break-in—a lapse of concentration in his double game that causes him to get caught in the robbery scam. A second revelation, that his supposed sale was to a legally incompetent client, only compounds his failure. Levene's performances, as a salesman and an actor in fraud, are what constitute his identity, but when he pushes the illusion a step too far, threatening the profit structure of the business, his whole world comes down around him. Realism in this play is a matter of listening closely, following cues and sustaining the illusion of a seamless performance; when the theatrical self breaks down, reality is felt most acutely by Levene as an absence of achievement, for which he must pay with suffering.

The obverse of *Glengarry Glen Ross* is *House of Games*, Mamet's film about a con game designed to bilk a fortune from a wealthy psychologist, Margaret Ford. After an opening sequence suggesting that psychoanalysis is itself an elaborate scam, Margaret goes to aid a troubled client by confronting Mike, the lender of the con artists, at the House of Games, a gambling room. She is quickly drawn in, ends up teamed with Mike in a poker game, and guarantees his bet; when he loses, she is about to write a check when she notices that the winning player's gun is a water pistol. The first plan to bilk her is revealed. The primary problem for Margaret in the film is the problem of depth, of how many layers of playing a scam might involve, and how many of them she is supposed to see through; the criminals here are performers, who can show or conceal the act of their own playing, so long as they are the only ones who know the limit of the play. The first play with the water pistol, like so many others, turns out to be a setup for the big sting on Margaret, in which she fronts eighty thousand dollars to Mike to replace money supposedly borrowed from the mob and lost. Margaret is sufficiently fascinated by Mike's con games to play with him, to be seduced by him, and to be so hurt by his ultimate betrayal that she murders him. In the end it is Mike who does not know the real limit of playing; when she threatens to shoot him, he calls her bluff, only to discover that the threat was real. Even then he will not stop playing, saying after the second shot, "Thank you, sir, may I have another?"[23]

The world in *House of Games* is as completely theatricalized as in the best modern metadramas, and the problem of authentic action within it becomes the problem of which reality to affirm, which of the performances to accept as true. What Margaret understands, which Mike does not, is that death—not just cash, and not realistic illusion—is only a limit of intentional performance for the one who dies; with his dying breath Mike pleads that he himself never *killed* anyone. In a world so full of lies, the metaphysical distinction is mere hairsplitting. Evil characters, as well as good ones, are constituted by their performances, and Margaret Ford, renowned psychologist, is no exception in Mamet's world. The thrust of realism in such a context, as with *The Verdict* or *The Postman Always Rings Twice*, may be the apparently simple matter of finding out the lie, finding out the theatrical pretense, though this may also eventually involve breaking down the characters' fictions through courtroom melodrama, placing speech under the additional obligations of an oath.

Hiding Out/Undercover

Often the theatrical game is not very elaborate in Mamet's work, just a matter of personal preservation through improvisation, or simple flight from a previous life. This latter is the context for Mamet's *Reunion*, in which a daughter seeks out the father who abandoned her and attempts to establish a relationship with him. Bernie, the father, has simply dropped out of his past relationships, drinking and occasionally trying to start again with a new family, which he eventually must leave. By the end of the play Carol, the daughter, seems to have persuaded him to forgive himself and to take a small role in her life that will help to ease her own loneliness.

In *Lakeboat* one of the crew members, Giuliani, is lost, and the remaining fellows invent an elaborate crime story about his adventures, his disappearance, and eventual death, when in fact he had simply overslept and missed the boat. Another character on the boat, Dale, is a sophomore English literature major, simply putting in time on a summer job until he can go back to school; a figure for the author, he becomes an audience for the narratives the crew members tell, allowing them to authenticate themselves while simultaneously reminding the audience, through his presence, that the play is based on the similar experiences of a young Mamet.

The most unusual of the plays that involve hiding out is probably *Lone Canoe*, the musical drama of a stranded English explorer from the early nineteenth century, living with the Athabascan tribe in the Canadian wilderness. More in tune with James Fenimore Cooper than with Emerson, this odd little play's hero, Fairfax, takes an Indian wife but is then discovered by a rescue party. Asked to return to England to explain the fate of his earlier party, Fairfax agrees to leave when a fight occurs between the explorers and natives; the tribal shaman wounds the man who led the English party, Van Brandt, and is in turn wounded by Fairfax. The party leaves, and while they wander through the lake country, Van Brandt dies. His journal reveals that he, not Fairfax, is wanted in England, so Fairfax returns to a forgiving tribe, ready to face a food shortage with the native community. This play draws out the common Rousseauian fantasy of the noble savage and the cultured man who discovers virtuous life in a simpler society. From a theatrical standpoint the plot is virtually transparent; Fairfax is free to choose who he will be by choosing which culture to belong to, and he chooses the more authentic, honest, and virtuous group of people. Fairfax rejects English society because he finds its values exemplified completely by the "natural" community of the Athabascans.

LYING ABOUT LOVE

In the politics of self-creation, one of the most dangerous acts is to give oneself over into dialogue, to admit a relation to another; such relations must, like the created self, be constituted sincerely, in declarations of genuine affection. Consequently Mamet's characters are reluctant to love one another, reluctant to admit it when they do, and apt to be extremely sensitive—hurt, angry, or morally outraged—when they are romantically deceived. It is the seduction more than the money that inspires Margaret Ford to kill her deceiver in *House of Games*, and similar dramas of intimacy are played out elsewhere in Mamet's work.

The early paradigm statement of this anxiety about honesty in relationships is surely *Sexual Perversity in Chicago*. The primary dramatic relationship in the play is between Danny and Deborah, as they struggle to establish their intimacy while simultaneously maintaining the personal identities and friendships that predate their relationship. Love, as a kind of contractual performance, is thus potentially transforming, even in a situation in which both fear of commitment and emotional honesty are obviously ideological, that is, "in Chicago." When Danny confesses his love, and Deborah asks him if love frightens him, he answers that it does; her response, "It's only words. I don't think you should be frightened by words," ignores the performative significance of the declaration, as if it were the same kind of speech as her earlier statement, "I'm a Lesbian," a lie designed to ditch Danny's first proposition. Deborah wants to create a bond hewed on less monumental speech acts, a contact established through the continuity of a dialogue with Danny; their conflict may be a simple difference over communicative preferences, but she, too, seeks authentic declarations:

Danny:	I try.
Deborah:	You try and try. You are misunderstood and depressed.
Danny:	And you're no help.
Deborah:	No, I'm a hindrance. You're trying to understand women and I'm confusing you with information. "Cunt" won't do it. "Fuck" won't do it. No more magic. What are you *feeling*. Tell me what you're *feeling*. Jerk.[24]

The italics indicate, here as everywhere in Mamet, a certain pressure on the word that emphasizes its performative significance. Similarly, Danny's curses merely perform anger and aggression theatrically; they have little referential value, yet they do work against any bond of shared understanding. The social alternative to the characters' efforts to constitute romance through authentic speech is a same-sex friendship, which in *Sexual Perversity in Chicago* is almost purely ideological, that is, based on a shared litany of what is supposed in the general culture to be true—in pornography, in child rearing, in casual observation—rather than what might be the case in any particular relationship.

The layers of theatricality and speech are more obvious and contradictory in *The Shawl*. In the first act a supposed clairvoyant, John, meets with a client and convinces her of his psychic talent. In the next act John reveals to his lover, Charles, that his gifts of spiritual vision and prophecy are based on educated guesses, confirmed by the client's wish for his credibility. What seem to be foundational speech actions—prophetic statements and observations of obscure truths—are the result of theatrical technique, and what seems to be dialogue—spiritual contact with the other world—is not. Yet genuine performative speech acts do exist in the play, as when Charles delivers an ultimatum to John: that if he does not convince the client to contest her mother's will and give the money to them, Charles will leave him. In act three when John's seance seems to be going according to plan, the photograph that the client brings turns out not to be a photograph of the mother but rather a test; when John identifies the photograph incorrectly, he puts the whole scam at risk, and can only redeem it through the image of a red shawl. This shawl eventually nets John a fee, though exactly how much the image—a likely guess based on a little simple research in an archive—will net him is not clear. Finally he must lie once again to the woman; in order to get his money, he must tell her he truly saw her mother during the seance. This lie may be a help to the client, and it even seems to coincide with what she remembers, but for John it is too late since Charles has already left, unable to accept the limits of John's vision.

Lying about love is less benign in *Oleanna*, where the title derives from Mamet's choice to write, as he often does, against a literary citation; in this case the framing texts are a quotation from *The Way of All Flesh* on the limits of moral vision and a verse from a folk song in which Oleanna names an ideal land, beyond the misery of the real world. The language of this play is the most fragmentary in Mamet's work—half of a telephone conversation, whole pages of simple phrases that trail off or are interrupted, abrupt and unpredictable changes of topic, etc. It seems to be the case that a confused female student, Carol, unable to understand the course material, gradually becomes frustrated with the male teacher's personal attempts to explain her situation and decides to accuse him of sexual harassment.[25] John's career, marriage, and whole identity eventually turn on her accusations, and by the end of the second short, intense act, he finally becomes violent. Here the quandary of interpreting the play falls upon a choice between two attitudes toward the dynamics of true performance. Was the young woman responding to a sexism situation which, in the final image, is ultimately revealed to the audience as the truth of the teacher's character, or was the teacher forced into a desperate, uncharacteristically violent and hateful act because of the enormity of her false accusations?

Oleanna seems to be written not toward any clear resolution but rather toward what has been called, in various critical arguments, the "proper statement of the question." If real human character exists prior to speech acts and is merely revealed by them, then John would seem to have been harboring criminal thoughts all along, and is perhaps innately guilty of some of the charges. If, however, his character is constituted through performed actions, then his hatred of Carol may be a new aspect of his character, an expression of his suffering and frustration. Similarly, the young woman may always have been constructed as simpleminded, that is, talked down to, in her experiences, like the way she is treated when she asks for help in the first act; her accusation of the teacher may be her new discovery of the power of expressive speech to transform her into a stronger person. Mamet does not presume to decide such conundrums in the play, and seems even to withhold the information that would make the job of interpretation easier for the audience. However, in light of the habit Mamet shows of writing against orthodoxies, and also in view of his often-stated position that women tend to manipulate speech, it would seem that even by problematizing the student's accusation, Mamet is writing against the current social trend toward accepting charges of harrassment without material evidence or convincing corroboration; the professor's life has already been shattered, his reputation and character apparently altered, before such questions of evidence have ever been considered. Mamet seems to attack the harrassment problem from the traditional Americanist perspective of the presumption of innocence and the burden of proof, and to imply that decisions made before such due process are probably unjust; the real truth in *Oleanna*, like the idea of utopia itself, is ultimately deferred.

FORMAL ILLUSIONS/THE TRUTH OF PERFORMANCE

Mamet also uses perspectives of formal manipulation to reveal theatrical structures. The truth within an illusive dramatic fiction can be revealed as a construction by showing the machinery of illusion making, which Mamet accomplishes not through layered Brechtian techniques but simply by moving the audience's perspective "backstage," showing the action of performance as if it were directed toward some other audience.

The most literal version of this *per angolo* technique occurs in *A Life in the Theatre*, in which scenes in various locations around the backstage of a repertory theater (played toward downstage) alternate with scenes that are supposed to be from actual performances (played toward an upstage drop that looks like a dark theater)—"in effect, a true view from backstage."[26] While the behind-the-scenes action is revealed, the onstage action is shown from a new perspective, in sympathy with the actors' frequent discussions of technique and effect. The play has no story, but the twenty-five scenes cohere in a representative impression of the life of a typical actor. The two characters, one young, one old, gradually reveal their limitations and their depth through everyday actions and their identification with their roles. Mamet's play flirts with the phenomenology of the theatre, with the paradox of acting and the body of the performer, as the characters continue to build their own identities while building fictional roles together. The drama seems to play especially well when the old actor is cast for closure, as an older, somewhat minor star: Denholm Elliot in London or Ellis Rabb in New York. In these cases the backstage scenes in rehearsal, after a show, or at the makeup table achieve a powerful illusion of authenticity and great sentimental appeal.

Another early Mamet play also debunks the performance by emphasizing its technique; in *The Water Engine* the onstage performance is of a radio play, so that the theatrical audience sees what the radio audience would only hear. Mamet is fond of the imaginative appeal of radio drama and originally wrote the play (about a 1934 Chicago inventor of an engine that runs on distilled water) for a national radio performance; in this case the era of the play's setting and the performance form were an interesting American historical match. When *The Water Engine* was produced theatrically, the conceit of the radio performance was simply placed onstage, and the theatrical audience asked to listen to the drama while they watched the spectacle of its studio production. The play's story is almost a fairy tale of good and evil, as the inventor is destroyed by dark figures from the big business world of automobiles and petroleum. By undercutting standard radio and theatrical techniques, Mamet manipulates form to emphasize the role of the imagination, aligning the audience's experience of imagining the play with the creative imagination of the inventor. The play finally appeals to the nostalgic, naive virtues of radio drama and of the simpler era that so many of Mamet's dramas try to recall. Through imaginative performance both actors and audience create the illusion of life in that era, though in this case everyone participates with full consciousness of the illusion.

The other major anti-theatrical play by Mamet is not about the theater *per se* but rather about Hollywood. *Speed-the-Plow*, written for a minimalist stage, is about the appalling ethics and greed involved in the behind-the-scenes manipulations of film producers and specifically about the arbitrary decision they make of which screenplay to produce. In the first scene, two self-described "Old Whores," Bobby Gould and Charlie Fox, celebrate over having attracted a major star to act in a formulaic sex-and-violence prison movie. Their artistic reasons for producing the screenplay are nonexistent, but they have a clear concept of "wealth." Most of the first act dialogue consists of sharing fantasies that money can fulfill. Hollywood, rather than Broadway, is the powerful commercial orthodoxy that the play condemns, while the only artistic alternative *in* the play is a visionary ecological novel, "The Bridge or, Radiation and the Half-Life of Society."

Mamet's 1983 play *Edmond*, however, remains outside the realm of specific indictments, utilizing a natural framework of American dissent and creating a kind of anti-allegory, a puritan cautionary tale in reverse, where transcendence comes not through a pilgrim's progress but through a spiraling fall, a submersion in the criminal underworld. Toby Silverman Zinman has recognized the Jewish background in *The Disappearance of the Jews* and the other Bobby Gould plays.[27] The strange peace of Edmond Burke in his jail cell at the end of the play is the result of an anti-baptism, a negative apotheosis which is still fully spiritual:

Edmond: Do you think there's a hell?

Prisoner:	I don't know. (*Pause.*)
Edmond:	Do you think that we are there?
Prisoner:	I don't know, man. (*Pause.*)
Edmond:	Do you think that we go somewhere when we die?
Prisoner:	I don't know, man. I like to think so.
Edmond:	I would, too.
Prisoner:	I sure would like to think so. (*Pause.*)
Edmond:	Perhaps it's Heaven.
Prisoner:	(*Pause*) I don't know.
Edmond:	I don't know either but perhaps it is. (*Pause.*)
Prisoner:	I would like to think so.
Edmond:	I would, too.
	(*Pause.*)
	Good night. (*Pause.*)
Prisoner:	Good night.

(*Edmond gets up, goes over and exchanges a goodnight kiss with the Prisoner. He then returns to his bed and lies down.*)[28]

The ending echoes that of *The Cherry Orchard*, where Firs lies down to await death. But the inexplicable breaking string of Chekhov has been cut from Mamet's adaptation of that moment, just as the spiritual symbolism of Edmond as everyman has been thrown into doubt.[29] By writing against genre, against religious doctrine, and against a canonical realistic text, Mamet again asserts himself by performing acts of artistic dissent.

Mamet's enormous commercial success in recent years brings a certain pressure to bear on his status as a figure of dissent. While still a relatively young writer, in mid-career, he is also one of the few of his generation to have sustained his project, to develop a distinct way of working and writing that meets with consistent acclaim. A recent issue of the *Dramatists Guild Quarterly* sought to acknowledge this status, though some of Mamet's remarks demonstrate a certain discomfort with his acquired intellectual credibility. About playwriting in general, for example, he argues: "It's a craft which has been practiced down through the ages, in the main, by whores like me; people who didn't know how to do anything else and were wandering around in the dark trying to express themselves, who somehow got good at it or got famous at it (perhaps not both) and so perservered. The purpose of literature is not to do good, but to delight us. That's why the writer writes it; it delights him or her to express it, or to be rid of it, and in some way delights the audience, appealing either to their self-esteem or to their prejudices, creating in them a new, happy understanding of the world."[30] As this statement reflects both on Mamet's talent and on his mission, this public declaration is surely a case of false modesty. Yet such self-deprecation is precisely what Mamet's public position requires, if he is going to maintain his status as an American writer, unique like others and therefore capable of critical self-expression.

In the creation of an illusion, whether of reality or of singular selfhood, the primary compositional technique is still to undercut, to construct an excess which, when pared away, seems to reveal the essential. As Mamet summarizes: "The main difference between somebody who wants to be a professional writer and somebody who doesn't is that the former knows how to cut. If you don't know how to cut, if you're a product of some school that didn't teach you that, you're not serious. If you're unwilling to cut viciously, just on the off chance that the audience might beat you to the punch line, you haven't been watching the audience. And if you haven't been watching the audience watching your plays, you're not a playwright."[31] Mamet's remarks are in the context of a public address, in which he was acutely aware of his audience as a community of American writers.

What Mamet tends to universalize, then, might be more carefully considered as a gesture specific to a particular cultural moment, and an expression which requires as its background a relatively stable cultural symbology. From a technical standpoint his primary advances over the old "selective realism" of the Group Theatre generation would seem to be his recognition of performance as a constitutive act, and his ability to dramatize the moments in peoples' lives when their performances seem to come undone, and so I have tried to suggest a working typology of those moments. Viewed through the critical lens of a theory of representation, a debunked illusion is merely one stage in an infinite regression, and reality is always deferred, always subject to a subsequent deconstruction. Yet viewed in the expressivist mode, which is one the deconstructive theorist often—inconsistently—employs, a gesture of undoing takes on the converse quality of having founded something singularly true. In an American culture that values such creative rejections, Mamet's dramas enjoy a remarkable affective power. But since cultures themselves are far from any security as critical absolutes, estimates of Mamet's significance will almost surely continue to change.

NOTES

1. There are four book-length studies of Mamet's work thus far: one reference guide, Nesta Wyn Jones, *File on Mamet*; two general surveys, Dennis Carroll, *David Mamet* (New York: St. Martin's Press, 1987), and C. W. E. Bigsby, *David Mamet*

(London: Methuen, 1985); and one treatment of his dialogue, Anne Dean, *David Mamet: Language as Dramatic Action* (Fairleigh Dickinson UP, 1989). No interpretive consensus on the significance of his work has emerged, though Mamet is now read internationally; see Martin Roeder-Zerndt, *Lesen und Zuschauen: David Mamet und das amerikanische Drama und Theatre der 70er Jahre* (Tubingen: Gunter Narr, 1993). My argument here is primarily an extension of the "language as action argument" through speech-act theory into cultural politics.

2. See, for example, William Demastes's chapter, "David Mamet's Dis-Integrating Drama," in *Beyond Naturalism: A New Realism in American Theatre* (Westport, Conn.: Greenwood Press, 1988), pp. 67–94. As regards realism in general I suppose I should admit the undue influence of Roman Jakobson, who thought the term so overfull of conflicting significance that its use was mostly rhetorical; see "On Realism in Art," trans. K. Magassy, in *Readings in Russian Poetics: Formalist and Structuralist Views*, ed. L. Matejka and K. Pomorska, pp. 38–46 (Ann Arbor: Michigan Slavic Studies, 1978).

3. This, among other things, causes many critics to dislike Mamet. Ruby Cohn, in *New American Dramatists, 1960–1980* (New York: Grove, 1982), repeats Edward Albee's observation that Mamet had "a fine ear, but there was as yet no evidence of a fine mind," and then went on to say that Mamet has a mind "so fine that no idea could violate it" (p. 46). Nevertheless, in the revision of her book she cedes to Mamet a major historical role, linking him with Shepard in the final chapter (*New American Dramatists, 1960–1990* [Basingstoke: Macmillan, 1991]).

4. David Mamet, "Realism," in *Writing in Restaurants* (New York: Penguin, 1986), p. 132.

5. See Sacvan Bercovitch, *The Puritan Origins of the American Self* (New Haven: Yale UP, 1975); his *The American Jeremiad* (Madison: U of Wisconsin P, 1978); and Bercovitch, ed. *Ideology and Classic American Literature* (Cambridge: Cambridge UP, 1986).

6. Sacvan Bercovitch, *The Rites of Assent: Transformations in the Symbolic Construction of America* (New York: Routledge, 1993), p. 311.

7. Bigsby comes close to this reading in the late pages of his chapter on Mamet in *A Critical Introduction to Twentieth-Century American Drama*, vol. 3: *Beyond Broadway* (Cambridge: Cambridge UP, 1985), when he argues that Mamet's realism is rooted in a "myth of decline" (p. 288).

8. Thorstein Veblen, *The Theory of the Leisure Class* (New York: Macmillan, 1899).

9. See for example Herbert Blau's first book, *The Impossible Theatre: A Manifesto* (New York: Collier, 1964).

10. Theatrical manifestoes have a difficult but continuing history; see for example Mac Wellman. "The Theatre of Good Intentions" *Performing Arts Journal* 8:3 (1984): 59–70; or Daryl Chin, "An Anti-Manifesto," *Drama Review* 27.4 (Winter 1983): 32–37, the latter in a special anniversary issue of manifestoes.

11. Mamet, "Decadence," in *Writing in Restaurants*, p. 58.

12. The construction of political correctness as an orthodoxy even allows conservatives, paradoxically, to grasp the rhetoric of dissent, as is evident in *Culture Wars: Documents from the Recent Controversies in the Arts*, ed. Richard Bolton (New York: New Press, 1992).

13. J.L. Austin, *How to Do Things with Words* (Cambridge: Harvard UP, 1962). The principal historian of politics to use this performative method is Quentin Skinner; for an overview see James Tully, ed., *Meaning & Context: Quentin Skinner and his Critics* (Princeton UP, 1988).

14. David Mamet, "WFMT," *The Cabin: Reminiscence and Diversions* (New York: Turtle Bay, 1992), p. 56.

15. David Mamet, *Some Freaks* (New York: Penguin, 1989), p. 3.

16. Rousseau makes his theory perfectly clear in the "Letter to D'Alembert on the Theatre," *Politics and the Arts*, ed. and trans. Allan Bloom (Ithaca: Cornell UP, 1960); for such a reading of Jefferson see Jay Fliegelman, *Declaring Independence: Jefferson Natural Language and the Culture of Performance* (Palo Alto: Stanford UP, 1993).

17. Mamet theorizes such a shared idealism in relation to the theatre in his "A National Dream Life," in *Writing in Restaurants*, pp 8-11.

18. See for example his remarks on entropy in "Decay: Some Thoughts for Actors," in *Writing in Restaurants*.

19. Jonas Barish, *The Anti-Theatrical Prejudice* (Berkeley: California UP, 1981).

20. Mamet, "Acting," in *Writing in Restaurants*, p. 129.

21. Henry Schvey, "The Plays of David Mamet: Games of Manipulation and Power," *New Theatre Quarterly* 4.13 (Feb. 1988): 77–89. See also, regarding *American Buffalo*, Thomas King, "Talk as Dramatic Action in American Buffalo," *Modern Drama* 34.4 (Dec. 1991): 538–48, and remember that to "buffalo" is to intimidate (Jack Barbera, "Ethical Perversity in America: Some Observations on David Mamet's *American Buffalo*," *Modern Drama* 29.2 [Sept 1981]: 270–75).

22. David Mamet, *Glengarry Glen Ross* (New York: Grove, 1984), p. 105.

23. David Mamet, *House of Games* (New York: Grove, 1985), p. 70.

24. David Mamet, *Sexual Perversity in Chicago and The Duck Variations* (New York: Grove, 1978), pp. 57–58.

25. There is a background for this conflict in Mamet's earlier work; see Pascale Hubert-Leibler, "Dominance and Anguish: The Teacher-Student Relationship in the Plays of David Mamet," *Modern Drama* 31.4 (Dec. 1988): 557–70.

26. David Mamet, *A Life in the Theatre* (New York: Grove, 1978), p. 9.

27. Toby Silverman Zinman, "Jewish Aporia: The Rhythm of Talking in Mamet," *Theatre Journal* 44.2 (May 1992): 207–15. In the same issue Carla McDonough reads Edmond in terms of American masculinity rituals ("Every Fear Hides a Wish: Unstable Masculinity in Mamet's Drama," pp. 195–205).

28. David Mamet, *Edmond* (New York: Grove, 1983), pp. 105–6.

29. The sound occurs in act two of Mamet's adaptation but not at the end. Anton Chekhov, *The Cherry Orchard*, adapted by David Mamet from a trans. by Peter Nelles (New York: Grove, 1985). Lue Douthit pointed out this absence to me.

30. Mamet, "Mamet on Playwriting," *Dramatists Guild Quarterly* 30.1 (Spring 1993): 8. Compare Mamet's stature, for example, with that of the playwrights with whom he was first compared in Peter Ventimiglia, "Recent Trends in American Drama: Michael Cristofer, David Mamet, Albert Innaurato," *Journal of American Culture* 1.1 (1978): 195–204.

31. Mamet, "Mamet on Playwriting," p. 12.

HOWARD PEARCE

Plato in Hollywood: David Mamet and the Power of Illusions

Mamet's *House of Games* and *Speed-the-Plow* explore ideas of worlds and identities, especially the idea of the artist. Focusing on the two female characters in these works, who manifest certain attributes of the artist, this essay explores how identity can be transformed and the way that such change is discovered through experiencing an alien world.

As Aristotle long ago observed, mimesis is a two-way street: as much as humans take pleasure in seeing representations of themselves, so much are they disposed to imitate what they see. As Plato's dialogues suggest, however, dramatic characters can take different forms, just as there are different ways of responding to art or to the dramatic experience: at one extreme there is the Socrates type who evaluates the performance by the standards of "thought, intelligence, memory ... right opinion and true reasoning," while at the other there is the Philebus type who abandons himself to the "mixed pleasures" involved in encountering the characters and events of a play (*Philebus* 11b, 50e). Contemporary philosophers, of course, continue to believe in the learning experience involved in theater, and indeed Hans-Georg Gadamer devotes a section of *Truth and Method* to this topic. As he sees it, drama as *Erlebnis* ("experience") provides "something of an adventure" and operates by interrupting "the customary course of events ... It ventures out into the uncertain" (69). As he further explains in *The*

From *Mosaic* 32, no. 2 (June 1999). © 1999 by *Mosaic*.

Relevance of the Beautiful, for this very reason theater provides "the alien shock that shakes our comfortable bourgeois self-confidence and puts at risk the reality in which we feel secure" (64).

For David Mamet as for Gadamer, the theater challenges our ideas of what is real, engaging us in a "marvelous adventure filled with ... risk and danger" (*Some Freaks* ix–x). Although Mamet is now most widely known as film writer and director (e.g. recent popular films like *The Edge* and *The Spanish Prisoner*), his stage career has also earned him recognition as a major playwright. *American Buffalo* in 1975 was the first of his critically acclaimed plays, followed by other successes such as *A Life in the Theatre, Glengarry Glen Ross,* and *Oleanna.* In addition, Mamet is known for his critical theorizing which has been dispersed in several volumes of essays, including *Writing in Restaurants, The Cabin,* and *Make-Believe Town;* and he has published fiction as well, notably *The Village* and *The Old Religion.* The diversity of his accomplishments, finally, also includes film directing, a role he performed in his *House of Games.* Both this film and the play *Speed-the-Plow* raise those questions about reality that are central to Mamet's drama, looking from one side and then the other at a woman's entry into a man's world. In *House of Games* the protagonist, the psychiatrist Dr. Margaret Ford, descends into the underworld to encounter Mike and his con men, whose base of operation is the bar and gambling house, the House of Games. From another perspective, in *Speed-the-Plow* the audience is engaged in the world of Hollywood entrepreneurs, Bobby Gould and Charlie Fox, who ritualize their treatment of a female interloper, the temporary secretary Karen.

Approaching these two characters, Karen and Maggie, as they encounter alien worlds and reveal themselves, needs to be illuminated by theoretical concerns—not only Plato's but also Mamet's and Gadamer's—about the existence and value of the aesthetic in a world of commerce and "serious" thought. As much as Plato sets up the antithesis of Socrates and Philebus, the philosopher and the aesthete, so much does Mamet undercut the distinction in a defense of the artist. Karen and Maggie must finally be seen in terms of this apologia. As I see it, since the occurrence of art in the world entails appearances—the illusions that Plato objects to in the artist as sleight-of-hand man—Mamet's habitual playing upon illusions must be recognized as a means of probing the reality of both his characters and their worlds. To present my case, after first looking at the two women in terms of theoretical issues I will follow first Maggie and then Karen in their encounters and their development. My moving in this way from the theoretical concerns toward a clearer and fuller view of these two characters is designed to show how they function as variations on the artist figure in themselves and in terms of their relationship to the audience. In observing that relationship with the audience, I will attempt to illustrate how the two women reveal the problematical nature of identity and involvement with others, with a view to suggesting how they represent the ironic role of the artist in the relationship with her world and audience.

Mamet's collection of essays *Some Freaks* begins with speculations on the artist as "freak," including his view of himself as "one of those freaks privileged to live in the world of the Arts" (5), and concludes with his speculations on the significance of the Superman character. As he sees it, it is Superman's embarrassment at his own duplicity—his "two false fronts: one of *impotence* [Clark Kent], and the other of *benevolence* [Superman]"—that keeps him in "constant hiding" and implies his having "relinquished any hope of sexual manhood, of intimacy, of peace" (179-80). According to Mamet, Superman's apologia might read: "I do good but take no pleasure.... I pray that my false-self attracts no notice: forget about me." Placed in a Platonic context, one might say that Superman's persona of benevolence and the power to see and safeguard the good, allies him with Socrates, just as Clark Kent's persona of impotence identifies him with Philebus, who in Plato's dialogue both intrudes and is summoned into the discussion several times, but is silenced by Protarchus, who tells Philebus that he is "no longer in a position to agree with Socrates or to disagree" (12a). A freak disqualified from entering the philosophical pursuit, Philebus is also like the artist, Socrates's Ion or David Mamet. His doubleness in the drama of this dialogue is an ambivalent withdrawal and assertion of his identity, grounded in his insistence that to be human is to be allowed to range from pleasure to serious thought.

This being human in a world in which identity and place are interdependent can also be thought of in terms of Heidegger's *dasein* wherein the activity of discovery involves moods and feelings as well as thought, and wherein being human demands a readiness to see afresh, to discover the alien in the commonplace and the familiar in the *unheimlich*, the "uncanny" (Heidegger, *Being and Time* 233). In *House of Games* and *Speed-the-Plow* Mamet presents situations in which attentive and empathetic response to character might uncover a sense of the sincere in an apparently cynical, game-driven world. In the deceiving worlds of these plays, the two women, Maggie and Karen, appear, whose identities emerge and change, and who are regarded by others as freaks and aliens. They themselves, however, journey toward an integration of the self as a realization of wholeness, and to a receptive audience they can be seen as offering the fullness of experience that ranges from Idea to sensual gratification, from philosophy to titillation, a journey toward the "mystic Conjunction of Opposites" (*Freaks* ix).

Socrates's world of flux is a condition wherein the serious and rigorous pursuit of knowledge is imperative but made difficult by the diversity and instability of what can be experienced. It is expected, however, that pursuit of the good and what is entailed in the good—the beauty of oneness, truth, changelessness—can attain that enduring and knowable idea. In Mamet's world, the possibilities of being are grounded in a perhaps inescapable uncertainty and illusion, which are more pervasive and intimidating than in Socrates's. Time and change disturb and disappoint the convictions that plot a sure journey toward discovery and understanding.

The versatility requisite in the worlds of Mamet's plays is not a matter of gaining power to build a rigid identity in an assured, fixed structure. Whereas the assurances of a protected structure speak the consolation of the familiar, keeping the identity secure and immobile, the call of adventure, even of the frivolous or the perverse, is an invi-tation into the strange otherness of a world not yet known, whose shadowy depths might reveal that what is to be discovered might not conform to what is expected according to ordinary understanding in a known world. This adventure toward discovery of identity and of other worlds is a "mixed pleasure," mimetic in Aristotle's sense of the way that "the habit of imitating is congenital" and that man "learns his first lessons through imitation" (*Poetics* 20). The negotiations with others, interpreting them as they interpret us, are matters of both self-creation and discovery of others. Moving into the openness beyond familiar structures might allow pleasure as well as knowledge.

To the extent that openness to another dimension of reality throws the familiar world and self into suspension, it invokes the metaphor of the *theatrum mundi*. In this light, it is possible to find something invigorating in Socrates's conclusion that "in laments and tragedies and comedies—and not only in those of the stage but in the whole tragicomedy of life—as well as on countless other occasions, pains are mixed with pleasures" (*Philebus* 50b). There is also something encouraging about Edmund Husserl's observation that the inseparability of the experiencer and intentional objects of experience "leaves open the possibility that what is given, despite the persistent consciousness of its bodily self-presence, does not exist.... It was, we afterwards say, mere illusion, hallucination, merely a coherent dream.... Everything which is there for me in the world of things is on grounds of principle *only a presumptive reality*" (*Ideas* 131).

As instances of the movement toward the possibilities of discovery and change, Karen and Maggie, of course, reveal something of the tentativeness and uncertainty that oversee any such event. Each bears in herself the ideas of the incompleteness of knowledge and the radical letting go that are vital to encounters in a world that might fragment and scatter the convictions brought into it. This destabilizing of assumptions helps in turn to account for the qualifications to which critics frequently resort in their interpretations of Mamet's plays. Ann C. Hall, for example, in interpreting Maggie's interest in Maria's cigarette lighter, extends a Freudian reading to suggest that "this action may hint at lesbian desires or Ford's fear of such feelings" (142). Yet, although her feminist psychoanalytical concern with the essentiality of conflict between the sexes avoids questions of another essence in relationships—i.e. love-union-reunion—she recognizes that in the end Maggie has eluded her: "she remains the sphinx. Her gesture is mysterious, and we are the inquisitors" (148). Citing Luce Irigaray, Hall concludes, of both *Games* and *Plow*, not only that "the females are enigmatic" but also that "such subtle disruptions" have in the real world "profound consequences" (158).

Maggie appears at the center of *House of Games* as protagonist. If her identity was in the beginning a secret perhaps kept from herself as well as from others, her apparent recognition and reversal have to do with her journeying from her world into the alien underworld of the con men; she is driven toward it perhaps by a curiosity that must be sublimated into care, perhaps by the crass desire to practice her own con in writing another book, perhaps by the need for love or the need to make connections with and participate in the game or the drama that includes others "as storytellers or as listeners" (*Writing in Restaurants* 107). These "perhaps" argue that if we cannot make the (liberated) Maggie of the final scene conform to a single logic known to convince in our world, then it may be because she has from the beginning contained mystery. Her freedom in the end is not only an apparent freedom from the rigid persona of the beginning, the erected and therefore in some way counterfeit structure of self, but also a freedom from those who would find themselves resolved in her and bring her into another counterfeit structure of understanding.

As Maggie moves deeper into that underworld (the metaphor of descent is operative in both plays), any reading of her *bildung* should take into account her movement through dimensions, from one reality into another: from one game whose lessons learned do not necessarily serve in the next; from one dimension of reality, the play's illusion, into another dramatized dimension; from one dimension that casts brackets around another dimension's certainties suspending but not necessarily refuting those certainties. As Gadamer explains, *bildung* should be understood as an acculturation, as a process of formation and development that nevertheless does not transcend and dispense with the *Bild*, the root of the idea that retains the concrete image or picture. Nor is the process merely away from the self: "What constitutes the essence of Bildung is clearly not alienation as such, but the return to oneself—which presupposes alienation, to be sure" (*Truth and Method* 14). The loss or withdrawal of self is a forgetting. The recovery is not of that secure identical self but of a self made possible by "keeping oneself open to what is other ... as the viewpoints of possible others. Thus the cultivated consciousness has in fact more the character of a sense.... It embraces its sphere, remains open to a particular field ... is active in all directions" (17).

Maggie's mobility is the expression of a need to experience or to become something more than the successful role she has created, a need that is provoked by three questions. The first is from the Woman Patient (a murderess), who cites a mentor as having said that "we all try to run from experience ... but that it will seek us out"(6). She challenges Maggie with the question, "Do you think that you're exempt ... ?" (Mamet's ellipses). The second is from Billy Hahn, another patient Maggie is trying to help: "What do you think this is? Some 'dream'? Maan, *you're* living in the dream, your 'questions," cause there. is. a. real. world" (10; punctuation as in original). And the third comes from Maggie's mentor Maria Littauer, who has earlier advised her to "Give *yourself* all those rewards you would like to have" (8): "What gives you satisfaction? ... you have something to do that brings you joy?" (30, 31). The questions are about who and what she is, and they challenge her to discover herself, to change, to find pleasure. They urge her to recognize that the world she thinks is real could be a dream and that she is not autonomous, that "experience" will "seek" her "out" What she sees and what she becomes is a matter of seeking experience by moving from her secure professional world into that world of the con men who, after an opening gambit, invite her to join them and begin teaching her tricks.

It is only after she has insisted on deeper involvement in their game, which is set up to include major crime (grand theft and murder), that she moves into a third dimension within the underworld, discovering that the game has been an elaborate sham. That third dimension is the world in which she has been engaged but now seen from backstage, the vantage point of the audience when it sees through the illusion of the stage, and from that new position, sees the trappings of the performance. Wishing herself, as she says to Maria, out of the dream—"What would I not give if this was a dream, and ... " (55; Mamet's ellipses)—Maggie comes to see that her participation in the events has been as in a *theatrum mundi*, that the world of the con men, who have been forthcoming in revealing their reality to her, has indeed been an elaborate orchestration for her. Discovering that Billy Hahn is driving the "vintage red Cadillac" (60) that they had "stolen" for their getaway, she goes to Charlie's Tavern at night, evidently to learn the full truth about their deception and/or to confront Mike.

"Sneaking into Charlie's through the back," she witness the actors who had roles in the drama they staged, for her as participant and audience, being paid for their performances and discussing the details of how well they performed. The "businessman/policeman" asks, "How come I always got to play the straight guy ... ?" (Mamet's ellipses). Like a disoriented audience, from backstage she sees actors appraising the roles they played, in a drama directed by Mike for her as an audience, and now interpreting her, the naïve participant. The relationship is a structure whose possibilities Mamet had found attractive for *A Life in the Theatre*, a play wherein the actors might perform for an audience that is, for the real audience, backstage: "Thus we see the actors' backs during their onstage scenes, and a full view of them during the backstage scenes—in effect, a true view from backstage" (*A Life* 9). As Maggie becomes the backstage audience, "Shielded by a stack of beer cases" (61), she watches and listens to the men; and she stands looking at them through the open woodwork of a booth, in effect a stage curtain or a visual frame that sets the other world apart.

This appearance of a reality behind the performance prepares her for the next-to-last scene, in which she casts, directs, and plays a role in a drama or con game that she devises for Mike. Her self-justification to Mike—"You raped me.... You took me under false pretenses.... You used me" (68)—elicits his counter-interpretation: "And you learned some *things* about yourself that you'd rather not know." His self-justification—"I never hurt anybody. I never shot anybody" (69)—and his naming her a "whore" (70) raise the same questions about identity that the Woman Patient had earlier proposed (29): whether someone can be made a whore and is not responsible for what he/she becomes, or whether, in becoming a whore, the becoming is what she already was. Mike's and Maggie's self-justifications are uses of language that, rather than resolving questions of motive, action, and reality, direct attention toward the unknown. The questions hover irresolutely over the final scene, where Maggie's stealing the cigarette lighter is an action that presents, before the audience's eyes, her withdrawal from their understanding and freedom from their judgments. In adopting Maria's words—"*forgive yourself*"—in autographing a copy of her book, has she gained new insight and a new lesson for life or is she merely providing a new rationalization allowed by her old Freudian psychology?

An audience trying to understand Maggie, to appreciate her, to identify with her, or to make use of her in a mimetic act of justifying the self or an understanding of the world, cannot bring her and her world of illusions to full interpretation and Aristotelean resolution of form. Attending her in her journey into and out of the underworld remains a "marvelous adventure filled with ... risk and danger" as well as pleasure. The world of the film is a "mixed pleasure" that is not like the figures that can be made "straight, or round ... which a lathe, or a carpenter's rule and square, produces" (*Philebus* 51c). That "mixed" experience involves "the pleasures of scratching" in which we might, like Philebus or Mamet's freaks, indulge ourselves. In the assumed innocence of simply enjoying the play or film, we share Maggie's desire to experience what can bring her and us an immediate if fleeting "joy."

These pleasures might lead us, however (we being like Maggie instinctive and irrepressible interpreters), to enter the world of ideas and, like Philebus, intrude ourselves into thoughtful debate about plays, about ideas, about reality; we might be encouraged to engage in both the aesthetic and in "philosophical" thought about "truth." Even though the ephemerality of the events seen on screen would mark them as Platonic eidolons, the aesthetic justifies itself in the retention of *bild* in *bildung*. Maria's cigarette lighter is early in the play such an image for Maggie, and it embodies ideas not only of experiencing momentary beauty but also of the enduring value that "will seek us out," that is bestowed and taken to oneself: "It's so beautiful. It's old and it's heavy, and it looks like someone gave it to you" (8). Like the beauty of the two cigarette lighters, so is Maggie's made a focus, a center of attention. Initially, when she picks up Maria's lighter, the image we are to see is: "Angle—Insert. Ford, holding the gold lighter, lights her cigarette." The play's final image is "Angle"—Maggie lighting a cigarette with the stolen lighter and smiling (72). She has found the "good things in life," including tobacco, that give pleasure. She is like Philebus, silent about what has been her self-realization, while she remains for the world to which she returns, as professional psychiatrist, the wise and caring Socrates, whose benevolence and knowledge are presented in a new book (that remains for the audience undefined).

While "Dr. Margaret Ford" is protagonist in her play, Karen in *Speed-the-Plow* is on the periphery: neither she nor Charlie Fox but rather Bobby Gould is the protagonist and who in the opening scene performs histrionically so that, like Willy Loman, attention will be paid to him. In a world of male conquest and caste, Karen is the woman; in the unassailable structure of Hollywood business she is a temporary secretary who needs instruction about the chain of command, about providing coffee, using the telephone, making reservations at a restaurant. Karen comes from an indeterminate outside, appears in this world uninitiated and unsponsored, and is drawn into a game of sexual conquest grounded in the calculated deceptions of life fabricated and played as a game. Ostensibly she is more "naïve" than Maggie; indeed she uses that word to apologize for her actions: "it was *naïve* of me" (39) and later she reflects upon the attribute: "I don't think it's attractive, and I don't think it's right. To be naïve" (56). Karen, however, might also be interpreted as using language to create a false image of herself, especially since she later confesses to Gould that she knew "what the deal was," that she knew he "wanted to sleep with" her (57) when he assigned her the task of giving the book he has been asked to consider a "'courtesy read'" (42).

Karen, moreover, sees through the superficial deceptions of Gould's game to read his character. She seems to have perceived something in him worthy of risking the venture in filming the book; accordingly, she is willing to give herself, perhaps to serve only by making coffee (52) to an improbable filming of the book's world in decay, *in extremis*, which she believes might not be *appreciated* but is *needed* by its audience. Gould seems to validate that perception of him not only in his own naïveté, his belief that she might, possibly, love "me for myself" (36), but also in his vulnerability to the book that she gives more than a "courtesy read." Reading it as the play opens and Fox enters excited about the *"Buddy* picture" (11), Gould blocks him five times by reacting to and reading from the book and asking Fox to read. Confronted by this thing that is "not quite 'Art' and ... not quite 'Entertainment'" (3), Gould characterizes himself as already fascinated by the book that does not meet Hollywood expectations; and he invokes tragic or heroic images from the past, from Euripides and Dante: "When the gods would make us mad, they answer our prayers.... I'm in the midst of the wilderness.... I have inherited a monster" (3).

Karen and Gould can be regarded as agreeing with Mamet in their naïve belief that this work about a world in decay by an "Eastern Sissy Writer" (23) would be good for a world that thinks it wants the buddy film with "Action, blood, a social theme" (13). Like them, Mamet thinks his world does not know itself or its needs, and he represents himself as sharing the world's ambivalent nature, as having both Philebus's genuine aesthetic instincts and Hollywood's crass love of entertainment and money. In *Writing in Restaurants*, on the one hand, he declares that "to work in the true theater ... is a great job in this time of final decay" (116); that, since "all plays are about decay ... the theater exposes us to the notion of decay, to the necessity of change" (111). On the other hand, in *The Cabin* he explains his attendance at the Cannes film festival in terms of "whore that I am" (144).

Karen and Gould, then, reflect that ambivalence of the playwright, inclining, on the one hand, toward Philebus and Clark Kent while reflecting, on the other, the attractiveness of Socrates and Superman. And they know, if not the truth, at least some questions about Art and Love, questions that turn and accuse Gould when he chooses a bad angel Fox, and abandons his good angel Karen. When in the play's last moment Gould has regained his status of power with Fox by the rules of their game, the Euripidean question re-emerges: if Gould "wanted to do good ... but ... became foolish" (81), was not his naïve "foolishness" with Karen a kind of madness by Hollywood standards, and was that madness perhaps a prelude to the moral or spiritual destruction that is evidenced by his abandonment of Karen and the "arty" novel for the commodity of entertainment? Perhaps what is considered "madness" in the real world's (Hollywood's) estimation is a true sanity and is the "purity" that Gould prayed for (43). Gould repudiates Karen and the question of art because he has found himself again, and he re-establishes himself in a cynical world by the restrictive definitions of reality and value that keep him safe with a sense of power in that world, which is a time of "final decay" that masks itself in illusions of personal power and control.

The convictions by which Gould interprets life are those of the Hollywood establishment, and he confirms its values. A naïve Karen enters it as a disturbing voice questioning Gould's certainties and his values and embodying in her character the ideas of uncertainty and possibility. Trying to fix her in the structure of their world's thinking, Fox defines her as either a "floozy" who would sleep with Gould for no "good" reason or an ambitious type who "would schtup you just to get ahead" (35). In anger and frustration he finally asks, "What is she, a witch?" (69), tacitly admitting that his crafty understanding has been unavailing. When in Act One she answered his question of whether this is "a good place to work" with a polite "I'm sure that it is," he mockingly replied, "How wonderful to be so sure ... to have such certainty in this wonderful world" (28). Her essential uncertainty is evident in her actions, however, as well as in the words she speaks. Asked by Gould to do merely a "courtesy read," she reacts instinctively, "But what if there is something in the book?" (42); when Gould declares that "this job corrupts you ... and everything becomes a task," she asks, "Does it have to be that?" (43).

The "purity" that she offers him is the acceptance of the world and the self as they are. People in this world are not gods or angels; as she teaches Gould at the end of Act Two, they might best be described in terms of the

words she has found in the book, "weak ... depraved ... frightened ... lost"
(58), and their need for "companionship" affirms both animal pleasure and
the need that can be called "love," that possible uniting with another. She
understands Gould's fear and dishonesty, she knows their affinity, and she
knows that if they, having come so near to death in a dying world, are open to
change, there is reason for hope in that "sometimes it reaches for us." The
idea of letting experience come to us, which must be learned by Maggie and
is affirmed here by Karen, also echoes that interdependence that characterizes
Heidegger's *dasein*, being-in-a-world. The "it" that "reaches for us" might
look like the "monster" that Gould says he "inherited"; the world might be,
as Gould defines Hollywood/reality, a "sinkhole of slime and depravity ...
garbage" (28–29). But Karen's question—"why is it garbage ... ?" (Mamet's
ellipses)—confirms not a contradictory understanding of reality as
immaculate benevolence but a readiness to see and become what is possible,
to entertain the possibility that can arise only if things and people can change.
Karen's development of a fervent belief in the message of the freakish book—
that everything "has been sent" to us "to change us" (48)—attests to the
book's having reached out to her in calling for a "return to the self" (58).

    The "return to the self" is a truth revealed in a book that, coming from
an alien voice far off in the East, postulates a world far different from the
world of sham and illusion that Fox and Gould make cozy for themselves.
But that book's language, so poetic—that is, metaphorical and "arty"—can
cause both Hollywood and the world of the play's audience to read the book
with contempt. Ruby Cohn, for instance, twice labels the books language
"maudlin, mawkish, and quasi-mystic" (117), but she also seems to be tacitly
responsive to a "pure" element in the language when she take from the book
the simple question that is the title of her essay. "How Are Things Made
Round?" Christopher Hudgins feels that there is significance and truth in the
ideas of the book but that these can be discovered only in spite of its
language: "though the language is overblown the idea of the line is a fine
testimony to" the book's genuine value (221). A prejudice against the
language of the book might be based in a manifold of subjective, social, and
aesthetic presuppositions. We might in our time still be rather embarrassed
about the exuberance of Romantic expression, or suspicious of what seems
too free in traces of the Longinian sublime; but we might also be disdainful
of the language of Freudian psychology, in which Maggie places her trust as
she sets out on an adventure in the underworld, the bar and gambling house
"House of Games."

    In the heightened language of the book, the metaphor of roundness is
spoken as a question: "How are things made round? Was there one thing

which, originally, was round ... ?" (3; Mamet's ellipses). Echoing the metaphor, Fox and Gould play upon the idea of the circle, as when Fox observes about their careers: "Yes, but the Wheel Came Around. And here we are. Two Whores" (26). Fox's and Gould's appeal to the notion of roundness is derived from a past world, the conceptions of the Wheel of Fortune and the Fall of Princes. If the "Two Whores" have risen because "the Wheel Came Around," then their world-business is to speed the plow, to make profit and prestige for themselves while they move upward on the wheel. Fox and Gould, in their industriousness and their commitment to art as commodity, echo, as Tony Stafford shows, the worthy farmer of Thomas Morton's *Speed the Plough*, a play Mamet ironically echoes in his title, since Morton's play treats seriously the substance and value of his characters' accomplishments. In keeping with Matthew Roudané's suggestion that there are traces of Emersonian thought in Mamet's work, we might also suggest that Fox and Gould inherit the illusion of Emerson's farmers, who thought that they "Possessed the land": "Earth-proud, proud of the earth which is not theirs; / Who steer the plough, but cannot steer their feet / Clear of the grave" ("Hamatreya" 9.35). For Fox and Gould, the answer to the question of how things are made round involves believing in the certainty of knowledge about the game and the predictability of actions in it: "It's a business, with its own unchanging rules" (29). In a world of circumstance and accident, however, the rise is not assured, and Gould's being afraid encompasses this awareness.

What he discovers through Karen and the book is that if we are in "the same state of decay as the world," then the world as he has trusted it is "a dream, and delusion" (68). In the book's world of purpose and design beyond our grasp, being brought down to "that lonely place, the low place ... under the bridge" (47), is a movement into deprivation and extremity that makes possible the reunification of self and the reunion of self with God and with another. Gould's glib allusion to Dante's wilderness in the play's opening and his impassioned echoing of the idea in Act Three—"I'm *lost*, do you hear me, I'm *lost*" (79)—imply that he is, in the book's interpretation of his life, at that low point, even if or indeed insofar as he has just been "promoted" in his real world, Hollywood. The structure of reality conceived in the book is Platonic; it directs an escape from the "gross infection rampant in the world" toward transcendent beauty: "silver is more powerful than gold; and the circle than the square or the triangle. He [evidently the protagonist in the book] thought of architecture" (73). This appeal to cosmic design in terms of architecture and geometry recalls the classical shape of the Ptolemaic system. In the Platonic view, Socrates's metaphors of ascent, like his images of pure form, involve a cleansing, a transcendence of the senses, in the rise toward knowledge on the journey up and out of the cave. Plato's answer to the question of how things are made round is to train the intellect for apprehension of beauty, truth, goodness, and the changeless roundness of the One.

The ascent toward perfect love and beauty in the *Symposium* is, however, a rise from the hiccuping, sneezing, and "silly jokes" of Aristophanes, and from his compelling image of "the real nature of man" (189a–b, d). The Aristophanic myth of human origins is another answer to the question about roundness. This "thing" for the Aristophanes of this dialogue is the being that was "globular" (189e), "whirling round and round like a clown turning cartwheels" (190a); having been split in half by Zeus, each partial being instinctively seeks its other half. As a definition of the human condition, this "clown" or "freak" suggests that in essence human beings require reunion, one with another, that the "innate love" that can "bridge the gulf between one human being and another" (191d) is of a sexual kind. Aristophanes's story voices Karen's belief, perhaps drawn from the book, that two human beings finding each other, whether their intercourse is named sex or love, is just such a minimal and essential action.

When Karen embraces the ideas in the book, it is not because of a belief that she has miraculously transcended her mortality but an acceptance of debility and need. She and Gould are "in the world. Dying" (59); her reading of the book merely for "courtesy" engendered hope that they might become better, "in *spite* of our transgressions," that Gould might "make stories people need to see" (59–60); their uniting is a beginning of possibility: "you prayed to be pure," she reminds Gould, "What if your prayers were answered?" Karen's answer to the question, her proposal that they "do something" that would "bring us alive," is silenced by Gould's decision to bring things round within the confines of his little world; and when he repudiates her she goes out—into the indefiniteness, the irresolution of a future. If the book has in fact been for her a discovery or confirmation of values, her return to her world is a return, like Maggie's, to a self transformed. Although she is not necessarily deprived of the assurances she found in the book, she is deprived of reliance on the text; unable to find in it the words to which she could give voice, she becomes again the dependent naif, fearing that she is being "punished for my wickedness" (80). Repeating the words spoken earlier by both Fox and Gould—"I don't understand" (59, 64, 79)—she knows that she does not "belong here," and her last words are "I hope" (80, 81).

Karen, like Maggie, seeks reality and truth in a world that must be read as text, as a constructed and already interpreted structure. Maggie, at the center of a world she has interpreted in her own text, discovers an alien world whose words are both true and false and whose actions direct her through illusion toward perception; her final performance is a wordless demonstration that leaves interpretation—of her new dress, of her stealing the cigarette lighter, indeed of who she now is—open. Karen, despite succumbing to the machinations of powerful men like Fox in the world of Hollywood, is left no less than Maggie with a privacy, a withdrawal from the audience's desire to know and interpret, and her failed attempt to retrieve the words of the book is an ambiguous performance no less than Maggie's final actions. What she tries to retain could be meretricious to the degree that the book's language is exalted and antithetical to the business language of Hollywood—where for Fox reading "coverage" reveals the truth and is preferable to reading a "talky piece of puke" (62). Yet howsoever improbably, the book might be able to reveal things brought round in a "vision of infinity" (58) that echoes the childlike vision of Thomas Traherne's poetry. Karen's retreat with an ostensible belief in a transcendent vision is like Maggie's return to her world of the professional psychiatrist: Maggie's assured and reassuring advice to "forgive yourself" and Karen's tremulous "I hope," pointing in opposite directions, reveal the characters' retreats from an audience's full understanding of how they might be interpreted.

Maggie and Karen might appear to be fragments of the whole human being, "two false fronts": Maggie representing the benevolence of Superman, and Karen the impotence of Clark Kent. They might, however, also be perceived as artists who, like Philebus and Ion and other freaks, never come fully and complacently into the circle of the *theatrum mundi* defined by the real world. Each seems to have found a satisfying or at least serviceable version of truth for herself. Like Philebus, they could tell more. Maggie with silent eloquence shows that she has moved toward an appreciation of Philebus's argument for pleasure. Rebuffed and silenced, like Philebus, Karen has shown what Philebus has been unable to argue, that the idea of sensual pleasure might be transmuted into the artist's pleasure and the satisfaction of making "stories people need to see," just as the pleasure of sex might be transmuted into love.

Mamet's artist, like Philebus, is a freak on the periphery of a world of commerce, a world built on an illusion of power that is generated out of a simple and self-assured reality. Such voices speak, equivocally, to a world that would disdain or condescend to the artist's aesthetic. The artist as freak or expatriate asks the indulgence by which the pleasure of art is not repudiated as being what Socrates contemns, the pleasure of scratching. This voice can express a hope in art for the idea of a "Place Where Three Roads Meet, the mystic Conjunction of Opposites into the Whole, the possibility of True Love" (*Freaks* ix). This voice can offer speculation about possibilities in free mobility and the hope for growth in change about the need for readiness on the part of artist and audience to be, like a character in a play, astonished.

Works Cited

Aristotle. *Poetics.* Trans. Gerald F. Else. Ann Arbor: U of Michigan P, 1970.

Cohn, Ruby. "How Are Things Made Round?" Kane 109–21.

Emerson, Ralph Waldo. *Complete Works.* Centenary Edition. 12 vols. Boston: Houghton, 1903–04. New York: AMS P, 1968.

Gadamer, Hans-Georg. *The Relevance of the Beautiful and Other Essays.* Trans. Nicholas Walker. Ed. Robert Bernasconi. Cambridge: Cambridge UP, 1986.

———. *Truth and Method.* 2nd ed. Trans. Joel Weinsheimer and Donald G. Marshall. New York: Continuum-Crossroad, 1989.

Hall, Ann C. "Playing to Win: Sexual Politics in David Mamet's *House of Games* and *Speed-the-Plow.*" Kane 137–59.

Heidegger, Martin. *Basic Writings.* Ed. David Farrell Krell. New York: Harper, 1977.

———. *Being and Time.* Trans. John Macquarrie and Edward Robinson. New York: Harper, 1962.

Hudgins, Christopher C. "Comedy and Humor in the Plays of David Mamet." Kane 191–226.

Husserl, Edmund. *Ideas: General Introduction to Pure Phenomenology.* Trans. W. R. Boyce Gibson. New York: Collier, 1962.

Kane, Leslie. *David Mamet: A Casebook.* New York: Garland, 1992.

Mamet, David. *The Cabin: Reminiscence and Diversions.* New York: Turtle Bay-Random, 1992.

———. *House of Games.* New York: Evergreen-Grove, 1987.

———. *A Life in the Theatre.* New York: Evergreen-Grove, 1978.

———. *Some Freaks.* New York: Viking Penguin, 1989.

———. *Speed-the-Plow.* New York: Grove, 1988.

———. *Writing in Restaurants.* New York: Viking Penguin, 1986.

Plato. *The Collected Dialogues.* Ed. Edith Hamilton and Huntington Cairns. Bollingen Series 71. Princeton: Princeton UP, 1961.

Roudané, Matthew C. "Mamet's Mimetics." Kane 3–32.

Stafford, Tony J. "*Speed-the-Plow* and *Speed the Plough*: The Work of the Earth." *Modern Drama* 36 (1993): 38–47.

LESLIE KANE

Gathering Sparks

"Spawned in America, pogroms a rumor, *mamaloshen* a stranger, history a vacuum ... "

—Cynthia Ozick

The period between 1982 and 1987 was an especially prolific one for David Mamet during which time *Edmond; Glengarry Glen Ross; Goldberg Street*, a collection of short dramatic works; *Writing in Restaurants*, the playwright's first collection of essays; and three minimalist works on the subject of Jewish identity, cultural identity, and bonds of memory, *The Disappearance of the Jews, Goldberg Street*, and *The Luftmensch*, were produced, published, or aired as radio dramas. These works articulate the ambivalence of confused cultural identity expressed in the attempt to recover the past, reestablish the bonds of memory, reclaim personal dignity, and confront anti-Semitism. Yet they have been largely ignored and dismissed by scholars as unimportant and/or unintelligible.

In 1989, during his writing and filming of *Homicide*, a work that also raises issues of Jewish assimilation and affiliation, which will be discussed in the following chapter, Mamet was inspired to revisit *The Disappearance of the Jews* in light of his growing interest in these subjects. *The Old Neighborhood*, comprised of *Disappearance of the Jews, Jolly*, and *Deeny* (formerly called "D")—the latter two works written in 1989[1]—unites three works in a single

---

From *Weasels and Wisemen: Ethics and Ethnicity in the Work of David Mamet*. © 1999 by Leslie Kane.

bill, through which Mamet explores "the personal terrain of memory" (Holmberg 1997b, 7) in three interrelated plays that complement one another in a subtle but compelling manner. Completed in 1989 and revised in 1997, *The Old Neighborhood* is central to the study of Judaism, ethics, and pedagogy in Mamet's work in the late 1980s and early 1990s and is a precursor to *Oleanna* and *The Cryptogram*, both informed by memory and the quest for and loss of home. Hence the trilogy serves as a pivotal link between the motifs developed in Mamet's earlier work, especially *Glengarry Glen Ross* and *Speed-the-Plow*, and that of the 1990s, which increasingly reveals his further exploration of identity, family, memory, and ethnicity.

In Mamet's view the structure of *The Old Neighborhood* is "an unusual form. It would be too grand to call it a trilogy," he suggests, "but it's something trilological. Three explorations of the same theme which make the evening partake of the dramatic, I hope, and also of the epic" (Holmberg 1997a, 9). Although he acknowledges that the term "epic" is somewhat surprising for these seemingly slight works, given its sweeping temporal and historical panorama and the journey that the character Bobby Gould makes to his boyhood home to visit family and friends after an interval of many years, *The Old Neighborhood*'s triple bill "generate[s] a unique synergism," as Richard Christiansen points out in his review of the world premiere, in which the plays "speak to each other and resonate, making up a whole that is greater than its parts" (1997). Tropologically and linguistically linked by Bobby's return to Chicago and unified by a trio of reunions through which he confronts his past—personal, familial, ethnic—or, as Mamet puts it "to close out some unfinished business" (Holmberg 1997a, 8), the play raises unsettling questions about "how to deal with a legacy that, as it slips through our fingers, shapes our lives" (1997b, 7). Searing the mind with stunning images and radiant poetry, the trilogy speaks of the loss of illusion and of faith, of the healing power of memory, of the redemptive power of love.

This chapter will also open a dialogue on the formerly neglected elegiac *Goldberg Street* in concert with a close reading of *The Old Neighborhood*.[2] Both are breakthrough plays whose tropes, emblems, and unmistakably Jewish characters provide stark evidence of the playwright's staging of conflicted Jewish identity in a luminous symphonic structure that particularizes and humanizes experience. The dyads and triads of this trilogy not only traverse the old neighborhood, they provide critical avenues to explore the sites of heightened conflict between professional and familial demands that inform Mamet's most recent and highly personal plays, screenplays, and memoirs. Anchored in place and deeply personal experience, this work may be among Mamet's most intimate in subject and structure, inspired as much by his maturity as a dramatist as his commitment as a Jew.

Visiting three individuals who have shared and shaped his life—Joey, his oldest, closest friend "since grade school" (1997a, DJ 28); Jolly, his sister with whom he is bound in pain; and Deeny, his first love—and who have remained *in* the Old Neighborhood as he, marrying outside the religion and venturing into the wider world, has moved away from place and whatever gave a sense of rootedness to his life, Bobby makes a journey that is educational, one disclosing familiar and forgotten truths. In each of these plays he engages a close friend or family member in dialogue, or more accurately, they engage him in conversation and the binding relationship of listener and storyteller providing a fitting venue for his airing confessions and questions about his prior decisions and future endeavors. As he reminisces with each of these individuals closely aligned with his youth, a structure perfectly suited to the "kitchen play, a reflective family oriented play" typical of the 1950s that Mamet has previously eschewed (Weber 1997, 12), Bobby's reunions serve as clustered border-crossings in which the dialogue straddles timelines and spans emotional terrain typically unexplored by this playwright, with the exception of his heart-piercing *Cryptogram*.

Whereas *The Disappearance of the Jews* dramatizes a conversation between two old friends who chew over old times, lost opportunities, and faded dreams, their longing for connection to their Jewish heritage and feelings of disappointment in themselves and in their marriages revealed or implied in the rich subtext, *Deeny* is an acknowledgment of lost love and a recipe for renewal. *Jolly*, the longer middle play, is the centerpiece of this trilogy, its remunerative questions into the nature of mothering, memory, guilt, atrocity, love, and legacy deeply affecting and unsettling. A poignant work, *The Old Neighborhood* is immediately recognizable as Mamet country by its idiosyncratic invective, comic irony, and raunchy profanity that make a unique backdrop against which "times past," the controlling figure of this play—and to lesser or greater degree all of Mamet's canon—are repeatedly projected. From the outset Mamet portrays Bobby Gould as grappling with regret, learning to face his past and value its lessons, the most notable that "his problems are rooted in rootlessness" (Feingold 1997). However, Mamet doesn't so much plot Bobby's story linearly as map it out on coordinates of character and place. Swirling around these points of reference the playwright coils Bobby's moody, ruminative, obsessive inquiries into the nature of memory, guilt, atrocity, love, and restoration, so that we perceive the trilogy's structure essential to Bobby's talmudic investigations into memory's inevitably incomplete record.

Analogous to Chekhovian scenarios that similarly evoke the vacillating, prismatic, confounding emotion of love tempered by joy, hope, disillusionment, and the searing pain of loss, and a seemingly quiescent surface that belies fluidity, Mamet's plays share a stasis more noticeable than in recent works.[3] And like Chekhov's plays, these works rely on the unspoken to reveal the distance between thought and meaning, between illusion and reality, between a person's conception of him or herself and the conceptions of companions, and between the speaker and the listener. But therein lies their intimacy, poignancy, and poetry. "[L]aced with a yearning to return to friends, and family, and a past ... and, perhaps, most of all to his neglected Jewishness" (Cummings 103), *The Old Neighborhood* reveals that in going back to native ground, Bobby, a landsman among landsmen, frees himself to move forward, for "'It is only through the great truth of returning to oneself,'" observes Lawrence Kushner, that one locates "'the light of life'" (1993, 32).

In a now familiar structure of playing with distances, Mamet positions Bobby Gould in transit as a marginal man on the brink of change who returns home for much the same reason that Lyubov Ranevesky returns home to Russia from Paris in Chekhov's *The Cherry Orchard*. As Mamet has observed, Ranevsky does not return "to *save*" the orchard and estate, but rather "To lick her wounds, to play for time, to figure out a new course for her life" (1987d, 122). "None of these is a theatrically compelling action," he reminds us, for the latter could be satisfied "in seclusion" rather than in the company of old friends and family. What is to be gleaned from "returning," is a universal sentiment that Bobby's sister Jolly ratifies: we all need comfort. Likening *The Cherry Orchard*'s structure to "the revue play ... the *theme* play," in which "a series of review sketches" are linked by "a common theme" (124), Mamet presages a structure he has adopted for *The Old Neighborhood*, with the distinct difference that this trio of plays, the first two episodic and the latter a single scene, has a through-line and a protagonist who, in the process of confronting his past and himself, undergoes a journey of self-discovery, a search for truth.

Bobby Gould, who reappears with varying surnames and dilemmas in *Speed-the-Plow*, *Bobby Gould in Hell*, *The Disappearance of the Jews*, and *Homicide*, his name inspired by what Mamet views as the most common American first name and recognizably Jewish surname, and admittedly the playwright's alter ego in this work,[4] is a man on the margin—a man on the brink of divorce, an outsider to tradition, a weekend traveler visiting the old neighborhood, a stranger to himself, an acculturated Jew. In each of these circumstances he bears the traces of biography. Speaking recently with Bruce

Weber, Mamet affirms in a comment he then deflects by humor "that he, like other writers tend[s] to write about their [his] youth" (1994 C10). Hence although the playwright cautions us that dramatic biography ends and must end "by reverting to fiction" or rather, "the dramatic elements must and finally will take place over any 'real' biographical facts," which are, finally, only a supervention in what we viewers can understand as a fictional drama" (1998, 29–30), this work is suffused with personal and cultural memory— Mamet's hometown, the neighborhood in which he grew up, a childhood scarred by rejection and violence.

Although *The Old Neighborhood* explores the motifs of love-hate bonds, of evanescence, of learning in the absence of reliable mentors or ethical elders, of the devastation wrought by unethical parental behavior that was so riveting in *The Cryptogram*, this play, which also depicts an unsettled character—whose mind is "full of thoughts" about what he "is *leaving* ... and what they're [he is] going *toward*" (1995b)—is similarly a memory play, but it is more clearly focused on history, as seen through the eyes of a disillusioned, deeply pained man disappointed in love and in life who returns home rather than escape from it. Principally concerned with the very uniqueness of American Jewish life—who or what defines a Jew, the responsibilities of Jewish men and women, the effects of deracination, the pitfalls of intermarriage, the illusion of assimilation, and the difficulty of maintaining ritual—*The Old Neighborhood* raises questions about the difficulty of being Jewish in America confronting both the issues of self-hatred and anti-Semitism in ways not previously addressed by Mamet. Drawing us into the vortex of swirling emotion that only occasionally breaks through the veneer of stability that Bobby struggles to maintain, the play announces its return to home ground from the outset by counterpointing past and present realities. That Mamet also returns linguistically to the "old neighborhood" is reflected in diction and discourse, the musical Yiddish rhythms, inverted word order, intimate vulgarities, dropped phrases, and the absence of verbs, whereby authentic sounds of home underscore Bobby's outsider status. For although he displays knowledge of this discourse, he is cut off from it, neither using it nor finding refuge in the past that is so vital an element in Joey's and Jolly's lives.

Characteristically, Mamet depicts his characters engaged in fictionalizing, novelizing, mythicizing, and embellishing their lives in vintage Mamet stories—"The Plaid Raincoat," "The Fucking Skis," and "The Rogers Park Broads"—but as Ben Brantley recognizes, their "fantasies of an alternative world, in which religion, family and erotic love have a formal, enduring substance" stand in opposition to lives lived in quest of these (1997,

B12). Moreover, *The Old Neighborhood* like *Oleanna* and *The Cryptogram*, manifestly illustrates Mamet's increasing interest in personal narratives that afford greater visibility to ethnicity. And his methodology here is especially impressive, where concision belies immense cumulative power. Employing a paradigm that Walter Benjamin illumines in his famous essay, "The Storyteller," Mamet draws upon reminiscence *and* remembrance. "Memory is the epic faculty *par excellence*," Benjamin writes, and "by virtue of a comprehensive memory can epic writing absorb the course of events on the one hand and ... the passing of these ... " (97) on the other. As "Memory creates the chain of tradition which passes a happening on from one generation to another," he adds, narrative assumes the form of "perpetuating remembrance" complemented by "the short-lived reminiscences of the storyteller" (98). Recalling a technique perfected by Saul Bellow in which "The fragmentary nature of flashbacks" precludes the work from "bogging down in the past" (Alter 1969, 108), *The Old Neighborhood* acquires a broad sweep. Set once again in an urban setting, the elegiac and eidetic play not only taps into the yearning for safety and connection, but the very uniqueness of American Jewish life, expressed in such issues as intermarriage, deracination, and what Alan Dershowitz terms the "Vanishing American Jew."[5]

Prior to its world premiere in 1997, only *The Disappearance of the Jews*, staged in 1983, has received critical attention.[6] For Dennis Carroll it is "one of the playwright's bleakest" (146); for Jeanne-Andrée Nelson, Joey and Bobby, the play's protagonists, whom she likens to Didi and Gogo in Beckett's *Waiting for Godot*, "seemed to have missed their appointment with meaning and identity" (464); and for Christopher Bigsby, "The play's title seems to suggest not simply loss of identity through assimilation," but the "erosion of the self which stems from the denial of history and of the power of the individual to intervene in his own life" (1985, 41). What none of these critics addresses, I believe, is that the act of reminiscence and remembrance that informs these works is a powerful act of will, however subtle. "To forget is, for a Jew, to deny his people—and all that symbolizes," Elie Wiesel argues; "[it is] also to deny himself" (1990, 9), whereas remembering, with its resonance for the Jew, is by implication a return toward self.[7]

Jocy Lewis and Bobby Gould, childhood friends in their late thirties and Jewish archetypal "stoop philosophers" in Mamet's *The Disappearance of the Jews*, are two such culturally and ethnically detached American Jews. Longing for a life of connection, value, and tradition but finding themselves detached from Jewish identity, family, and each other, Joey and Bobby fabricate their own connection—however temporary—through memories and myths in which they functioned, or imagined functioning, as a dynamic duo. Rich in Jewish tradition, humor, irony, and discourse, the comedy of *The Disappearance of the Jews*, releases by "the superimposition of the tragic upon the trivial" (Shechner 1979, 234) and the sensual upon the serious, portraying assimilated American Jewry in transition, whose portrait is colored as much by persecution to which the Jew has been historically—and recently—subjected as the habit of self-irony.

Mamet situates his obviously Jewish characters in a hotel room in Chicago where together they recreate a panorama of the largely Ashkenazi Jewish community of their youth—Chicago's South Side from Seventyfirst Street to Jackson Park, and Rogers Park, the site of major Jewish migration from the West Side in the early 1950s.[8] Mamet employs the Chicago landmarks of the Conservative synagogue, Temple Zion, Rodfei Zedek, the delicatessen Frankels, the Jewish cemetery Waldheim, and the Ravenswood line of the "El" train to stake out authentically "the corner(s) of their world" (Mamet 1992a, 125–26).[9] And although he signals his return to the home turf that has served as setting for numerous works through recognizable Chicago iconic emblems, such as the Cubs and Marshall Fields Department Store, allusions to Jewish historical landmarks, such as the shtetl, the Lower East Side of New York City and Maxwell Street in Chicago—better known as the "New" Old World—and Hollywood, the site of development of the motion picture industry, and Europe under the Nazis evoking the Holocaust and the death of six million Jews, provide a cultural backdrop for the fixed and fluid continuum of Jewish experience anchored not in place but in time. Their visiting these "monuments" of their common past has, as Pierre Bourdieu observes in another context, "all the clarity of a faithfully visited grave" (31)—a ritual that we learn Joey and his wife Judy regularly perform— binding the men's time travel to the past to the grave of parents and grandparents, an excursion that bears little likeness to the promiscuity and propinquity of their youth. But as much as Bobby's and Joey's recollections of their youth reveal a kind of "anthropologically focused tour to ancient sites," it exposes "an underlying insecurity in contemporary Jewish life" that bears directly on their collective identity and unease (Kugelmass 44).

Employing an episodic structure of seven scenes, Mamet conveys the passage of time that has made these men older, if not wiser. Mood, method and motifs are immediately signaled by reminiscence, narrative, and controversy, such that they communicate Bobby's and Joey's disquietude through "Their macho posings and posturings, what's said, what's held back" (Siegel 1997, 4). "What I remember ... what I remember was that time we were at Ka-Ga-Wak we took Howie Greenberg outside," Joey begins, but in trying to identify Howie Greenberg, "Red hair Braces," (1997a, DJ 3–4), Bobby and Joey immediately widen their frame of reference and establish sharply opposing memories in an ethnically coded dialectic marked by their argumentative tradition. Bobby's rejoiners are representative: "I got to tell you something, Joey, it was not Howie Greenberg. Howie never went to Winter Camp. (*Pause*) Am I right? (*Pause*) Am I right? Jeff went to Winter Camp. Tell me I'm wrong. (*Pause*) You fuckin' asshole ... " (DJ 5)

Inspired by a prank that they played on Howie Greenberg—or was it Jeff?—at Camp Ka-Ga-Wak, they recall an even better time with two Jewish girls, Debbie Rubovitz and Debbie Rosen, whom they met in Rogers Park. Reminiscent of Bobby Gould and Charlie Fox in *Speed-the-Plow*, the two friends engage in a "high stakes" bet to determine which of "The Rogers Park Broads.... Some Jew broad ... Some folk dancer" slept with Bobby. "For five bucks, which was mine.... For ten bucks?" (DJ 11, 16), Bobby dares his friend in a line that reveals that neither remembers these finer points of their youth, although both have the larger picture in focus. Such an erotic memory triggers Joey's questions about Bobby's wife, and the seemingly casual way in which the playwright juxtaposes the profane and mundane and the present against the backdrop of the past—or from a Jewish perspective, views past and present as synchronous—is distinctively Mametic. In contrast to the easy banter of two guys sharing war stories of the women they have bedded, in other words, safe territory and topics, Bobby is noticeably reticent. Although his parsed responses yield little about the source of his distress, suddenly piqued at Joey's questions, he explodes, exposing a man both vulnerable and seething with "rage ... simmer[ing] below the surface" (Shalhoub qtd. in Marx 108). "You been reading 'Redbook' ... ? What is this all of a sudden ... (*Pause*) You want to know how she is? She's fine," thus cutting off further inquiry, but whether or not Bobby is "fine" remains to be seen (DJ 17).

In an even more outrageous fantasy of masculine prowess, Joey imagines himself "a great man in Europe ... Reb Lewis, he's the strongest man in Lódz" who "'once picked up an ox.' (*Pause*) Or some fucking thing" (DJ 28–29).[10] Rewriting history, Joey believes he was built to be "hauling stones," "Building things," or working the land instead of "schlepping all the time with heart attacks, with fat, look at this goddamn food I sell ... that stuff will kill you ... "(DJ 29). And how he would have worked in Lódz. An urban center of Polish Jewish life in the late 1800s, to which many shtetl Jews gravitated, often just prior to their migration to America, Lódz figures importantly in Jewish history as a barbed-wire-enclosed labor camp where between the years 1940–1944 two hundred thousand men, women, and children died of starvation and exhaustion, and the men quite literary worked like oxen dragging dead bodies to open pits before all perished in liquidation camps (Howe 10; Adelson and Lapides 197–98). But Joey's image of greatness and imagined physical strength in the shtetls (the Jewish villages in the Pale of Settlement that have been "painted with a fresh coat of romanticized nostalgia" since the end of World War II [Desser and Friedman 25]), gives rise to an even more fantastic theological image of Bobby elevated to the status of a learned man, a rebbe: "I'll tell you where I would of loved it: in the shtetl.... You, too. You would of been Reb Gould. You would have told them what Rabbi Akiba said ... (34).[11]

Implicitly referring to the aggadic narrative tradition that has long been the method of choice employed by Jewish theologians from biblical times to the present to communicate halakah—the set of rules for the way in which Jews are "to walk" in life, to behave in business, in family life, and in the synagogue—Joey remembers (or imagines) that biblical narrative island was interpreted "not by a clear presentation of its theme or meaning, but by the telling of a new tale about an aspect of an old one," which in turn, "discloses by answering one question and conceals by raising new questions" (Kepnes 213). With the mention of Rabbi Akiba, a learned, beloved rabbi martyred in death by flaying at the hands of the Romans, Joey implicitly suggests that a learned man, one wiser than he, like Bobby—"Mr. Wisdom," as he teasingly terms his laconic friend—would metaphorically extract the meaning of Jewish historical existence and his own, thus connecting him personally to a cultural and ethnic history. In such an idealized world, instead of "the doctors, teachers, everybody, in the law, the writers all the time *geschraiying*, all those assholes, how they're lost," suggests Joey, "They should be studying talmud ... we should come to them and to say, "What is the truth ... ? And they should tell us.... what this one said, what Hillel said, and I, I should be working on a forge all day" (DJ 29). Reb Gould, he imagines, would be studying Talmud and conveying "the truth." Sprinkling his speech with Yiddish phrases, some of which are not entirely understood by the audience, Joey employs an idiolect, like that of *Glengarry*, *Speed-the-Plow*, or *Oleanna*, that confirms the authenticity of the world evoked.

Whatever deprivations the shtetl entailed, it encompassed a world of values, order, and meaning that gave members of the community a sense of belonging and purpose. Thus, Joey's lyric romanticism of the shtetl reflects the manner in which American Jews typically hold East European Jewry at a spatial, spiritual, and temporal distance that, as Jack Kugelmass notes, is "a representation of the essential Jewish self uncorrupted by the compromises of the many" (41). Therefore, in a world of disconnection and disappointment, such as Joey's, his repeatedly distancing himself from his present reality, responsibility, and perceived entrapment in business and marriage and glorification of the past signal a longing for community and connection barely satisfied in fantasy. Further, as Joey's musings on marriage underscore, the gulf between Bobby's and his middle-class marriages and a lost world known only to assimilated American Jews through fantasy and photos is vast. In this context, the world of the shtetl represents an intact world of ritual, spirituality, and community[12]—a world apart from the dominant culture—that by definition sharply contrasts with contemporary American life, adding yet "another layer of complexity to a never ending discussion on what it means to be a Jew" (Kugelmass 50).

Bobby, who has an overabundance of complexity in his own life, imagines shtetl life in far more profane, pragmatic, and erotic terms, ponders the feasibility of sex in the shtetl or outside it with Polish whores:

> *Bobby*:   You think they fooled around?
> *Joey*:   Who? In the shtetl?
> *Bobby*:   Yeah.
> *Joey*:   The guys in the shtetl?
> *Bobby*:   Yeah.
> *Joey*:   I think it was too small. (DJ 34)

Hence, however tempting Bobby's dream of adultery, Joey's sense of history tells him that sex with "some young Jewish thing" has more merit than with Polish whores, his shocked remark—"Inside the shtetl?"—questioning what kind of a Jew would even think of defiling his own home. Their conversation darkens when Joey admits reluctantly and, in effect, shattering the sexual fantasy, that if a Jew "wanted to go out and fuck around who'd have you? If you stayed home [in the shtetl] you would be found out. I think. (*Pause*) But on the other hand who's to say what could go on. At night. In Europe" (DJ 36). It is a question that surely suggests infinite possibilities of nocturnal pleasure and plunder. Inspired by Bobby's reverie, Joey scripts a scenario in which he imagines his wife Judy stricken with an incurable disease, his grief and libido assuaged by "Some young, the daughter of one of my customers, the orphaned daughter ... is this what you're saying?" (DJ 37), the elliptical rhythm, the absence of verbs, and observational nuance of Yiddish calling attention to the fact that as a "culture" that "exalts reasoning, no less than faith ... Jewish wit hinges on logic to celebrate illogic" (Rosten 1989, xviii).

Although the phrases, "Who's to *say* what could go on. At night. In Europe," promise adventure, illicit pleasure, and freedom implicitly unavailable to the unhappily married Bobby and Joey struggling with monogamy and the reality of disconnection within their own homes,[13] Joey's delight at imagining a liaison with a sweet young thing is a vespertine vision more menacing than pleasurable. Setting us up with a bawdy, long-running joke, whose echoes may be found in dyads of men sharing stories about propositioning or bedding women in *Lakeboat, Sexual Perversity in Chicago* or *Speed-the-Plow*, Mamet strips the reminiscence of shtetl life of even a hint of romantic nostalgia with a "laugh" line that hits us broadside with its implicit reference to anti-Semitism in its myriad, mundane, and horrific permutations. Countering the illusion of illicit pleasure with the reality of plunder and pillage in the shtetl, Joey's comment—"Is this what you're saying"—and its pregnant pause permits us to enjoy the fantasy, on the one hand, only to find ourselves walloped by the recoil. For the veiled reference to nighttime raids connotes night terrors far removed from a night of pleasure, given the recollection that pogroms took place under cover of night to plunder, pillage, and prey upon unsuspecting Jews long before the SS "night-knock" rousted them from their homes during the Holocaust.

Conversely, Bobby's fantasies of power and potency are inspired neither by intellectual esteem traditionally accorded a rebbe, a teacher of ethics and moral behavior, nor by carnal knowledge. Nor is he particularly interested in reliving the American Jewish immigrant experience on Orchard Street in New York City, or Maxwell Street in Chicago, the "folk past" of pushcarts idealized in Joey's postnostalgic vision of an intact community, a romanticized portrait at odds with that depicted in Abraham Cahan's *Yekl*, Mike Gold's *Jews Without Money* and Henry Roth's *Call It Sleep*, classic novels of the urbanized immigrant experience. In fact, like Maxwell Street, Orchard Street lacked stability and cohesion precisely because it was the place where "old country Jewish ideals" battled a "powerful disinheriting America" (Klein 189, 222).

In his fictionalized account of American Jewish history, Bobby echews nostalgia for glamour and power. He would have "loved" to have been a maven and mogul in "Hollywood" in "the twenties" in an industry run solely by "five smart Jew boys from Russia," convinced that "they had a good time there" (DJ 38–39). As I discussed in my analysis of *Speed-the-Plow*, Jews utilized their commercial savvy to create a world apart in Hollywood. Far from the urban Jewish life of New York City, it lacked all semblance of religious ritual. Thus, in retrospect, we note the irony of Mamet's depicting Joey searching for cultural anchorage in the shtetl and Bobby, an assimilated Jew, finding his historical place in a de-Semitized Hollywood. However, that both seek refuge in a distant past strongly intimates that they are both "undergoing crises of faith and family" (Christiansen 1997, CN1).

As in previous dyads, Joey's and Bobby's banter quickly turns to quibbling, and once again Joey's interrogatory rhythms, which are themselves reflective of his Yiddish inflected speech, characterize his discourse. In fact, Joey speaks English laced with Yiddish, or what remains of the language, punctuating his points with such juicy phrases as "this shit is dilute, this is schveck this shit" (DJ 29). But when Bobby rattles off the names of the Hollywood moguls "Mayer. Warner. Fox." from memory, Joey is at a loss. Mulling over the name "Fox," Joey admits to thinking it "a goyish name" (DJ 40), which sets in motion a game of ethnic "Trivial Pursuit": "you know who else was Jewish?" (DJ 41). "'You know who's Jewish ...,'" writes Mamet, "was a recurring phrase at my house," one that ratified that a person, *particularly* in the entertainment industry ... had 'passed' ... into the greater world from the lesser" (1989b, 12). By association, then, Joey tries to top "Mr. Wisdom" by besting him with his knowledge that "Charlie Chaplin was Jewish" (DJ 40–41). Linking a story that brings them both back to their youth, the traditional visits to buy shoes at the neighborhood shoe store, Miller-White Shoes, and the Charlie Chaplin reference, Joey reveals that Mr. White was not only Jewish, a fact he had long doubted, but that he was "the shamus [a sexton] at Temple Zion thirty years" (44). His point is that "People fool you" (41), a resonant remark whose intent is both humorous and ironic, as the conclusion of the trilogy amply reveals. Chaplin, who both Joey and Bobby (and apparently Mamet) concur was Jewish—in fact, it is one of the points on which they do agree without argument—was generally believed to be Jewish. Mamet cites him among the cultural icons to which Jews refer in framing a Jewish identity: "We have our rare ballplayers, we have our tales of Charlie Chaplin and Cary Grant.... we have our Jewish food.... and we have our self-deprecating humor" (1989b, 12–13). Indeed, Chaplin was blacklisted by the House Un-American Affairs Committee, was concerned about Jewish issues, as his films from *The Immigrant* to *The Great Dictator* attest, and was "influenced by Jewish humor," but in the case of Chaplin, like Bobby's wife Laurie, about whom we learn much more, "people fool you": the mythos surrounding that individual—Chaplin was not Jewish—is more convincing, or in Laurie's case more worthy, than the truth (Desser and Friedman 9–11; Robinson).[14]

However, Bobby's fantasy, so unrelated to his life and a marriage ripe for divorce court, returns them both to the present and the nightmare reality that plagues each in differing ways. Joey's lament, "Life is too short" elicits a story that has in fact fueled his fantasies and memory, that he has not only dreamed of changing his life by murdering his family, he believes he has. "I can't tell you, Bobby ... I have a pistol, I can end it any time" (DJ 48). Like

Teach, a man with a gun, Joey is just a Jew stuck in a store living on dreams. Trapped in his delicatessen selling "heart attack" food, Joey seeks the power and freedom that he lacks through a criminal act—murder, mayhem, and adultery—and alternatively prays that ritual will enrich his tedious existence. Worst of all, he fears that he is going to die like this—a disconnected "schmuck" powerless to realize his potential. For "Men get together under three circumstances," observes Mamet: "to do business," "to bitch," and to have "*fun* with each other" in the company of other men in which "one is understood ... not judged ... [and] not expected to perform" (1989b, 87– 88). These men have clearly come together "to bitch," comforted by the fact that in an atmosphere devoid of shame, each "at some point [will] reveal that, yes, *they* are weaklings, too." If men "are *not* sensitive to women," acknowledges the playwright, "we are sensitive to our own pain and can recognize it in our fellows" (87). Hence, recalling the rationale for the choice of setting for this work, Mamet states, that "the scenic element essential to the dramatic thrust of the play ... is that this is a place [a hotel room] where these two guys can be alone and be intimate with each other" (Savran 143).

Sympathetic to Joey's pain and increasingly honest about the depth of his own, Bobby echoes Joey's desire to radically change his life by obliterating his marriage. "I should never have married a *shiksa*," he confesses (DJ 18). Initially, Joey makes a joke at Bobby's expense, teasing him about his dating non-Jewish women. "Yeah. I know," he says. "Cause that all you used to say, 'let's find some Jew Broads and discuss the Midrash ...'" (DJ 18). However, Bobby's cryptic remark acquires broader significance when, in answer to Joey's provocative "Mr. Wisdom ... speak to me" (DJ 18), Bobby gives him an earful. Prior to his leaving for a visit to Chicago, a touchstone of identity, Bobby and Laurie have discussed and obviously disagreed about their son's ethnicity, a subject that initiates a discussion on the "law" from the maven, Joey, who knows. To Bobby, on the other hand, the issue is simple and settled: "The kid is a Jew" (DJ 20), regardless of Conservative and Orthodox Jewish law that recognizes the boy as Jewish only if his mother is Jewish. As their banter reveals, Joey and Bobby may be close in age but light years apart in religious philosophy. Yet they are quibbling over a matter of far more importance than which of the Debbies each slept with or whether it was Howie Greenberg or Jeff they threw in the snow, an illustration, suggests Allen Guttmann, that "The anxiety accompanying the discussions of Jewish identity is greatest among secular Jews and least among Orthodox." Whereas the former have no idea who they are, "the latter have no doubt" (11).

Enraged by Joey's point of law, the typically terse Bobby is suddenly loquacious: "They start knocking heads in the schoolyard looking for Jews,

you fuckin' think they aren't going to take my kid because of, 'cause he's so
blond and all. 'Let's go beat up some kikes ... Oh, not that kid ... (DJ 21–22).
Beyond the painful realization that his fair-haired son, who is not even
considered a Jew by Conservative or Orthodox law, will nonetheless be the
victim of anti-Semitism in the schoolyard is the harsh lesson that Bobby has
learned, that anti-Semitism begins at home—*his* home. Like Joey, Bobby has
a harrowing tale to tell, but it is no fantasy. "Well, listen to this Joe, because
I want to tell you what she says to me one night. 'If you've been persecuted
so long, eh you must have brought it on yourself' " (DJ 22).[15] That Bobby's
ethnic dislocation has come full circle is manifest when he appears to
intellectualize, even condone, his wife's anti-Semitism. "Self-hatred arises,"
writes Sander Gilman, "when the mirages of stereotypes are confused with
realities within the world, when the desire for acceptance forces the
acknowledgment of one's difference" (1986, 4). Revealing the discourse of
the majority, "saturated with the imagined projection of the Other" (13)—in
this case the fallacious myth that Jews are responsible for the hatred directed
against them—Bobby's self-hatred is reflected in his conceding, even for a
moment, that Laurie's premise has merit, that "it got me thinking," and that
he remained silent in the face of her challenge (24).

If we've missed that point in Bobby's silence, Joey, who has been
pondering Laurie's statement and his friend's reaction, brings it to the
forefront of our consciousness. Mamet uses the opportunity to highlight
subtly that each friend assumes the role of mentor to the other, dispensing
lessons to live by and asserting Jewish values, privileging compassion and
respect, on the one hand, and assertion of pride in one's heritage and identity,
on the other. Notable, as well, is that Bobby and Joey dispense these lessons
in a manner consistent with their characters, which simultaneously rivets
attention to the studious intellect and the performance artist. Hence,
although both Joey and Bobby live lives of quiet desperation, devoid of the
power, potency, and confidence that colors their fantasies and characterized
their youth, an empowered Joey, still mulling over Bobby's wife's remark and
finding not a kernel of logic in Laurie's statement, rejects the sophistical
reasoning for what it is. "Wait a second. If we've been oppressed so long *we*
must be doing it" (DJ 22, emphasis added). Typically at his best in crafting
imaginary scenarios, Joey sets forth his sage wisdom in a mind-numbing
monologue with classic Mamet flair, counseling Bobby to jettison such a
premise from his mind (much as Roma advised Lingk in *Glengarry* to ignore
his wife's advice), challenging him to reject his guilt, self-flagellation, and
self-hatred, and encouraging him to question a relationship disrespectful of
his identity as a Jew. In doing so Joey draws upon the history, tenacity,

eloquence, and wit of his ancestors, both in the literal and figurative sense, to convince his friend of 30 years of the wrongheadedness of his thought, and in so doing manifests what Wiesel has defined as "the importance of friendship to man's ability to transcend his condition" (1990, 238). Illustrating that "the stoic ideal is goyish, having a tantrum is Jewish" (Whitfield 1984, 127), Joey is in rare form:

> Ho, ho, ho, ho, hold on a minute, here, ho, Bobby. Lemme tell you something. Let me tell you what she feels: she feels left out, Jim. Don't let that white shit get into your head.... they got, what have they got, you talk about community, six drole cocksuckers at a lawn party somewhere: "How is your boat ... " Fuck that shit, fuck that shit, she's got a point in my ass, what the fuck did they ever do? They can't make a joke for chrissake, I'll tell you something, you are sitting down, the reason that the goyim hate us the whole time, in addition they were envious is; we don't descend to their level.

> *Pause*

> because we wouldn't fight ... Because we have our mind on higher things.

> *Pause*

> ....

> My dad would puke to hear you talk that way.... your father, too, to hear you go that way. What are they doing to you out there? (DJ 24)

Tucked away in Joey's tirade is the key phrase, "white shit," which in his hysterical vitriol is easily missed. However, as Itzkovitz observes, the ongoing debate of the early twentieth century in America and of late has swirled around the issue of the "white" Jew, raising the question inferred in Joey's offhand, ostensibly insignificant remark: "Does a Jew who *is* able to appear white ... remain a Jew?" (182). Itzkovitz puts the question regarding the Jew's whiteness to the test, wondering whether "the Jew's performance of whiteness—the self-erasure of the Jew's Jewishness"—not only "enables his or her smooth assimilation" but is a reflection of the border-crossing, one that illustrates that assimilation is concomitant with "passing as white" (184).[16] And as that clearly is what Bobby has attempted to do, he suddenly finds himself listening not merely to Joey's tales but to his wise counsel.

In like matter and on the related subject of race, Mamet reverses course, and it is Bobby who challenges Joey's brazen braggadocio that one could prove his manhood in Europe during the reign of the Nazis by "standing up," presumably in the Chicago definition of the phrase as one who is faithful in the broadest interpretation of the term[17]—"the stand-up guy" sanctioned by Don in *American Buffalo*. Joey is not wrong that the posture of the Jew is one of conscientious objector, that is, having the courage to recognize inhumanity and speak out on it. And the Holocaust is the one subject, as Dershowitz has noted, that typically aligns Jews (1991), if for no other reason that it taught the harsh lesson that, like the boys who would pick out Bobby's son in schoolyard because he was a Jew, the Nazis incinerated "cosmopolitan," assimilated Jews along with shtetl Jews. It was and is race, not Jewish law, that determines how the Jew was or is seen by others, as Bobby's wife Laurie has made abundantly clear. In vehemently objecting to Joey's glib "Fuck the Nazis ... I'm saying, give a guy a chance to stand up," Bobby matches fact with Joey's fiction, proving how he has earned his moniker. "That's romantic shit," he tells him (DJ 31), reflecting at once Mamet's proneness to unequivocal statement and Bobby's impatience with Joey's bold front.

One of the lessons to be learned from the study of the Holocaust, Bobby explains with his characteristic conciseness, is that "You don't know"—nor can we know—what went on in Europe "with the Nazis" (DJ 32, 30). In lieu of the nexus of guilt that typically aligns the comfortable American to European victims of Nazism, Joey's preposterous claim that he would have had the courage and strength to endure the concentration camps, though unintended offense, is nonetheless pernicious, defaming the memory of Holocaust victims and survivors of Nazism, and Bobby calls him on it, just as Joey similarly rejected Bobby's self-hatred. Joey's impropriety so disturbs Bobby, a man of few words, that he reiterates his objection several times; in short, "it's profaning what they went through" (DJ 31).[18] And because the character has little to say, that which he does say gains greater impact, both in this play and in *Jolly*, the second of the trilogy, in which his loquacious sister threatens to drown out his thoughts and speech. An empathic figure, Bobby imparts a cautionary comment to his friend, affirming that his is a recondite wisdom, a heightened sensitivity to persecution, which in *Jolly* Mamet reveals is in part the result of a protracted exposure to brutality and oppression where he learned first hand the price of sacrifice that does not occur on behalf of anything. Moreover, Bobby's insistence on respect owed the dead and the survivor illustrate that although he is an acculturated Jew who has ceased to observe practice and prayer, he is attuned to what David Roskies terms the catastrophe of "memory of past destruction" (1984, 14).

That they are changing and have changed is the *other* narrative implicitly conveyed in this play. When Bobby is particularly withdrawn, Joey observes, "you never fuckin' changed you know that, Bob. 'Fuck you, I don't need anyone, fuck you ... '" (DJ 17), by which we assume he refers to Bobby's stoic silence, but both have grown older and wiser, learning, among other things, that there is no statute of limitation on anti-Semitism. In reflecting upon their youth, expectations, and identity, Bobby and Joey, disconnected from wives, families and those whose "questions are answered with ritual" (DJ 52), have in speaking about their spiritual alienation, rekindled personal memory, (re)established cultural bonds, and reflected the desire for enhanced spirituality. Joey's complaint that "Everything, everything, everything ... it's ... I'll tell you; it's a mystery ... (*Pause*) Everything is a mystery, Bob ... *everything* ... And we have no connection" (DJ 51-52), echoing the guilt, confusion, and alienation experienced by assimilated American Jews, is belied by *his* connection—brief in time and long in memory—to Bobby. Deeper still are the bonds of ethnicity, education (spiritual as well as sexual), tradition, and Jewish history.

Although critics are quick to dismiss these characters as accepting of the emotional and ethnic malaise in their lives, Beckettian pals who "refus[e] to take action while they wait for something to validate their lives" (Holmberg 1997b, 8), *The Disappearance of the Jews* amply illustrates that their contemplative mood comprised of both reminiscence and remembrance does not signify acceptance, nor does it acknowledge the "disappearance" of the Jews, as the playwright told me.[19] Conversely, given the context of their talking about the difficulty of maintaining connections (to Judaism and Judaic practice), in other words, of finding ways to foster (ethnic) identity and pride, their discussions explore the literal and metaphysical aspects of "returning home." In this manner they not only visit the past, they participate in rewriting the present,commencing a process of healing. Thus, although Bobby is an acculturated Jew *outside* tradition, the potential exists for him to find his back *into* a body of collective history "through his very consciousness of being outside it" (Alter 1969, 29). Or as Thorstein Veblen precisely puts it, "by loss of allegiance, or at the best by force of a divided allegiance to the people of his origin" the marginalized Jew "finds himself in the vanguard of modern inquiry.... [Yet] it does not follow that he [who goes away] ... will swear by all the strange gods whom he meets along the road" (1948, 474, 478), an observation that has broad application to Mamet's experience. As numerous critics, theologians and sociologists have noted, the disappearance of American Jews through acculturation, assimilation, and intermarriage has been a prediction solemnly intoned for the past several decades. As Robert Alter observes in "The Jew Who Didn't Get Away," with or without demographic data—the method by which the John in *Oleanna* sought to illustrate trends—one finds, instead, "the stubborn insistence" of a surprising numbers of American Jews gravitating back to religious practice, a trend that might be termed "a glimmering of an American Jewish culture" (1986, 281).

In *Jolly*, the second play, and the most devastating of the three, Mamet dramatizes Bobby's reunion with his younger sister Jolly. Here the playwright revisits the territory he charted in an autobiographical reminiscence, "The Rake," the lead article in *The Cabin*, a collection of reminiscences dedicated to Mamet's sister Lynn. She has written a play about a dysfunctional family entitled *The Lost Years* (1995) in which the character of the sister characterizes their family as "the reigning champions" in the "'Dysfunctional Family Olympics'" (15).[20] In *Jolly* Mamet forges a link between Bobby's and Jolly's familial experience of disjunction, dysfunction, and cruelty and the emotional events that currently overwhelm him. And he has never come closer to revealing the dysfunctional family or dramatizing the rationale for Bobby's self-imposed exile from the old neighborhood. In a rare use of invective, scatology, and irony, Jolly, we soon learn, has never been jolly by any stretch of the imagination, for her life—"A rich 'full' life" as she puts it (J 52)—has long been denied any whiff of the mirthful or the joyous. And while she is jocular after a fashion, Jolly is true to her name only in her ability to "jolly along"—to gladden, encourage, and uplift—Bobby's flagging spirits and self-worth.

Set in Jolly's home, the three-person, three-scene play takes place over the course of less than one day. It opens on an evening discussion among Bobby, his sister Jolly, and her husband Carl that is already in progress. Bobby has returned to Jolly's house, where he is staying for a brief visit after an absence of many years, and the initial scene finds him engaged in dialogue, or rather responding to Jolly's expository stories and diatribes in the informal, seemingly comfortable surroundings of her home. Like the conversation between Bobby and Joey in *The Disappearance of the Jews*, the dyad between sister and brother initially appears "deceptively casual and meandering" (Holmberg 1997b, 8). In fact, when the play opens, Jolly is recounting a telephone conversation with her stepfather to her brother, whose planned visit to Waldheim Cemetery with Joey, though neither confirmed nor denied, suggests a credible explanation for Bobby's somber mood obviously exacerbated by his sister's tale of the stepfather's brutal conversation with her.

As Jolly describes their stepfather's disapproval of the way in which she is raising her daughters, establishing the parameters for a trenchant discussion of parenting, both in the present and in the past, Bobby, who has been mostly restrained in his conversation with Joey, quickly builds to a wrathful rage. Advising her that she must cease all communication and connection, "all *meetings, dialogue*.... You should take an oath never to talk to, meet with" (J 4-5), he taps a reserve of repressed bitterness. But when she protests," ... but the children ... " Bob's response is instantaneous and even more adamantly obsessed with the protection of Jolly's children: "And the children most especially.... are we going to expose another generation to this ... this" (J 5), his disjunctive speech breaking under the weight of his anger, the words "another generation" providing minimal Mametic back story. Subtly framing the play as an exploration of their linked past and troubled lives, Mamet signals that like *The Disappearance of the Jews*, *Jolly* is a memory play; however, here the memories evoke little laughter and immense pain. With the barest brushstrokes Mamet paints a picture of divorced parents, stepparents, and siblings, of resentments, jealousy, preferential treatment, and mostly the cold reality that the memories and experiences of siblings sharply differ. As they rake up the past and reopen old wounds, or confront ulcerated ones, announcing, as in *The Cryptogram*, the journey in time, the play further reveals that Bobby's transient status naturally accelerates and condenses the revelation of family stories and personal dilemmas so that the unfolding of these appears in the natural flow of a compressed visit dredging up in a mere twenty-four-hour visit and within the safety of their relationship a seemingly endless ocean of pain. As Mamet tells Terry Gross, Jolly and Bobby "go back through the 'attic,' as it were, of their childhood, which was apparently not a very—not a very diverting time" (1997).

Bobby's anger, so well controlled—or hidden—for much of the time that he spends with Joey, even eerily suppressed as he related dispassionately his wife's heinous accusation that Jews deserve the persecution brought against them, here he is almost uncontrollable at times, his vacillating between despair about what effect his leaving his failed marriage will have on his own children, and his recollections of the rejection and confusion he felt as a boy, "the psychological sleight of mind" by which his parents "project[ed] their inadequacy onto their children" (Lahr 1997b, 73–74). Hence, Bobby's outburst to Jolly, "That's their swinish, selfish, *goddam* them. What *treachery* they have not done, in the name of ... " (1997, 7) breaks off, as many of his comments do, evoking her support, their common memory, and the impossibility of his finishing his sentence:

Jolly: ... I know ...
Bob: ... of 'honesty.' God *damn* them. And always 'telling' us we ...
Jolly: ... yes.
Bob: ... we were the bad ones ...
Jolly: ... Well, we were. (J 7)

Thus even as the text elicits through reminiscence the presence of strangers—the *sheigetz*,[21] the gentile man that their mother married, stepbrothers and sisters—and the absence of mentors, Mamet simultaneously evokes through fragmentary flashbacks that Bobby's and Jolly's lives are still held hostage to the past, their resentments and repressed feelings as much a part of their marriages as they were a part of their parents'. As Jolly justifies furthering the communication with their stepfather to herself, her husband Carl, and her brother, reminding Bobby and implicitly informing us that he was not living at home during her most painful and unprotected years, and neither did he care for their dying mother, nor visit Jolly during a period that has again been a trying one, Mamet leaves open the question of whether Bobby, like the maligned Carol, even returned to Chicago for his mother's funeral. Thus, while she sketches in the details of the most recent telephone conversations with her father, sharing with Bobby the current example of her father's parsimoniousness (emotional and well as financial), Jolly illustrates that this latest exchange is consistent with her father's longstanding criticism of her, revealing a woman "almost gnawed away by unappeased anger over her childhood, her mother's death, her stepfather's maneuvers over the estate and at Bobby" (Feingold 1997), the most loved and least available of the two children.

Sharing a gem that they both relish, Jolly ignites another round of vituperative rage directed at the offstage stepfather who, it seems, is undergoing therapy, which Jolly ridicules as so much "psychobabble." Continuing her story, she adds, "Oh, oh, he said, he's learning—you're going to love this: "learning to live 'facing his past'" (J 14). Indeed, learning to confront the past and move on to face the future emboldened or saddened by its lessons is the larger subject of *The Old Neighborhood*, for as the playwright amply illustrates, release does not come from the mundane but from matters of the soul. "The theater," he writes, "exists to deal with problems of the soul, with the mysteries of human life, not with its quotidian calamities" (1998, 27). Overarching the mundane details of family, business, and the

activities of a family weekend—popcorn, pancakes, Monopoly, and movies—
is Jolly's running narrative, a circuitous and often hilarious tale that
progressively closes in on anguish tearing at the soul. In typical Mametic
fashion, however, spare speech cuts to the quick, exposing profound sadness,
anxiety, disappointment, and despair, and "conflicting layers of past and
present selves," as Brantley has it (1997, B3).

 Unique in *Jolly*, however, is that Mamet has afforded this character a
distinctive dignity and discourse rare in Mamet's depiction of women. A
raconteur of unique talent with a flair for the dramatic, Jolly peppers her
stories with profanities not heard since *Glengarry Glen Ross* through which we
feel the full thrust of her fury, frustration, and anguish. Much of this early
scene is a running monologue occasionally interrupted by Bobby's
interjections—"Fucking leeches" (J 15) or "What in the hell *possesses* a man.
To *treat* you like that" (J 29)—and interrogatories, and Jolly's husband Carl's
reverberant instruction, "Tell him," compelling Jolly to speak and constrain
the listener in the binding role of narrator. Mamet's paradigmatic
counterpointing of a taciturn figure and a voluble one, which indicates the
conscious suppression of information or evasion of speech and moves the
fiction forward toward the revelation of facts repeatedly engulfed by the
flood of emotion that overtakes Jolly and listener alike, is especially effective
in this scene. One telephone call leads by association into another in a
continuing saga that reflects in Jolly's inimitable vernacular and fictive style
facts about which Bobby has little or no knowledge, namely that all her
requests for financial assistance during a period of dire fiscal exigency, the
result of her husband's unemployment, have been roundly rejected by the
stepfather who is kept dramatically alive as a pivotal figure, as is the dead
mother, through lively and frequent allusion to these offstage personae.
Framed in equivocations and legal jargon such that despite Jolly's urgent
need for funding her stepfather not only refuses to "*invade* the trust....," but,
as she explains, continuing her story, "it gets worse" (J 21, 25). Or more
accurately, the picture comes into greater focus as Jolly sketches in the sordid
details of her petition for assistance and recognition of her claim to her
mother's estate. Her stepfather's outright rejection deems both petitioner
and petition unworthy. Similarly, Jolly's solicitation of iconic emblems of her
mother's life and legacy—an armoire, an old mink coat, antiques with all the
resonance of history and heritage—is disregarded and denied by the
patriarchal figure empowered to facilitate her repeated appeals: "And so I *told*
him," Jolly continues her dramatic narration of her telephone call to the
stepfather with appropriate mimesis:

He'd say, "waaaaalll ... : that's a very special *piece* ... uh. Huh huh."
What do I get? NOTHING. NOTHING. Nothing. Some
cheap ... and it doesn't *matter.*... But she was my mother. And I
was there when she was dying. *I* was there. *I* was there. He'd drop
her off, and I was left, an infirm woman.... And that sonofabitch
that *cunt* that *cunt* that Carol. DIDN'T EVEN COME TO THE
... the *funeral.* And who gets the armoire? (J 17)

Indeed, as Arthur Holmberg notices, "Among the many surprises lying in
wait in *The Old Neighborhood*" is "that David Mamet, bulldog of male
invective, attacks ... patriarchy," as he has done in *The Cryptogram*, "for the
psychological damage it inflicts on women through contempt" (1997b, 9).
Furthermore, in choosing Jolly as that character who has both the voice and
the vocabulary to win our attention, Mamet emphatically illustrates the high
cost of disrespectful discourse to men and women alike.

Fusing *mamaloshen*, the Yiddish that comes easily to her lips with its
bawdy vulgarity, Jolly, clearly without benefit of the counseling she mocks,
channels her substantial rage into narrative. Contrasted with this discourse
is a language of affection also rare in Mamet's canon; Jolly not only
deciphers the coded phrases that intimate with few words the depth of her
brother's pain, she communicates her profound love for him. Repeatedly
using that wonderful Yiddish phrase (of varying spellings) "Bubeleh"—or
the shorthand, "Buub" for which there is no apt English equivalent other
than that it bespeaks unconditional love, and when used by his now-
deceased mother cloaked judgment. For Jolly, however, the word is not only
a natural expression of affection but a marker of the dual worlds in which
she functions as an angry, hurt adult badly scarred by horrific memories and
recent history—a woman who labels any uncaring action, whether in the
past or the present, as an unethical exchange—and conversely a caring
mother, wife, and sister who is one of Mamet's most fascinating women and
dedicated teachers.

Counterbalancing to some degree the painful heritage of abuse
dredged to the surface of the play, Jolly is a figure of reconciliation whose
life-affirming and sustaining family activities nurture Carl and her daughters
in an effort to initiate a new legacy, notably through giving the gift of
herself—in playing games with her children, home cooking (its echoic
allusion to Roma's and Levene's shtick that glorified home cooking in
Glengarry Glen Ross), and inventing weekend ceremonies that have the full
force of ritual. Additionally, Jolly implicitly conveys that despite—or because
of—the burden that she carries, she at least sets an ethical example for her

daughters, lessons to which they may refer after her death. Simply put, as Jolly tells Bobby, linking her past experience and current choices, she creates in a different model: "If they [their parents] had loved us. Mightn't they have *known* what we might want. I know what *my* kids want" (J 36). Thus it is with delight that she playfully makes Bobby admit that he slept well in her home because it is "Safer than Anyplace in the World" (J 57). "You see, Bob? Do you see? This is a *family*" (J 39), though in a surprise ending Mamet reveals how tenuous the concept of "safe haven" is for them or any of us, no matter how appearances and reiterated code words may shore up the illusion.

As a child Jolly felt her home was anything but safe. Her recollections of rejection—of literally being kicked out of bed by a stepsister, an iconic sign that signals her exilic, unprotected condition within the home—are linked to her mother's rejection of Jolly's plea to recognize the validity of her claim and her place in the primal family. Although Bobby readily acknowledges that the family treated Jolly "like filth," Jolly's disturbing childhood recollection is a case in point that implies her lingering resentment of her beloved brother who left her to face her oppressors alone:

> ... Do you know, you don't know, cause you weren't there—when they first came. *Mother* told me, I was ten. So she was eight; she was going to sleep in my bed. She took up the bed, as she was a "creeper," you know. I'm a rock. You put me in a bed. And unmoving. Morning. She was all over the place. And I went and told Mom that I couldn't sleep. She said, "she is his daughter, and this is the case.... If you can't sleep, sleep on the floor." (J 10)

In retrospect, it is an event that opened the floodgates for all manner of verbal and physical abuse inextricably bound to this test of a mother's love, or rather the failure of the mother to protect Jolly from the intruder in her bed and, by extension, in her home. That the support was nonexistent, in fact, that the event was marked by the withdrawal of support, solace, or expression of affection—the ripping away of the proverbial blanket, that emblematic token with associations that we recall from *The Cryptogram*—is the most graphic indication of childhood abuse that finds form or phrase in *Jolly*. Like the "white shit" in Joey's monologue, Jolly's three-word phrase— "you don't know"—nearly missed in the narration of her horrific experience, represents the gulf of experience between a sister and the brother she adores who is physically, emotionally, and psychologically out of touch with her life. In sharp contrast to the brutalization of Mamet's sister portrayed in "The Rake," Jolly's psychological trauma is the only one at issue, for even as they differ, as Brantley also notices, Jolly's and Bobby's past is "their central defining reality, its particulars recited and repeated like a litany" (1997, B3).

Awakened in the middle of the night by uneasy dreams and disquieting thoughts, Bobby and Jolly continue their conversation in scene 2, their intimacy attenuated by the lateness of the hour. From the outset their conversation turns to a distant time when as Jewish children they celebrated Christmas. "One thousand generations we've been Jews and she marries a *sheigetz* and we're celebrating Christmas" (J 44), Jolly notes with little humor, as brother and sister recollect their mother's marriage to a gentile that stripped life of all familiar traditions and customs and supplanted them with a loveless life, a despised, violent stepfather, the trial of coping with the spectacle of Christmas, and the ritual of unwanted gifts that came with disclaimers but dared not be returned. Yet, in contrast to scene 1, Bobby and Jolly assist one another is recovering the past, each scripting forgotten details of the other's story in a scene that is alternately bathed in pathos and brightened with humor, although undergirding the scene, and occasionally rising to the surface of the dialogue, are the sadness, haunting memories, and troubling thoughts that have awakened both siblings. Bobby recalls "A plaid ... a ... a plaid something" and with the aid of his sister weaves a hilarious, touching story of his being given an unwanted plaid reversible raincoat from Marshall Fields that he so detested that he returned it, trading it in, and "Oh my God. Jol. For, what, then, a year ... ?.... For a *year*," he remembers being hounded, 'Where is that raincoat, Bubby ... ?'" (J 33-34). Desperate to stop the questions, he went to Marshall Fields "TO SEE COULD I BUY BACK THAT COAT.... And that woman at Fields. Sent to fucking *Germany* to see, could they replace that raincoat" (J 35).

The conversation goes "round and round," picking up the threads of subjects picked up and dropped earlier in the evening or in the scene, one that merges immediate past and ancient history. Jolly is apparently obsessed with convincing her brother that Carl, the man her family rejected as unsuitable for her, their despised daughter, is a prince and she a nurturing mother. As she speaks incessantly, however, her words are reminiscent of the two ways in which Pinter has described silence, as the absence of speech and a torrent of speech.[22] Implicitly, the play suggests that neither her marriage nor her life is a fairy tale but rather a daily struggle, a point underscored by Carl's irritation with Bobby when he queried Carl earlier in the evening about how Carl—an outsider who inherited their miserable misfortune by marriage—can endure the saga that is their family's history.

Like the protoganists in *The Disappearance of the Jews*, Jolly and Bobby are storytellers with vivid memories, pained lives, terrifying nightmares, and fantasies of an alternative world. That these two adults dwell on their deprivation "with such virulence after so many years dramatizes its lasting psychological significance" suggests Holmberg, wisely noticing their seemingly insatiable need to pick the scabs off the scars (1997b, 9). Jolly, for her part, has two stories to share with her brother that concern their mother. The first is a memory of her mother's continuance of the gift-giving rituals to which she and her brother were subjected as children. Disregarding either the wants or the needs of the recipient for the "Big Present," her mother ignored Jolly's specific appeal for money for shoes for the girls, no doubt a link to a similar, earlier request, though on a vastly different scale, to her stepfather for assistance to cover basic needs. This allusion also serves as a narrative transition to Bobby's and Joey's conversation in the first play of *The Old Neighborhood* about Miller-White Shoes and Joey's recent visit to the shoe store they had frequented as children.

The second story is a recurring nightmare that since her mother's death continues to savage Jolly's dreams. Whereas she embellishes the shoe story, Jolly demurs on the subject of the nightmare until the following morning just prior to Bobby's departure when juxtaposed to the figure of security, her childhood recollections of an intact world—of grandparents, of fathers who returned at the end of the day, of holidays spent as a family, of favorite foods, of Jewish ritual—flood the conversation and bring her fear and pleasure as a child into sharp focus. The technique not only builds anticipation, it arouses curiosity, intimating that in one who is rarely silent on any subject, her choice to defer discussion belies a nightmare so troubling that she prefers postponing rather than uncovering it. Further, it intimates that Jolly so cherishes the time with her brother that she delays until a future time a tale that will undoubtedly mar her visit with him. Setting the scene, Jolly picks up the dropped threads of the shoe story sharply paralleling that of the unwanted raincoat. "I'd say Shoes. They need shoes," she goes on, but at "The end of her stay, she would give them, God Bless her, these, two *incredibly* expensive, what are they, 'vanity' sets" (J 42–43). Jolly's best tales are of the "fucking *skis*" and the red bookbag that, unlike Bobby, she did not have the courage to return to Marshall Fields and resentfully carried for three years, much as she still shoulders the burden of that memory. In this case, it is Bobby who prompts Jolly in her performance of the story of "The Christmas Skis," cueing her with the line "What Is That Behind The Door" (J 44), that in scene 3 takes on new meaning as we come to understand how much is hiding behind the facade of stability and security that Jolly works so hard to maintain.

The late-evening encounter, however, proves an opportune moment for a more intimate line of questioning and confessions that finally draws brother and sister into a discussion of the marital problems that have sent Bobby to Chicago in search of the safety and comfort of Jolly's love. Maintaining a respectful distance from her brother's personal life Jolly nevertheless uses this opportunity to question her brother's future intentions, and he appears to surprise himself by revealing a previously unacknowledged decision that he has no intention of returning to his destructive marriage and anti-Semitic wife. Whether that decision is the result of discussions with Joey or Jolly or both Mamet characteristically leaves open to our interpretation. Conversely, Jolly's expression of unequivocal support, regardless of Bobby's decision, illustrates the lessons she has learned from manipulative, exploitative, sadistic relationships that rewarded her with love or gifts as they served others' needs and disposition. Yet, the stability of her love for him is bested by the chaos of her life which receives substantial clarity as she relates a story of going the wrong way on a one-way street, one which validates the fragility of *her* state of mind and her entrapment in the past. This provides the perfect transition to Bobby's fragile emotional state tacitly conveyed in his long silences and sudden rages. Through intimation rather than explanation, Mamet reveals the depth of Bobby's anguish in a single, disjunctive statement that, like Levene's allusion to his daughter in *Glengarry*, implies how much more pain remains unspoken. Coming from him, Bobby's expression of grief—"Oh, God, I get so *sad* sometimes, Jol. I can't, it seems, getting up from the *table* ..."—yields one of the play's most poignant moments and anguished revelations (J 53).

Scene 3, which takes place on the following morning, sets up the scenario for Carl's departure for work and Bobby's for places unknown. Yet brother and sister cannot say goodbye. The play's briefest scene, it packs a powerful punch as Jolly's long-delayed narration of her nightmare has yet to be aired. Juxtaposing her memories of the intact world of her childhood before the divorce that has deeply scarred her with that of the nightmare, Mamet achieves a stunning contrast in images of exterior and interior space, of a protected world and an appalling one, of a life of connection and deception, of affection and enmity through which we make "the discovery," as Lawrence Langer writes, "that memory is not only a spring, flowing from the well of the past, but also a tomb, whose contents cling like withered ivy to the mind" (1991, 69). Whereas the two earlier scenes counterbalance Jolly's expressions of anger and outrageous invective, this scene is unrelentingly painful as we witness a woman for whom no amount of fictionalizing and romanticizing can render this picture anything but bleak. Like the world of values and cultural history to which Bobby and Joey retreat in their fantasies, Jolly, too, locates pleasure in the distant past, retrieving at will the world of her early childhood enriched by connection, ritual, observance, and love. When Jolly tempts Bobby, "We could go back" (J 61), the emblems associated with safety are to be found *way back* in a home imbued with love and tradition, both familial and cultural, an intactness that preceded a family fractured by divorce and de-Semitization and a childhood savaged by cruelty. In that idealized time "Dad would come home every night, and we would light candles on Friday, and we would do all those things, and all those things would be true and that's how we would grow up" (J 62). In short, in the ceremonies and rituals, the sights and the smells of the old neighborhood, Jolly finds a prescription for happiness and the pain of loss. While the pull of the past, especially cultural memory, is a source of strength in Mamet's domestic plays, it may well be that the remembered past is illusory, even trustworthy, and that Jolly's idealized home precludes her full engagement in her present reality.

In contrast, her recurring nightmare strips away the fantasy and thrusts her into the swirling world of disempowerment that she has struggled to escape. Revealing betrayal and the language of lie that gives life to it, Jolly's riveting narrative binds listener and audience to the nightmare vision: "I'm having this dream. How's *this* for dreams ... ?" she asks, drawing Bobby into the tale.

> They're knocking at my door...."Let me in," and I know that they want to kill me.... *Mother's* voice from just beyond the door: "Julia, Let Me In." "I will not let them hurt you.... " the sweetest voice. "You are my child ... " and it goes on.... "You are my child. I *adore* you." ... I open the door, this sweetest voice, and there is Mom.... *(Pause)* And she wants to kill me. *(Pause).* (64)

A stunningly dramatic moment, Jolly's matter-of-fact narration is a shocking conclusion to this play, which reminds us, "as Freud suggests," writes Mamet, that "there is the *manifest* dream, the dream we remember, and ... the *latent* dream—the dream the manifest dream is intended to obscure, the dream we would rather forget ... which is too unsettling" (Mamet 1996f, 59). As emotionally wrenching as anything that Mamet has written, *Jolly* is a deeply moving, complex work, which reveals that memory is a double-edged legacy that both binds us to the past and shapes our lives.

In *Deeny*, the briefest, most circuitous, and subtlest segment of *The Old Neighborhood*, Mamet dramatizes Bobby visiting his first great love Deeny about whom he queried Joey in *The Disappearance of the Jews*. Learning that she lives in Chicago, has been recently divorced, has inquired about Bobby, and works in a local department store selling cosmetics, Bobby apparently hopes to find something in this reunion. *Deeny* is in essence a monologue, whose impression of a single voice is supported by the laconism to which Bobby has retreated. Indeed, Bobby's responses are principally monosyllabic and few in number in contrast to Deeny's stream of consciousness. She speaks about her professional success, about a garden she intends to grow but never plants, about early frosts, predictions, the unhealthy aspects of cigarettes and coffee, smudge pots, and "the folly of passion and the function of rituals" (Holmberg 1997a, 9). Buried under layers of metaphor and understatement, Mamet has created, as it were, a scene reminiscent of that between Dr. Astrov and Yelena in *Uncle Vanya* (a play Mamet has translated), in which apparently nothing and everything is communicated between two people.

"D," an affectionate term for Deeny, whose name comes up in myriad contexts in *The Disappearance of the Jews* yet is never acknowledged in this play, is a shorthand of former lovers. Having learned from Joey the Marshall Fields department in which she works, Bobby, reunited by design or by chance with those with whom he had close relationships before marrying, decides to see Deeny. Whereas the depth of their relationship, in contrast to that of Joey and Jolly, remains unspoken, its tangible impression of loss is nonetheless felt. Typically, Mamet cuts directly to the scene of Bobby and his former girlfriend sharing a cup of coffee (which, ironically she disparages even as they drink it, making a joke of which she, too, is aware), leaving the audience to draw its own conclusions about his and her motivation, the seriousness of their former relationship, the wisdom of his seeing her in his emotional state, the price of an encounter that may further exacerbate his emotional distress, if only by setting him up for further disillusionment. Unlike the two earlier plays, however, Bobby and Deeny do not dredge up the history of their relationship or bicker about the facts of their separation. Neither do they reminisce. Yet, "the more she talks, the more we realize that nothing she's saying is tangential" (Siegel 1997, F4).

Juxtaposing the spiritual and the mundane, the "higher" things of ritual integral to the maturation of a young man with planting—both of which "force," as she puts it, new life—*Deeny* contains some of Mamet's most moving lyrical poetry. This representative exchange reveals the impact of Bobby's visit to the world of his youth, implicitly suggesting how distanced he and Deeny are from that time. But unlike his other reunions, Bobby listens attentively to her without apparent anger or angst. As she speaks about Oriental faiths, ritual, and change,[23] Deeny, like Joey, alludes to the subject of "spiritual practice." Finding her references to faith enigmatic,

Bobby becomes lost in the maze of her ideas, which makes his attentiveness to her telling remark on loss, bereft of nuanced sentimentality, all the more remarkable: "It's just something somebody says is true. And you say, 'Yes. I'll believe that that's true'.... But having lost the feeling that things will right themselves. (*Pause.*) What? It becomes harder ... "(D 10). Attuned to the fact that in his exceedingly vulnerable state he may not want to hear her clear-eyed vision of loss she hesitates but after she queries him three different times, she segues into a discussion of planting a garden that has more to do with why we act or fail to act, even on those decisions that we feel will bring pleasure and benefit. It is a beautiful interior monologue, but Bobby is lost in thought, or rather stuck on the one thought (as Joey was earlier on Laurie's statement) he has been pondering as she continues speaking: " ... that things will not come right" (D 11).

In a different key he had expressed a similar view to his sister when Jolly inquired about whether he intended to return to his wife Laurie, revealing his distress that the impact of his decision to leave the marriage would be hardest on his children, just as he and Jolly have themselves endured the scarring experience of divorce. Despite its ostensible indirection, the power of Deeny's rambling speech is cumulatively effective, for at play's end it becomes apparent tat her monologue is "futility spill[ing] out a stream of small talk for larger purpose: to awaken the affair, to reestablish a connection, to inspire new love" (Christiansen 1997). She, too, is needy, bitter, hopeful, resigned. And although it does not appear so at first glance, the seemingly nondirectional speech is both a protective stratagem against his anticipated rejection of her and a loosely constructed narrative that for a time holds his attention even if it does not rekindle love. Yet, "When the final goodbye comes," her "Goodbye, then, love," quite startling in its contrast to the meandering conversation, confirms a deep, first love that "tolls like a death knell. But with the parting, one feels not only sorrow, but also release, the release that comes with the possibility of rebirth" (Holmberg 1997b, 9) implied in those gardens waiting to be planted.

Hence, as Bobby leaves the woman he once loved and the old neighborhood, his time expired and quest concluded, one is left to wonder whether the lessons he has acquired from Deeny, a message of faith in the possibilities of life, together with those he acquired in his reunion with Joey and his sister, will cultivate healing and renew the ethnic ties sought in this return home. At play's end we are left to ponder the ethical exchange and the recognition that Bobby has achieved. To the playwright that exchange is "something very gentle. Perhaps it's on the order of one can't go home again, or perhaps not" (Holmberg 1997a, 8–9). In either case, Mamet does not send us out of the play uplifted by this reunion; rather, with a glimmering of hope we intuit that in returning home Bobby has found, as Michael Lerner has it, "a path to healing and transformation." For as the playwright has written in another context, " When something shines through ... when you are *done* with it.... you see the sadness less" (1991a, 292).

Inspired by a story of the persecution and extermination of his mother's relatives in a forest during World War II, David Mamet's *Goldberg Street* is a minimalist gem—no longer than one scene of *The Disappearance of the Jews*— in which father teaches his daughter about her ethnic identity, her history, and her responsibility as a Jew. In dismissing the play as "nearly cryptic," "utterly aporetic (*what* are they talking about?)," and "heartbreakingly moving," Tony Zinman reflects a common response to Mamet's minimalism (213). Conversely, while the stories themselves may be cryptic, the play is not.

"To be Jewish," Wiesel reminds us, "is to remember—to claim our right to memory as well as our duty to keep it alive.... For memory is a blessing.... creating bonds between present and past, between individuals and groups" (1990, 10). Analogous to the plays in *The Old Neighborhood*, this is principally a memory play, animated and informed, as are the others, by biography. What they are speaking about is education and ethical behavior, namely the responsibility of the older generation to teach the younger about a history of persecution, the moral imperative of religion founded an ethical principles, and the importance of each Jew's believing in and contributing to what Mamet describes as "the *excellence* [of] Jewish Culture" (1989b, 9). And dominated by interrelated experiences that reveal the binding relationship of story, *Goldberg Street* manifestly illustrates Benjamin's premise that "*Memory* creates the train of tradition which passes from one generation to another" (98).

We overhear a seemingly aimless conversation between a Jewish man and his daughter in which he recounts through the medium of two complementary midrashic stories (resonant with cultural connotations) memories of two incidents of his youth, each of which occurred in the woods, that continue to haunt him in old age. One event apparently took place in Bregny, France, where he fought in World War II and where he remembers soldiers armed with semiautomatic weapons hunting "deer"; the other, when he and his unit were lost in the woods during training maneuvers in Arkansas. The former is an implicit reference to the brutality of "the hunters" whose persecution of Jews is tellingly chronicled in Martin Gilbert's *The Holocaust*.[24] Lynn Mamet recalls that she and her brother both have a distinct memory of a family remembrance of "a brace of trees into which the men [of her mother's family who remained in Poland] went and from which they did not return."[25]

The latter story is an overt example of anti-Semitic behavior directed against American Jewry. The father relates an incident that occurred when he was a young soldier. When his platoon became lost in the woods, he volunteered to use a compass to lead the group back to their base

> I said, well, I'd never *held* one.... but I supposed I ... took it. Read it. Followed the map. Led us back to camp.... It was a joke. For anti-Semitism in the army. Then. Even now.... They scorned me, as I assume they did, for those skills they desired to possess. (33)

Because he had the survival skills, he was ridiculed; because he was wiser— or fool enough to volunteer in the army—he was awarded a Unit Citation[26]. "Reading a compass was easy enough," recalls the father, "if you just take away the thought of someone coming to help you (*Pause*)" (33). However, confronting the unit's anti-Semitic behavior exceeded his ability. Even with the passage of time, period left intentionally vague by Mamet, the man is pained by the knowledge that he could read both the compass *and* their minds; and knowing they thought him "ludicrous," the soldier was nevertheless willing and "glad to go" (34), not unlike the children in *Jolly*, drawn into the games of the grownups.

While fertile, the metaphor of the compass as a navigational tool pointing toward magnetic north is a paradoxical one whose meaning becomes increasingly apparent throughout the play as the father points his daughter in the direction of ethnic pride. The term "north" in Jewish tradition, observes David Fass, is a richly symbolic one whose myriad interpretations depict it as the locus of the powers of the universe, the source of evil and destruction, the source of justice tempered by mercy, and "redemptive transformation" for the exiled Jew of the Diaspora (473). Therefore, although the father's thought is never verbalized in its entirety, his obsession with fixing his priorities and behavior, as if they were in disrepair, assumes the double meaning of fixing a point on a compass to find the way to the "pride *in myself*—for the alternative is to say that I am not a man, or that I am impotent or *stupid*" (32), in other words, the schlemiel (or "*schmuck*," as Joey describes his impotence) who allowed himself to be mocked by other American soldiers in Arkansas. The lesson that the man wishes to teach his daughter is that one must have pride in oneself, belief in one's ability to influence the direction and actions that one takes, and responsibility for "those things where one *cannot* refer to someone" (32). Echoing the same idea in "The Decoration of Jewish Houses," Mamet exhorts Jews: "We are a beautiful people and good people, and a magnificent and ancient history of thought and action lives in our literature *and lives in our blood*" (1989b, 13).

Creating a broader field of focus and thereby uniting recent journeys and events distanced by decades, the daughter encourages her father to relate the story of his returning to Europe sometime after the war. Lacking in precise details, his enigmatic narrative sketches a story of reunion and remembrance, which by all implications took place at or near the American Cemetery in Normandy, "right by the cliff" (34). "They remembered you. (*Pause*) They remembered what you'd done" (34), she immediately recognizes, but this memory, too, strikes a chord for the father, for it triggers a mythos that all this talk of old times has not altered: "Patton slapped that Jewish boy. They said ... (*Pause*)" (34). Differing from several fictions in this short piece, for which the man has ample personal experience, this tale is drawn from common knowledge, though incomplete. In the absence of back story what is striking about the father's clipped phrase is that when he fought the majority of the "men" *were* all boys, as, presumably, was he. Even with the passage of time this anecdotal story triggers his memory; in the remembrance of things past, certain events and facts remain crystalline, "I knew they thought me ludicrous" (34) as vivid a humiliation as the Plaid Jacket or the fucking skis.

In fact, as the father correctly remembered, while touring military hospitals in Sicily in August 1943, General George S. Patton slapped and verbally abused two soldiers suffering from combat exhaustion, charging them with being cowardly shirkers, a coded term that had long attached itself to the Jew (Gilman 1991b, Hertzberg, Dinnerstein). Whereas the first incident may have gone unnoticed, in the latter incident, which occurred five days after the first, the soldier, responding to Patton's query about the nature of his ailment, said that he believed he was suffering from nerves. Patton slapped the soldier with his gloves, called him a "yellow bastard," and kicked him in the behind. Emerging from the tent, he was heard by correspondent Noel Monks to shout, "There's no such thing as shell shock. It's an invention of the Jews" (Knightley 320).[27] According to Martin Blumenson, the first reports of the incident in the American press failed to note that the soldier was of Jewish descent and that Patton had called him yellow-bellied or yellow-streaked Jew. Two weeks after the incident, the published story about the soldier being Jewish was retracted—he was, in fact, a member of the Nazarene Church—and Patton apologized publicly for his derogatory comments about Jews (791). Subsequently he claimed that his intention was merely to shock the soldiers out of their battle fatigue, but the event incurred the wrath of his superiors and nearly ended his career. The event has been mythologized among Jews as illustrative of the kind of anti-Semitic smear campaign to which Jewish soldiers were submitted which maligned their character and presumed cowardice under fire. Thus, long after the retraction, Jews maintained the belief that Patton's behavior was motivated by anti-Semitism. Hence the man's remark, "Patton slapped that Jewish boy. *They said ... (Pause)*" (34, emphasis added), retains that element of doubt and renders proof that the event has evolved, like Chaplin's identity, into an intact mythos. The father double-backs to his purpose to impart some worthy lessons, instructing his daughter to remember her identity and to acknowledge it with pride. With the benefit of age and lucidity the father acknowledges, "They sent me for a joke.... Our shame is that we feel they're right *(Pause)*" (34).

Not unlike those of second-generation American Jews, Mamet's childhood was "expunged of any tradition.... The virtues expounded were not creative but remedial: let's stop being Jewish, let's stop being poor" (Lahr 1983, 476). In *Goldberg Street*, however, the virtues expounded are creative, namely the "fixing" of priorities alluded to by the father, such as the criticizing of Jewish self-hatred and the denouncing of anti-Semitic behavior. Thematically linked to *The Disappearance of the Jews, Goldberg Street* picks up the subjects of impotence, spiritual malaise, and anti-Semitism raised and drooped by Bobby and Joey in the first play of *The Old Neighborhood* and focuses attention on assuming the central responsibilities of the Jewish parent sounded in *Jolly:* teaching ethical conduct and performing timeless, sustaining ceremonies. Although the father may have received his citation many years ago for reading the compass correctly, it is only now that he has begun the journey toward redemptive transformation. Indeed, observes the father wisely, "But sometimes ... *(Pause)* And sometimes, also—you must stand up for yourself.... At some point (1985, 31).

Although *The Disappearance of the Jews,* and *Deeny* are self- contained works, *The Old Neighborhood*, is aggadic as well as elegiac. Comprising the rich tapestry that is American Jewish history, its threads link past to evolving present, a point signified by generations of grandparents, parents, and children situated on and offstage. By recasting *The Disappearance of the Jews* in a larger frame, Mamet's dramatization of Bobby Gould's return to his home in *The Old Neighborhood* acquires immediacy and the weight of history. Thus the trilogy, Mamet's first, merges the minimalism of *Goldberg Street* and the dazzling language that we identify as Mametic, its clear articulation of culture encompassing the double-bind of legacy as blessing and burden in a teaching moment that envisions an ethical contract between individuals within or outside the margins of family, both seminal and communal.

NOTES

1. Lynn Mamet told the author that *Jolly* was inspired by a lengthy telephone call that she had with her brother during the filming of *Homicide*, interview 10 October 1990.

2. The world premiere of *The Old Neighborhood*, under the direction of Scott Zigler was 11 April 1997, at the Hasty Pudding Theatre, Cambridge, Mass. This production, featuring Tony Shalhoub as Bobby, Vincent Guastaferro as Joey, Brooke Adams as Jolly, Jack Willis as Carl, and Rebecca Pidgeon in the role of Deeny, was produced by the American Repertory Theatre, Cambridge, Massachusetts, in its "New Stages" series. *The Old Neighborhood* transferred to the Booth Theater, New York, opening 19 November, with Patti Lupone as Jolly and Peter Riegert assuming the role of Bobby Gould. Other cast members reprised their roles in a production directed by Zigler.

Although the play was written in 1989, Mamet made numerous changes to the manuscript before and during the rehearsal process for the world premiere. Therefore, the unpublished version cited serves as the principal reference for this chapter; alphabetical lettering in parenthetic references denotes non-continuous pagination in this manuscript.

3. The trilogy's notable reliance on the unsaid is dramatized in sentences that abruptly stop or drift off, the avoidance of subjects, and the counterpointing of quiescent and loquacious characters. Its seeming stasis recalls the plays of Chekhov in its coalescence of phenomenal and psychological experience, particularly apt for these small, seemingly slight works. On the use of the unspoken and the unspeakable in Chekhov's plays, see my chapter in *The Language of Silence* (1984, 50–75).

4. Interview with Mamet, 12 March 1992; this subject was also taken up in our discussion, 30 September 1996.

5. The literature on this subject is vast. See in particular Alan Dershowitz, who addresses the issue of intermarriage in *The Vanishing Jew*.

6. Most interpretations of *The Disappearance of the Jews* read this reunion and the subjects discussed as aimless discussion about that which is lost. Roskies's explication of the paradigmatic narrative of "rebellion, loss, negotiated return" in the Jewish experience is especially valuable in this context (1995).

7. The Talmud suggests that "Returning home" is, as Lawrence Kushner writes, "the easiest thing to do, for it only has to occur to you to return and you have already begun." See his "Coming Home" (1993, 31–33).

8. I am indebted to Bonnie Meltzer and the collaborative efforts of the Boston and Chicago offices of Facing History and Ourselves for their assistance in identifying numerous landmarks alluded to in *The Old Neighborhood*. See also Mamet's essay, "71st and Jeffery" (1992a, 125–28).

9. *Referring to Mamet's Duck Variations*, Steven H. Gale observes that the familiarity of the characters attests to their "stable relationship" achieved over time

(208), a point whose validity is similarly demonstrated in the disjunctive speech of two men in *The Disappearance of the Jews* whose friendship spans 30 years, a recurrent paradigm in the discourse of siblings and lovers.

10. Joey's fantasies of physical strength are ironic in that he imagines himself in the image of a famous American heavy-weight champion, Joe Louis. Neither is he as comic as his namesake Joe E. Lewis, a Borscht Belt comedian of the 1950s and 1960s. Implied is Michael Gold's 1930 novel, *Jews Without Money*, set in the Lower East Side of Orchard Street about which Joey rhapsodizes, a place of yearning and evanescence that is literally the "World of Our Fathers," the immigrant experience that Howe records in his encyclopedic study.

Given its context, Joey may have unknowingly confused "Lodz" with "Luz" in its varied biblical meanings. In this regard Schwartz's "The Aggadic Tradition" is valuable (esp. 86–87).

11. Rosten maintains that the term *rebbe* is applied to one who is a spiritual leader—"rebbe, a rabbi, spiritual leader, or teacher" (1989, 429); "Reb," on the other hand, is a term of address similar to sir or mister. Unlike rebbe, it is never used alone, but must be followed by the *first* name of the individual, as in Reb Yankel. That Joey does not know this serves to deepen the irony and confirm his paltry knowledge of *shtetl* life, namely that his Yiddish/Yinglish is disconnected from history. Mamet has developed a strong interest in *shtetl* life and the Holocaust.

12. The huge undertaking to preserve, compile, and identify photographic images of a lost shtetl world as a way of recovering what can be recovered of shtetl life is addressed in Kugelmass's essay.

13. Holmberg contends, on the other hand, that monogamy is a subject of significant importance to Joey, who wants to commit adultery (1997b, 8).

14. See in this regard David Robinson's well researched biography of Chaplin. I am indebted to David Desser for suggesting that I follow my instinct here.

15. What for Joey is a haunting nightmare about the loss of manhood is literally that action—the murder of his wife and children—for which the character, Grounder, is arrested in Mamet's *Homicide*.

16. This remark was made to Mamet. It is of sufficient importance that it appears in *The Disappearance of the Jews* and *Homicide* and recurs, either directly or indirectly, in numerous Mamet essays, among them "Decoration of Jewish Houses" (1989b, 7–14); "In Every Generation" (1996a).

17. On the subject of "whiteness" see Gilman (1991b, 96–100, 173–74); Pelligrini's essay, "Whiteface Performances: 'Race,' Gender, and Jewish Bodies" is also excellent, though the scholarship on the subject is vast. The allusions to non-white status also find form in Pinter's screenplay for *The Trial*. See my essay, "Peopling the Wound: Harold Pinter's Screenplay for Kafka's *The Trial*" (1997).

18. Macy, interview.

19. Speaking with Barry Davies about those who would disparage the memory of Holocaust victims, Pinter remarks, "People were dying.... What the hell were they [non-Jews] talking about" (16).

20. Lynn Mamet's *Lost Years*, directed by Mike Nussbaum, had a staged reading in Los Angeles in 1995. A fascinating play, it inverses the scenario of *Jolly*, delineating the sister as more critical of her sister-in-law and more supportive of her brother trapped in a marriage from which he cannot extricate himself. And whereas

the character Laurie, Bobby's wife, is depicted in Mamet's play in a typical minimalist sketch, this character looms large in *Lost Years*. I am grateful to her for the opportunity to read it.

21. Lynn Mamet characterized her stepfather (about whom Mamet writes in "The Rake" [1992a, 3–11]) as a *shegeitz*, "one of those white bread types" (interview, 20 September 1991). The term *shegeitz*, which Mamet uses in his latest revisions of *The Old Neighborhood*, is the masculine form of *shiksa*.

22. See his "Writing for the Theatre" (1990).

23. Mamet spoke with Jay Carr about the Eastern view of decay, which he views as the initial, requisite step in rebirth: "The decay still holds. It's still our life. But the confronting it is a way of getting over being frightened by it—admitting rather than denying it" (1988).

24. See Gilbert's monumental study for numerous references to this paradigm, especially in the early years of the Holocaust.

25. Lynn Mamet, interview 20 September 1991.

26. During my interview with Harold Palast, the patriarch of the Mamet family, he recalled that when he was assigned to a base in the United States during World War II, he was taunted in like manner and told directly by several officers that he should go to Europe because it was "his war."

27. See Hertzberg's discussion in *The Jews in America* on the American Jewish need to prove loyalty in service that dates to the American Civil War (136–38).

C.W.E. BIGSBY

David Mamet: all true stories

In an essay on 'Fiction and Reality' Mario Vargas Llosa spoke of the effect of abolishing the novel in Spanish America for three centuries as those in power set themselves to create 'a society exonerated from the disease of fiction'. Their failure he ascribed to the fact that the realm of fiction was larger and deeper than the novel. As he explained, they could not

> imagine that the appetite for lies—that is, for escaping objective reality through illusions—was so powerful and rooted in the human spirit, that, once the vehicle of the novel was not available to satisfy it, the thirst for fiction would infect—like a plague—all the other disciplines and genres in which the written word could freely flow. Repressing and censoring the literary genre specifically invented to give 'the necessity of lying' a place in the city, the inquisitors achieved the exact opposite of their intentions: a world without novels, yes, but a world into which fiction had spread and contaminated practically everything.

It was an observation designed simultaneously as an assault on the corruption of the state and as an explanation of the nature of much South American fiction. Magical realism, he implied, was a natural product of societies which 'still have great difficulty ... in differentiating between fiction and reality'.[1] But America, too, is a fiction. More than most societies it existed as idea before being realised as fact, and fact had then to be pulled into line with myth. As a character in David Mamet's *The Water Engine* asks: 'What happened to this nation? Or did it ever exist ... did it exist with its freedoms and slogan ... Where is America? I say it does not exist. And I say it never existed. It was all but a myth. A great dream of avarice.'[2] What Vargas Llosa says of South American countries—that they are 'in a deep sense more of a fiction than a reality'—is equally true of America. His description of his own country as an 'artificial gathering of men from different languages, customs and traditions whose only common denominator was having been condemned by history to live together without knowing or loving each other' is close enough to an American anxiety to find an echo for Vargas Llosa's remark that 'Le Perou, ce n'est pas Perou.'[3] America, too, is not America. It is compounded of myths to do with freedom and equality, of yeoman farmers and sturdy individuals, of spirituality and material enterprise. It propounds a dream of increasing wealth and perfectibility; it propounds a singular identity forged out of difference. It talks to itself in the dark for reassurance about its special status. No State of the Union Address is complete without its celebration of a special grace which has made it the peacemaker, the international frontiersman, the one bright light in a dark world. No wonder American writers, from Cooper, Hawthorne and Melville to Fitzgerald, Faulkner and West have set themselves to explore its myths. No wonder playwrights, from O'Neill through Miller to Shepard and Mamet, have done likewise.

David Mamet explores the myths of capitalism, the loss of that spiritual confidence which was once presumed to underpin individual identity and national enterprise alike. The language of liberal concern and humane principle echoes through plays in which rhetoric seldom if ever matches the reality of character or action. Nor are rapacity and greed presented as the decadent products of history. In America, he implies, they were its motor force. Sam Shepard is more ambivalent. His characters are scarcely less the alienated products of their society than are Mamet's. The characters in *True West*, surrounded by the detritus of a technological society, planning petty thefts and engaging in spasmodic bouts of violence, seem close kin to the figures in Mamet's *American Buffalo*. The peepshow in Mamet's *Edmond*, in which characters are physically separated from one another and sexuality is alienated as product, has its echo in Shepard's film *Paris, Texas*. For both writers the urban world is bleak and denatured. But Shepard is drawn to the mythical world of heartland America as his characters act out mythic roles, the embodiment of a culture hooked on dreams. There is no reality outside the imagination of those who perform their dramas in a world which is an extension of their own psyches. Reality is never stable in Shepard's plays. The America his characters manufacture serves the purpose of their own needs, which are rooted less in history than in a private set of anxieties or images. Like Mamet's characters, however, Shepard's seek to close the spaces in their lives. They are obsessive. A single dominant idea determines their actions. The frontier they explore has less to do with the landscape they inhabit than with their own state of mind. The country of which they are alienated citizens is one contaminated with fiction.

The Brazilian writer João Ubaldo Ribeiro prefaces his novel *An Invincible Memory* with the observation that 'The secret of Truth is as follows: there are no facts, there are only stories.'[4] It is tempting to suggest that much the same could be said of David Mamet's work or of Sam Shepard's. The reflecting mirrors of their plays throw back images not so much of a substantial reality as of a world transformed by the presence of the mirrors. Their characters live mythically. They live by exclusion. In the case of Mamet's characters what is excluded is everything that does not sustain the myth; in the case of Shepard's, everything that cannot be pulled into the vortex of emotion. In both cases, though, story, myth, fantasy have a power which renders the banality of surfaces null.

In some ways Mamet's first film as director, *House of Games*, can stand as a paradigm of his plays. A group of confidence tricksters conspire to rob a woman, a psychiatrist, of her money. In an elaborate 'sting' they trick her into surrendering her money in the belief that they need her help and that she is in some ways guilty for their situation. When she sees through the operation she is told that there is 'nothing personal' since it is 'only business'. Offering to let her in on their methods so that she can study what she calls 'the *confidence* game' they then ensnare her once again, winning her trust by apparently offering her their own. Their game merely reflects hers as psychiatrist. As she confesses, 'It's a sham, it's a con game.' The implied motto of them all is that identified by one of the conmen: *semper fidelis*, a motto on which he adds his own gloss—'Don't Trust Nobody.' But this warning is itself a ploy designed to win the confidence of its victim who ultimately reverses the sting by herself employing those methods of deceit which she has learned. We leave her a murderess who has killed with impunity, a successful woman whose act is to steal.

House of Games stands as a paradigm in that in play after play Mamet presents us with characters who turn moral virtues into vulnerabilities, justify criminality in terms of business, generate plots and perform roles with consummate skill, trade friendship into advantage and generate a language out of phase with experience. Like a blend of Eugene O'Neill, Arthur Miller and Tom Stoppard, he combines a concern with the underside of the American dream with a powerful social vision and a brilliant linguistic sensitivity to create plays of genuine originality.

Mamet's is a world in which people are not what they seem. The petty gangster in his film *Things Change* is not the Mafia leader he is taken to be; the card-players in *House of Games* not simply gamblers. They are all, like the figures in *A Life in the Theatre*, actors. It is not that they conceal substantial selves beneath their masks. They are their masks. They exist in and through their performances. Everyone, it seems, exploits everyone else and when it appears otherwise, as, briefly, in *Speed the Plow*, this proves illusory. Reality is deconstructed. It is not that human needs or fears are denied. Quite the contrary. Mamet's tricksters freely acknowledge them; they show a perception, a sympathy, an insight which is startling. It is simply that such an awareness is a tool of the trade. Just as advertising, pornography or Hollywood make fundamental human needs serve the purpose of commerce, so Mamet's confidence-men do the same. In doing so, of course, they thereby acknowledge the reality of those needs as they do the equally powerful impulse to exploit them. They also show the power of the imperial self, which wishes to subordinate other people, to colonise their imaginations as do Madison Avenue and Hollywood. It is, as the supposed psychic in *The Shawl* correctly identifies, the sense of 'loss', the need to 'believe', a feeling of 'fear', a desire for 'order,' which brings his victim to him and delivers her into his hands. It is, as he says, a question of trust, of confidence, but, and here is another twist to the tale, he, too, feels the same things, knows the same needs. As an actor is tied to his audience, and derives not only his living but his meaning from that relationship so, too, are Mamet's salesmen, confidence-men, tricksters. They are wordsmiths whose lies are transmuted into a kind of truth by those who need a story which will give meaning to their lives. As Ibsen's characters cling to their 'life lies', or Tennessee Williams's characters flare into life within the magical circle of their own inventions, so Mamet's embrace the fictions which are paraded before them by the new priests of a post-industrial society, selling reassurance, forgiveness and grace to those in terror of an empty universe or an empty life. The final irony is that those salesmen/priests are themselves in search of grace and have to discover it in the sheer professionalism of the performances which they deploy, in the insights which are the weaponry of their particular trade.

David Mamet's theatre essays are full of references to truth, authenticity and reality; he speaks of responsibilities, values, the community.

Discipline, work, dedication are assumed to generate an experience that can engage human aspirations and acknowledge deep psychological needs. Words hold a magical power to command experience; they are the tacit meeting-point where desires and fears are embraced and controlled. His plays are something else. In them authenticity is more usually traded in for performance; reality is a construct devised by those afraid to believe themselves its product. The language of communality and mutual responsibility is deployed by those who have no faith in it other than as a tactic to ensnare the unwary. Words have no weight except as elaborate mechanisms of deceit. His is a world full of petty criminals, dubious salesmen, gangsters, actors, urban cowboys, speaking a language which shatters on its own uncertainties. In this world, indeed, language is intransitive, gestures are incomplete, relationships self-serving and temporary. The individual has no substance beyond the masks he wears. And yet somewhere in this inchoate swirl of inauthenticity there is a truth—about human need, about the human capacity to construct meaning out of chaos— and that truth is as much the essence of his drama as is the caustic analysis of the collapse of purpose and value.

Mamet began writing in the 1970s, a decade which had the air of the day after the party. Kennedy's commitment to defend any friend, fight any foe, his call to the service of one's country, had devolved into a squalid war which killed 50,000 Americans and spiritually maimed as many more. The political idealism which led a generation onto the streets to fight racism and into the Third World to fight poverty ended in the 'me' decade, in which self-interest and self-exploration were offered as values to those embarrassed by their time on the barricades. A Vice-President had been indicted for corruption, a President of the United States forced to resign for betraying his public trust. It was hard to relate the My Lai massacre (and the rush to absolve those responsible), or Watergate, to American values or to accommodate a murderous hightech war waged against a low-tech enemy to American myths of the city on the hill, the beacon to the world, the land of the self-sufficient individual. Even the sexual freedoms of the sixties were reinterpreted in the light of a new conservatism and feminism. Every decade is liable to be a reaction to the one which precedes it (the political earnestness of the thirties to the supposed political frivolity of the twenties, the moralising consumer-oriented fifties to the wartime freedoms and relative austerity of the forties), but the sixties, which finally died around 1972, left a more ambiguous legacy than most.

Viewed in one way, Mamet's attempts to breathe life into American values, by exposing the extent to which they had been betrayed and subverted, might make him seem a product of his times. After all, the renovation and reassertion of American principles was going to be high on the political agenda, at the level of rhetoric if not reality, for the next decade and a half, and there is something of the civics teacher about David Mamet, as there is a sentimentalist. The theatre essays often look back to his own early years as, implicitly, he seems to identify a time when corruption had not yet started. As he says in an essay ostensibly about the theatre, but in fact an assertion of moral no less than theatrical 'First Principles', in a

> morally bankrupt time we can help to change the habit of coercive and frightened action and substitute for it the habit of trust, self-reliance and cooperation. If we are true to our ideals we can help to form an ideal society—a society based on and adhering to ethical first principles—not by *preaching* about it but by creating it each night in front of the audience—by showing how it works. In action.[5]

But though he talks about Americans as being 'recipients of the boon of liberty' this is no sixth-grader or America firster for, he insists, Americans 'have always been ready, when faced with discomfort, to discard any and all first principles of liberty, and further, to indict those who do not freely join us in happily arrogating those principles'.[6]

David Mamet addresses a public world which carries the impress of history and myth and a private world invaded by public values. For Arthur Miller the past is holy. It has to be addressed and embraced. His plays are full of revelations and confessions which redeem if not the characters then the idea of the moral self. Mamet's characters have no functional past. They are stranded in the present. The past is inert, disfunctional, like the discarded objects in Don Dubrow's resale store in *American Buffalo*. It does not inform the present except as the origin of a now degraded language or as the source of a set of decayed and disregarded values. His characters look out over a polluted lake (*Duck Variations*) or encounter one another in a junk store (*American Buffalo*), a wrecked office (*Glengarry Glen Ross*), an alienating singles bar (*Sexual Perversity in Chicago*) or the brothels and peepshows of a decadent city (*Edmond*). The dominant image is one of decay. Like the celebrants of some religion whose principles have long since been forgotten, they echo phrases drained of meaning by time. The Constitution, vaguely recalled, is seen as a justification of greed, the frontier as a cover for rapacity. Individualism has collapsed into an alienated solitariness and enterprise into crime. Revolutionary rhetoric has dwindled to aphasia, love decayed to an aggressive sexuality and brotherhood to simple paranoia. His characters come together as conspirators in temporary alliances which form and dissolve and which are motivated by greed and egotism. Men and women meet across an all-but-unbridgeable divide and deploy a language as secondhand as anything in Don Dubrow's store. Yet there is redemption. It lies in the persistence of need, in the survival of the imagination, in the ability to shape experience into performance and in a humour born out of the space between the values of the characters and those of the audience.

His plays feature man as an endangered species. His characters have forgotten how to make contact and have ceased to ask themselves the reason for their existence. Theirs is a life without transcendence, spiritually arid, emotionally bankrupt. Yet the plays themselves expose the deformed logic of such characters as they do the desperation with which they struggle to conceal it with platitudes and self-revealing appeals. Mamet is every bit as much a moralist as Arthur Miller. It is just that he seldom if ever allows his characters to perceive their own failures or to identify the implications of their personal betrayals. In Mamet's case the membrane between the self and an alienated and alienating society has become permeable. That self has accordingly been invaded by the language and assumptions of an aggressive capitalism in which value is determined by price and relationships turn on commodity exchange. The fantasies of adspeak and the media world define the parameters of experience and provide the vocabulary of a need easily satisfied by consumption—the possession of an object (*American Buffalo*, *Glengarry Glen Ross*) or a person (*Sexual Perversity in Chicago*, *The Woods*). Yet there is, Mamet insists, an irreducible reality. There is 'a way things are irrespective of the way we *say* things are',[7] and we become aware of that in the moment when a residual human need makes its presence felt. In both *American Buffalo* and *Glengarry Glen Ross*, no matter how briefly, characters place a personal relationship ahead of personal advantage. Just as in Edward Bond's *Saved* or *Lear*, the smallest gesture assumes a disproportionate significance. His characters desperately wish to connect. They have simply forgotten how to do so. Their need has been alienated from them and offered back as sexual encounter or business relationship. But we are offered a glimpse of selflessness as, in *American Buffalo*, Don's concern for his young helper, Bobby, momentarily overcomes his self-interest and, in *Glengarry Glen Ross*, the victim of a confidence trick apologises to the trickster for reneging on the deal and a salesman refuses to buy himself goodwill through betrayal.

The central theme of Mamet's plays is loss. His characters look for some kind of meaning to random events and try to generate order out of a threatening chaos. Their paradox is that they fear those who might neutralise their solitariness: they deceive those from whom they demand trust. They are the victims of self-generated ironies. They know and deploy the language of a humane and moral world. They acknowledge the reality and persistence of fear and need. Yet that language is deployed with a cynical awareness, that knowledge exploited in the pursuit of advantage.

In *The Education of Henry Adams*, Adams conceded that 'The human mind has always struggled like a frightened bird to escape the chaos which caged it.'[8] History was evidence of that failed enterprise, science a gesture of faith. The myth of human progress was itself born out of denial. If progress, then direction, if direction, then purpose, if purpose, then meaning. Once that meaning lay in a relationship with the natural world and through that to some underlying and unifying principle. Then technology and tools seemed to promise mastery before, in a post-industrial world, the self becomes a primary value, hedonism a logical result, power and money, as Spengler predicted, a means and an end, and experience aestheticised. Mamet's characters inhabit this last world. Nature has failed man or man nature. Lakes, in his work, are polluted, woods associated with mildew and decay. The great technological achievements of the nineteenth century, celebrated in Chicago's World's Fair Century of Progress Exposition, a point of reference in two of his plays, have turned into junk. Money is, in many of these plays, a motivating force and a metaphor. What can be taken by force or by guile acquires a greater significance than that which is freely given. Daniel Bell, in his book *The Coming of Post-Industrial Society*, identified the loss of a sense of transcendence as a primary fact of such a period. Indeed he has summarised a process which in Mamet's work is collapsed into metaphor. For most of history, he insists '*reality was nature*, and in poetry and imagination men sought to relate the self to the natural world. Then *reality became technics*, tools and things made by men yet given an independent existence outside himself, the reified world. Now *reality is primarily the social world* ... what does not vanish is the duplex nature of man himself—the murderous aggression, from primal impulse, to tear apart and destroy; and the search for order, in art and life.'[9] This is Mamet's world. These are the contradictions which he dramatises. He is the poet of post-industrial society.

In *The Shawl*, first presented in 1985, a woman in her late thirties visits a man who claims to be a mystic. In fact a confidence trickster, he understands what drives her to consult him: 'you want me to exhibit my *power*. Is this not the truth? ... For the question is WHAT POWERS EXIST? ... This is a rational concern. *Is* there an order in the world?'[10] This was equally the question debated by the two old men in *Duck Variations*. Even the petty criminals in *American Buffalo*, alarmed at the chaos of which they are the primary evidence, look for a rational principle behind seemingly arbitrary events and themselves generate a plot whose own structure hints at coherence, no matter how farcical or contingent. The final irony of Mamet's plays, however, is that the very faith which makes individuals vulnerable to exploitation and deceit is primary evidence of the survival of a sense of transcendent values for which otherwise he can find no social correlative. That might seem to suggest a sense of the absurd but Mamet will not permit that irony to become the only note sounded in his plays. Something in the relationship between Don and Bobby survives the reifications of *American Buffalo*; James Lingk is not simply ridiculous, in *Glengarry Glen Ross*, retaining his faith in the man who duped him. In *The Shawl* confidence trickster and victim share more than their roles in an elaborate fiction. They need one another for reasons which go beyond the drama of deceiver and deceived which they enact. Indeed there are hints that some non-rational connection between them may exist, that beyond language there may lie a surviving instinctual mutuality.

For David Mamet, the closest analogy to the theatre and the cinema is the dream. As he has explained,

> Even in the most rational plays, the element which has the power to move us is not the rational element or the polemic element but the mythic element. It is the unresolved, not the resolved conflicts which matter. We see this in our everyday society and in the decay of disparate mechanisms: Government, Religion, Theatre. We have seen them decay into rational organisations, each one of which thinks its purpose is the same: to determine by force of reason what is right and then do it.[11]

The logic of theatre, he suggests, should be that of the dream, addressing anxieties and needs which the rational mind sublimates. So, too, with the cinema which is, he insists,

> the least literal medium. The great film makers are those who understand that it is the medium that most closely approximates to the nature of dream. Because anything can happen; because you can't perceive distance in a movie; because the light that falls on people is quite artificial ... as film makers became more acquainted with the nature of the camera, they discovered cutting

and juxtaposition of images the better to tell the story. They understand that in the juxtaposition of the temporal and the plastic, they could conjoin things in a way that could only happen in one other place: the Dream ... The great movie makers evolved at the time of Freud's thinking: Eisenstein, for instance, the vast power of whose films comes from the ability to juxtapose simple and uninflected images.[12]

An ironic and entirely self-conscious homage to Eisenstein and his deformation of reality occurs in his script for *The Untouchables*, as a pram bumps down a flight of Potemkin-like steps in a sequence whose temporal logic is disturbed. But his plays are apt to play similar games, whether it be the carefully focused juxtapositions of *American Buffalo* and *The Water Engine*, the jump cuts of *Sexual Perversity in Chicago* and *Edmond* (the one exploring fantasy, the other nightmare), or the overlapping on and off stage performances of *A Life in the Theatre*. The tendency to 'read' his plays naturalistically, to praise or deplore them in terms of their literal accuracy, he sees as in part a result of ignorance—not knowing how petty gangsters, street corner voyeurs or salesmen speak, critics tend to see his poetic restatement of their language as the thing itself—and in part a resistance to metaphor. He is no detached naturalist, dissecting the body politic, but a writer offering images of alienation, moral dislocation and spiritual decay for which those characters offer a dramatic correlative. He resists equally realism, which he sees as mundane, and a self-conscious experimentalism, since a play 'concerned essentially with the *aesthetic* politics of its creators may divert or anger, but it cannot enlighten'.[13]

In the concluding decades of the twentieth century a number of writers have begun to move, in their work, towards a concern for spiritualism. The failure of ideology to inform or shape the world satisfactorily, of psychology convincingly to offer a secular route to self-understanding, or self-interest, of materialism or the rituals of social form to offer a structure to experience or a destination worthy of the journey, left them standing at the doors of faith. It was a logic which unfolded in as heterogeneous a group of people as George Steiner, Doris Lessing, Iris Murdoch, Alice Walker and August Wilson. The rise, internationally, of religious fundamentalism, though plainly at odds with the non-doctrinaire, non-authoritarian politics of such writers, may have been responding to a similar process. David Mamet has, perhaps, been on a similar pilgrimage. Not for nothing does he quote from Ecclesiastes in his essay 'A National Dream Life'—'For man also knoweth not his time: as the fishes that are taken in an evil net, and as the birds that are caught in a snare; so are the sons of man snared in an evil time when it falleth suddenly upon them.'

What his plays all, in very different ways, explore is the damage that has been done to the spirit, the loss of meaning in the lives of those who have been taught that such meaning lies in the alienated products not of their labour but of their desires. The theatre, with its roots in the church (and he as a child performed exemplary religious dramas), offers another version of the community gathered around the domestic table. For the moment other roles are laid aside and the audience share an experience which, in the case of his own plays, takes us beyond a model of theatre as mirror to the times. In a sense you could say much the same of the work of Arthur Miller and Tennessee Williams, neither of whom, like Mamet, could identify a social mechanism to reshape the social world whose alienation had in part generated their drama. Like Eugene O'Neill before them they were liable to use the word 'soul' in explaining that human quality placed under most pressure by modern society: in that sense Mamet seems a natural inheritor of a basic theme of the American theatre. He is prone to refer to the human spirit: 'Every reiteration of the idea that *nothing matters* debases the human spirit ... Who is going to speak up for the human spirit?' His answer is 'The artist. The actor' who works on 'that stage which is the proponent of the life of the soul'.[14] The theatre, he insists, affords an opportunity uniquely suited for 'communicating and inspiring ethical behaviour'.

Mamet's plays, unlike his theatre essays, are neither polemical nor didactic. His spiritual concerns have not led him, as at times they have led Doris Lessing or Alice Walker, to generalise his characters to the point at which they dissolve individual identity in the generality. His concern with unity does not lead him to unhinge the door of time, as it does them, though the poet is invoked as ironic commentator. He is committed to the moment, to characters who exist in time and who must find their redemption in the present, like the audience who confront them in the theatre: 'The magic moments, the beautiful moments in the theatre always come from a desire on the part of artist and audience to live in the moment, to *commit* themselves to time.'[15] He is interested in what binds people together. The fact that his characters use scatological language, inhabit a diminished world, are scarcely able or willing to decode or respond to one another's needs, has led some critics to see him as committed simply to rubbing our collective noses in the squalor of contemporary existence. In doing so, however, they miss a greater commitment. As he explained, Kafka once observed that 'one always has the alternative of ignoring and choosing not to participate in the sufferings of others, but ... in so doing one commits oneself to the only suffering that one could have avoided'.[16] Since the very condition of theatre is 'that which *unites* the actor and the house, a desire to share something',[17] the theatre stands as a paradigm and metaphor. This does not, of course, suggest that theatre is immune to egotism, ambition and falsity. *A Life in the Theatre* offers a comic demonstration of art decayed to artifice and harmony broken by rivalry. But the need for such unity sounds like a constant note beneath the dissonance. As he observed in an essay which he wrote about that play: 'We certainly all need love. We all need diversion, and we need friendship in a world whose limits of commitment ... is most time the run of the play.'[18] Reminding us that, for Camus, the actor is the embodiment of the Sisyphean nature of life he also implies the extent to which the actor stands as an image of those temporary alliances and desperate performances which are the stuff of daily life.

Hemingway observed that all true stories, if continued long enough, end in death and yet the story, as Scheherazade knew, is itself a defence against death. Not only in childhood fairy-tales is there an ever after. So long as the story continues, so long as there is a teller and a listener, we are not alone and we have imaginative control over our experience. At the heart of all Mamet's plays are story-tellers whose stories shape their world into something more than random experience, decay and inconsequence. That is why even his most morally reprehensible characters command his respect. They are in the same business as he is. They create drama and by so doing give themselves a role.

Shaped into myths such stories become the structuring devices of a society, a way of encoding its values, of shaping its dreams which, Mamet insists, are the figures of our desire. The theatre is concerned with such stories. They are both its means and the focus of its analysis.

An early play, *Dark Pony*, has all the simplicity of a bed-time story. A tale told by a father to his daughter, it tells of a pony who can always be summoned to the rescue. The words 'Dark Pony' themselves have a magical effect, language being able to hold fear and anxiety at bay. Yet even here the story is stained with the need of the teller, a need more sharply defined in *Reunion*, its companion piece. This is a portrait of a man who holds his life together, rather as does the protagonist of Hemingway's 'Big Two-Hearted River', by an act of radical simplification. As a reformed alcoholic, a member of Alcoholics Anonymous, he will have learned a take one day at a time. His language is similarly foreshortened. Simple declarative sentence follows simple declarative sentence. He seems consciously to avoid the complex sentence as he does the complex thought. Indeed the speeches in the early part of the play seem to fall into a short-lined, non-rhyming verse form.

There are few conjunctions, a fact which accurately reflects a life of many beginnings, of actions that have never generated continuous meaning. The reappearance in his life of his daughter, a daughter whose own life is unsatisfactory, is a threat because it reminds him of causality, of time that has passed without meaning emerging, because it hints at a story which ends badly. This may or may not be the relationship which was the focus of *Dark Pony* but either way it is a reminder of the incapacity of story to keep the real at bay, of the inchoate nature of experience which story is designed to deny.

Even here, in these early plays, then, the story carries a virus. Bernie's narratives in *Reunion* are of random violence, those in *Dark Pony* shaped by the unexpressed need of the teller. There is a vacancy to these lives, an emptiness circled around with words, and that void is reflected, too, in the space between speaker and listener. Private need is never quite enough to close the gap between those who feel alienated from themselves and from others. These first plays could apparently scarcely be simpler. A third, *Duck Variations*, consists of an inconsequential dialogue between two old men, an exchange whose unmentioned subject is death. They are conversation pieces. There is no movement, no plot except the unravelling of character. *Reunion*, *Dark Pony*, *Duck Variations* could be radio plays, except that the unbridgeable physical space between the characters is a clue to another gulf, psychological, spiritual.

Sexual Perversity in Chicago is also a conversation piece, except that this time there is a neurasthenic rhythm, an urban pace to a play in which random energy is substituted for a purposeful life. Owing something to Mamet's experience of Chicago's Second City revue group, it consists of a series of short, rapidly presented scenes in which two urban males, Bernie and Danny, discuss their sexual fantasies and attempt to act them out with two women equally bemused by sexuality in a world in which it has become fetishised, an alienated product of commodity exchange, a key component of a myth of consumption. Much of the play's humour derives from the characters' failure to understand themselves or other people, the ironic space between a confident language of sexual aggression and a fumbling incompetence when confronted with the reality of potential relationships. Bernie's view of women is pornographic, metonymic: 'Tits and ass.' He acts as mentor to the apparently more naive and sensitive Danny. It is an approach born less out of desire than fear. Safely mythicised as willing collaborators in their own seduction, women cease to threaten. Safely displaced into fiction they lose their power to engage his confused and vulnerable emotions. Accordingly, when Danny finds himself involved with a real woman he is unable to function, incapable of adjusting to the complexity of relationship.

Sexual Perversity in Chicago explores a world in which language generates action and public myths invade private lives. Mamet dramatises a world drained of beauty, purpose and meaning, a world in which aggression is a mode of communication and words have become denatured. Its principal currency is sexuality but a sexuality devalued, counterfeited, to the point at which it neither buys immunity from solitude nor offers satisfaction for needs. The singles bar becomes an effective image of a society in which alienated individuals market themselves, seeking the very companionship they fear, as they substitute lifestyle for life. Lacking real intimacy, they substitute only simple physicality.

Mamet has talked of his struggle to construct a play which consists of something more than a series of short scenes, but in fact the style of *Sexual Perversity in Chicago* could hardly be more apt. Its discontinuous scenes accurately reflect the fragmented experiences of his characters who have no plot to their lives and are terrified alike of causality and commitment. Past and future are transformed into fantasy. Only the present moment has any force and that is void of meaning. The broken rhythm of their exchanges is itself an expression of the intransitive nature of language and experience alike. The play won an award as best new Chicago play an Chicago is plainly its setting as it is of his first two-act play, *American Buffalo*, a work which ultimately established his national and international reputation.

American Buffalo is set in a junk store in Chicago. The characters are surrounded by the detritus of the city's Century of Progress Exposition which, in 1933, looked back over a century of development and forward to the following hundred years of achievement. The characters inhabit the ironies which stem from the juxtaposition of material progress (whose products have turned into junk or simple curios) and moral regression. The apparently naturalistic set is charged with significance, just as much as that of a Tennessee Williams play. Indeed Mamet has rejected those readings which would reduce the play to simple naturalism:

> I don't think it's a naturalistic play at all. It's a fairly well stylised play. The language is very stylised. It's very strict rhythmically. Structurally, it's classical. It's divided into two acts. It takes place in twenty-four hours and adheres to all the unities. Certain things about the play are misleading. For example, the fact that it has lot of four-letter words might make it difficult to see that it's written in free verse. The fact that it takes place in a junkshop might make it easier to mistake it for a kitchen play. The fact that these three people happen to be thieves might make it easier to say that

this is not a play about ourselves because the playwright isn't employing traditional theatrical devices of character.[19]

For him, though, character and setting offer a metaphor which the audience is invited to decode in terms of their own experience. It is a play 'set deeply in the milieu of capitalism', an idea which he suggests has exhausted itself. Speaking at the time of the London production of *Glengarry Glen Ross*, also its world premiere, he described capitalism as an enabling myth rooted in greed. Quoting W.C. Fields's observation that you can't cheat an honest man, he indirectly identified a central motif both in that play and in *American Buffalo*, a play in which petty criminals plan to rob a man who has purchased a buffalo-headed nickel for $90. Previously unaware of its rarity value, they now assume that even this purchase price must have understated its value. Greed breeds resentment and provokes criminality; but the point is that, morally speaking, the criminality is seen by Mamet as implicit in capitalism. When one of the three, an emotionally unbalanced and paranoid man called Teach, defines free enterprise as 'The freedom ... of the individual ... To Embark on any Fucking course that he thinks fit ... In order to secure his honest chance to make a profit',[20] he is hardly wide of the point.

The planned crime, however, never occurs, as Godot never comes. It simply provides a future objective, a marker which, once passed, will be replaced by another. In effect the characters simply pass the time torn between a paranoid suspicion of one another and a desperate need for contact. Indeed, the characters form a kind of family group, with Don, the store-owner, as the father, and Teach as his son, a kind of half-brother to the mentally damaged Bobby. Somewhere in that relationship is real affection as well as need, but in the world of *American Buffalo* values are inverted. Criminality is described as business, theft as an extension of national principles. Only in the fantasy world of their planned crimes do they come together, gain significance and status. Rather like the figures in O'Neill's *The Iceman Cometh*, they project themselves into fictions which alone can grant them meaning.

We know little about the characters in *American Buffalo*, but that is the essence of Mamet's approach. For him 'leaving out ... is the whole trick'.[21] In part that is a reflection of fundamentally simplified lives, a series of radical denials whereby normal human responses have been suppressed along with the language which describes those responses. In part it is an aspect of Mamet's attenuated realism:

We don't want to hear where he or she went to college unless that is essential to what they are trying to get ... leave it out ... no

matter how revelatory of character it seems to be there isn't any
character except action. Action and character are the same. The
character in a play can't reveal anything more about his character
by telling things gratuitously about himself than a character at a
party can reveal anything gratuitously about himself.[22]

And if that sounds remarkably like Pinter then we have Mamet's assurance
that 'he was the greatest influence on me, as a young actor and a young
student and a young writer. Absolutely!'[23]

Ostensibly, the play concerns a developing criminal conspiracy
rendered increasingly farcical by the thieves' incompetence and by their
evident fear of the action which they propose with such apparent confidence.
They have no idea how they will break into the apartment where the coin
collector lives nor how they will locate and open the safe or even identify the
coins which they assume, on the basis of little or no evidence, will be stored
there. An accomplice fails to arrive, having been mugged on his way to the
store. Don, otherwise so assured, assembles a team of misfits and
incompetents. Teach insists on his commitment and courage and then arrives
late, possibly in the hope that that courage will not be put to the test. In fact
the crime is an irrelevance. What they are doing is passing the time, enacting
their need for purpose to their lives, for companionship. They do so by
creating a fantasy, a fiction, a story, elaborating the details of a man about
whom they know nothing and of his apartment, of which they are wholly
ignorant. Within the story they feel both secure and alive.

Beyond the parameters of the story, however, is a threatening world.
Police cars circle the block while every gesture has to be inspected for its
concealed menace. As played by Al Pacino in New York or Jack Shepherd in
London, Teach is a highly neurotic individual, hypersensitive to slights,
neurotically alert to condescension and threat. Every gesture is over-
interpreted. His model of the world is one of naked competition in which
advantage to one must spell disadvantage to another. He sees himself as a
frontiersman for whom survival is a prime necessity and life a process of
seeking supremacy over others. The motive for the crime is less financial
reward than punishment for what is presumed to be the customer's
momentary advantage. The play, in Mamet's words, is 'about the American
ethic of business'. His point here and elsewhere is that the morality of
institutions is not that of the individual, that corporate morality justifies
unacceptable behaviour. Here, Teach sees the planned crime as 'business' and
as such not subject to normal restraints. Indeed, when he suspects that they
may have been betrayed by the young man, Bobby, he beats him viciously

and is himself beaten in turn by Don. It scarcely needs Teach's confused references to American principles to remind us that the slaughter of the buffalo—a central and ambiguous symbol in the play—was itself justified as a business activity, as, incidentally, was the harrying of the Indian who found himself inconveniently situated across the pathways of an American progress celebrated in the Chicago Exposition. Indeed the Chicago setting is a reminder that this city ('hog butcher to the world', as the pig-sticker among the assembled junk perhaps reminds us) was itself created out of business (trade with the Indians) and was home to Al Capone who turned crime into business as, Mamet suggests, others turned business into crime.

Teach, Don and Bobby, known to one another by their first names but denying the intimacy which that implies, are surrounded by the remnants of America's promise. They have inherited a language evacuated of meaning and principles distorted and deformed by greed and suspicion. They deploy the rhetoric of American revolutionary virtues but deny them in practice. Indeed Teach is barely in control of language as, like a Pinter character, his vocabulary outstrips his comprehension. He deplores the rising tide of violence, while arming himself and threatening to unleash a murderous assault himself, a paranoid response which is perhaps not without its political implication in a play in which he carries weapon, 'Merely as a deterrent.'

But beyond a social critique of American business values, *American Buffalo* is a play about failed relationships, about the gap between people whose need for contact is as real as their evasion of it. There is a real affection between Don and Bobby, albeit one betrayed when it conflicts with business. Teach has as great a need to be 'well liked' as had Willy Loman, except that he can never permit anyone access to his inner life or acknowledge the genuine sense of vulnerability which he feels. Bobby, too, desperately craves affection. Not the least of the ironies of the play, however, is that need can never align itself with action. The characters never quite allow themselves the openness necessary for genuine contact. Something has destroyed their sense of being part of a community of selves. If this is in effect a kind of family then it is as broken as are the families in *Reunion*.

Mamet's dialogue is fragmented, its syntax broken. His characters often converse in incomplete sentences, substitute nonsense words, find language draining away in the face of experience. In part this is an accurate reflection of how conversation works, but it is something more than that. Despite his observation that American speech falls naturally into iambic pentameters, the shaping of his prose is quite conscious. As an actor at the Neighborhood Playhouse in New York he had learned the significance of rhythm. From Stanislavsky he had derived the conviction that 'rhythm and action are the same ... words are reduced to the sound and the rhythm much more than the verbal content and that's how we communicate with each other'.[24] Praised for dramatic conversations which seem simple transcriptions of demotic prose, in fact he contrives that language with great care. The spaces which open up in the language of his characters open up equally in their lives. Their linguistic incompletions reflect psychological and social incompletions. This is an intransitive society in which thought and feeling fail to leap the gap between individuals who fear the very communication they seek. To communicate fully is to become vulnerable and the fear of vulnerability is finally greater than the fear of isolation.

Mamet's characters are liable to reverse themselves within a matter of seconds. Thus Don defines business as 'common sense, experience, talent', only to redefine it moments later as 'People taking care of themselves.'[25] Teach insists that he never complains about those who cross him, after an obscene tirade against someone who has. Such reversals are the sign of a self-cancelling language.

Teach's language turns round on itself with a comical bathos. When their co-conspirator fails to turn up he suggests that he 'should be horsewhipped with a horsewhip'.[26] Language here is a closed system, self-consuming. The disproportion between cause and effect (what Teach takes as a hostile inflection precipitates a cascade of violent but essentially meaningless obscenity), between rhetoric and fact (Teach describes his decision to carry a gun as 'A personal thing of mine. A silly personal thing',[27] inadvertently borrowing the trivialising vocabulary of manners), underlines the failure of language to give them any leverage on experience, while stressing the gap between word and meaning. The one character who appears genuinely selfless—Bobby—speaks the least and though he tells a critical lie (alleging that he had seen the target of the planned robbery leaving his apartment) he does so out of love for Don.

For the most part dialogue consists of brief, sporadic bursts, monosyllables, simple questions, abbreviated statements, as though no thought can be sustained. Even in the context of this aphasia, however, the last pages of the text are particularly spare. Only one or two speeches exceed a single sentence. For the only time in the play Teach is called by his first name, indeed a diminutive of his first name. After an orgasmic outburst of violence they are left, their plans in ruins, with nothing more than one another. Teach begins the process of blotting out memory, erasing action, thereby detaching himself from responsibility for that action. He places a paper bag on his head ('I look like a sissy'), behaving like an animal signalling his subservience to the pack leader, Don, who is left alone, as the play ends, with Bob. Some ritual has been completed. The tableau is of two men, like father and son, briefly together, no longer even separated by language, an echo of the opening scene but now uncorrupted by the greed and paranoia which had generated such disharmony.

Roland Barthes speaks of 'the shudder of meaning' which language generates sometimes completely independently of its formal coherence. Just so you might describe the sounds produced by Beckett's characters, whose words circle around a void which cannot be named. Just so you might describe Mamet's characters who deploy a language whose literal meanings are lost to them but who communicate with total clarity their sense of need, loss and fear, their defensive aggression.

American Buffalo opened at Chicago's Goodman Theatre in November 1975, reaching Broadway fifteen months later in a production featuring John Savage, Robert Duvall and Kenneth McMillan, where its reviews were, in Mamet's words, 'mixed to mixed'. Its language, its tenuous plot, its deracinated characters, its disturbing metaphor of social alienation left critics confused and uncertain. Seizing on what they took to be his naturalism, they responded to it as in part a message from the lower depths and praised or rejected it for its authenticity, or otherwise, of language. In fact, like a super-realist painting, the play presses language and character beyond a surface precision. Nor is this an account of a deterministic social environment. The failure of Mamet's characters to understand themselves or one another is scarcely a product of environment, fate or genetics. They have created their own context by conspiring in their own irrelevance and generated their own identities through taking as real and substantial what in fact is only myth degraded into fantasy.

Nearly a decade later, in 1983, Mamet wrote what is in some senses, intellectually, a companion piece to *American Buffalo*. *Glengarry Glen Ross* is set in and around a real estate office and was inspired by Mamet's own experiences in a Chicago real estate agency: 'I sold worthless land in Arizona to elderly people.'[28] The characters in this play are indeed confidence men, tricksters, and that very phrase is a key one for it underlines a vital ambiguity in human experience which seems always to have fascinated Mamet, for the confidence trickster depends on a human need to believe which in turn creates a sense of vulnerability. It also implies a greed which invites exploitation. The epigraph to the play is the shopkeeper's slogan: 'Always be closing.' A closing-down sale implies that the buyer has an unfair advantage over the seller. The response is greed rather than pity. As indicated earlier, not for nothing has the salesman or confidence trickster emerged as a central figure in American writing, from Melville's *The Confidence Man* and Twain's

'The Man Who Corrupted Hadleyburg', *Huckleberry Finn* and *The Gilded Age* through Sinclair Lewis's *Babbitt*, O'Neill's *The Iceman Cometh*, Miller's *Death of a Salesman*, Inge's *The Dark at the Top of the Stairs*, O'Hara's *Appointment in Samarra* to Ellison's *Invisible Man* or Updike's Rabbit Angstrom books. He becomes the image of a society hawking dreams for hard cash, selling a model of the real, of the ideal, for a two-dollar bill. When they sell real estate it is not the real that they sell. In some ways, perhaps, it is a reflection of an ambivalence rooted deep in the culture, a reflection of the eighteenth-century constitutional debate as to whether America should commit itself to the pursuit of happiness or the possession of property. O'Neill saw it as an American desire to possess one's soul by possessing the world.

There is, however, a function which goes beyond this, for the salesman is a story-teller and no matter how corrupt the salesmen in *Glengarry Glen Ross* they are consummate story-tellers, actors of genuine skill who respond to a deep human need for reassurance, companionship, order and belief. And if we are left at the end of the play with a powerful sense of betrayal, of human need turned against itself, corrupted by a society which has made money a value and exploitation a virtue, we are also left with a sense that the victory of materialism is only provisional. There is a residual and surviving need not addressed or satisfied as there is a faith not wholly destroyed by betrayal. As Mamet has insisted of one of the victims of the real estate salesmen, he 'wants to believe in someone, that's all he wants. So, finally, at the end of the play, even though he's been robbed of his money, or almost robbed of his money, the important thing is that he won't even believe that because he wants to believe in someone, that he's found a friend.'[29] Likewise, when one of the salesmen is in a position to betray one of his friends he fails to do so 'because it's more important to him to keep a promise'.[30] These are fragile foundations on which to construct an alternative society, but in the context of the play such gestures have to be sufficient.

Glengarry Glen Ross concerns a group of real estate salesmen whose company has imposed a ruthless regimen. The most successful will receive a Cadillac, the runner-up a set of steak knives; the loser will be fired. It is neat paradigm of a competitive capitalist society. The key to success lies in securing the addresses of likely buyers. Since priority is given to the successful, this is a world in which success breeds success. Such is the pressure that it encourages unscrupulous methods with respect to the clients and ultimately with respect to the company. Increasingly desperate, one of the salesman, Shelley Levine, breaks into the office and steals the address list of potential clients. The crime is investigated by the police. The salesmen's own fraudulent activities, by contrast, in deceiving their customers, is regarded simply as good business, sanctioned by the ethics of a world in which success is a value and closing a deal an achievement.

The play is in two acts, the first being divided into three scenes, each of which takes place in a Chinese restaurant. The second is set in the real estate office, following the robbery. It is in part a play about power. Just as Pinter (to whom the play is dedicated) once observed that in all human relationships at any given moment one will be dominant, the other subservient so, here, the first act consists of three conversations whose sub-text is to do with power and its manipulation. In the first Shelley Levine confronts David Williamson, whose job it is to assign the addresses, or 'leads'. They speak in a code impenetrable to the audience, deploying the jargon of the trade. As a result, other signals are foregrounded. As Mamet has said: 'if you see a couple in a restaurant talking at the next table and you can't quite hear what they are talking about but it's evident that what they are talking about is important, that fact, and the fact that you don't quite understand the vocabulary, makes you listen all the harder'.[31] It also means that the audience fall back on, and hence are sensitised to, tone, rhythm, volume.

Williamson says little: most of his speeches are restricted to a single word, an incomplete sentence. Levine's, by contrast, betray a growing hysteria. For the most part, Mamet restricts his stage directions to the word 'pause' or the simplest indication of movement, but Levine's speeches are sprinkled with italicised or capitalised words and with obscenities. He is the petitioner afraid to stop speaking in case the answer is the one he fears. It is Williamson who breaks off the conversation, leaving Levine alone. In the second scene, Dave Moss tries to ensnare his fellow salesman, George Aaronow, in a plot to steal the 'leads' from the company office. A conversation which begins with the camaraderie of prejudice ends with Moss threatening his colleague as an accomplice to a crime as yet uncommitted, on the grounds that 'you listened'. Language becomes a trap: simply to listen is to become guilty; as the skills honed on salesmanship are turned against one another. Having wrung a promise from Aaronow not to betray him in the event of his committing the crime, Moss himself is immediately guilty of such a betrayal.

Betrayal, indeed, is a central theme in a play in which human need is turned against itself, the third scene offering a particularly telling example of this process. Two men in a restaurant booth discuss morality, authenticity and need, or they appear to do so, since the conversation is in fact remarkably one-sided. Only in the final sentences does it become clear that one is a salesman and the other his mark. In a reversal of the first scene, power lies with the speaker. The potential client is permitted only an occasional word. The skill lies in the mixture of hokum and truth offered by the salesman, Richard Roma. He acknowledges the centrality of loss, deplores greed, identifies the reality of insecurity, as in a later scene another salesman closes a deal by urging the need to believe and insisting on his need to 'convert' his clients. Then, in a deliberately bathetic climax, he begins his sales pitch: 'Listen to what I'm going to tell you.' The story begins.

These are consummate story-tellers; actors of genuine accomplishment. When the need arises they can improvise a drama or create stories of total plausibility. It should not be assumed that their ethical failure loses them Mamet's sympathy nor yet that of the audience.

Not for nothing was Thorstein Veblen an early influence. It was the bohemian radical who, in *The Theory of the Leisure Class*, underlined the extent to which, for the businessman, 'Freedom from scruple, from sympathy, honesty and regard for life, may, within fairly wide limits be said to further the success of the individual in the pecuniary culture.'[32] It was in Veblen that Mamet could have found the salesman apotheosised as the quintessence of dishonesty. There, too, he would have found a surviving religious commitment generalised in the direction of a concern for the human spirit. In Veblen's work, as in Tolstoy's, he could and did find an instinctive hostility to the institution which seemed to absolve the individual of his moral responsibility. Indeed, to list the writers most frequently quoted by Mamet—Veblen, Tolstoy, Freud, Kafka, Bettleheim—is to identify certain constants: a concern for the individual alienated from his own nature and from his fellow man, a fascination with the desire to find pattern in chaos, and a belief in the centrality of story, this last, in a sense, subsuming the others. For it is the stories his characters tell, the myths they elaborate, the performances they stage, which constitute their attempt to deny that alienation and discover form in mere contingency.

For Mamet the natural focus of drama seems to be the irreducible component of the speaker and the listener. This is true not only of such plays as *Reunion, Dark Pony, Duck Variations, The Woods* and *A Life in the Theatre*, but also of *Sexual Perversity in Chicago, American Buffalo, Glengarry Glen Ross* and *Speed the Plow* in which the characters group themselves into pairs. It is the relationship between two individuals which not only provides the skeletal sub culture of his plays, the basis of a tension which generates its electrical charge, but also offers a mirror of the relationship between the writer and his audience.

For Mamet 'the artist is the advance explorer of the societal consciousness'. [33] But, more than that, in so far as the theatre offers a model of social action, of meaning generated through and by the interaction of individuals who serve a meaning beyond their own, the artist can become an agent of moral if not social change. What is celebrated is mutuality: 'We live in an unhappy nation ... one way to alleviate the moral pall and the jejune super-sophistication of our lives is by theatrical celebration of those things which bind us together.'[34] Yet celebration is scarcely the keynote to his drama. Relationships are seen as attenuated, exploitative, competitive, destructive; society is dramatised as a series of temporary and self-serving alliances, a community held together only by the mutuality of need and ambition, and dissolved when it ceases to serve its purpose. Betrayal is a constant possibility. The fact of the dramatic portrayal of an alienated and alienating world is thus played against the assumption of alienation. There is a redemption in the form which seems beyond the imagination of the characters. The irony is very consciously deployed by Mamet, as his plays sustain that very sense of moral coherence denied by their action. The need is acknowledged by characters who reach out to one another, who conspire in sustaining a myth which will offer them meaning even if it closes down possibility, but they can find no way of turning need into satisfaction. They seem victims of their own capacity to refuse the consolation of relationship. The theatre itself, however, is an assertion of possibility. What cries out from these plays is need. The problem is that their characters have learned to distrust the very source of possible grace: 'The urge to support each other's social position has atrophied ... we expunge direct reference to that which *we* desire most, which is love and a sense of belonging'[35]. This, rather than planning a robbery, devising a new machine, buying real estate property, is the real subject of *American Buffalo*, *The Water Engine* and *Glengarry Glen Ross*. The rituals which his characters enact, from *Sexual Perversity in Chicago* to *Speed the Plow*, are the remnants of a need for shared experience which had once been reflected in religion, ideology or myth.

If his characters pervert language, distort values and divert profound psychological needs into temporary social objectives, this is no more than do those who direct national policy or construct the fantasies of commercial and political life. But because we are permitted to see a space between the evident need of such characters for meaning and companionship, and their equally evident denial of both, we become aware of the inadequacy of their response. The English playwright David Hare has said that the theatre is ideally designed to expose the social lie, as word can be played against action. Mamet deploys it to suggest the disproportion between need and fulfilment for, as he has explained, 'My premise is that things do mean things; that there is a way things *are* irrespective of the way we *say* things are, and if there isn't, we might as well act if there were.'[36]

Mamet has spoken of himself as an outsider. As a child of immigrant Jewish parents he feels that he has inherited the role of observer. Whether true or not it seems possible that it does have something to do with his almost irrepressible optimism. If that seems a strange way to describe the work of a man who has produced a series of plays which seem to add up to an excoriating assault on American values it is because too often the plays are only seen in terms of pathology. The fact is that, outside of a fellow Jewish playwright, Arthur Miller, it is hard to find anyone in the American theatre, or, indeed, American literature, who has quite as much faith in fundamental American principles, as well as quite such an acute awareness of the threat to individual identity implicit in the compromise of language and the denial of community. The comedy, which is a vital component of his work, depends for its effect precisely on the persistence of those very values in the audience which are being denied by the characters on the stage. It is a comedy generated by contradiction, a comedy at the expense of characters who have evacuated a saving irony from their lives. Laughter and judgement are related and the fact of judgement is an affirmation of values. Perhaps there is something Jewish, too, about an apprehension of such a rhythm of moral ebb and flow. What is true politically and morally is true, too, metaphysically. 'All plays', he has said, 'are about decay. They are about the ends of a situation which has achieved itself fully, and the inevitable disorder which ensues until equilibrium is again established.' This, he insists, 'is why the theatre has always been essential to human psychic equilibrium. The theatre exposes us to decay, to the necessity of change.'[37] Mamet does not write tragedies. Nobody has ever died in a Mamet play, except offstage and by report in *The Water Engine*. His concern does, indeed, lie with the tenuousness of our social state, but as much as any writer of tragedy he is committed to a belief in fundamental values which can only be betrayed at great social as well as psychic cost.

Mamet returned the Century of Progress Exposition of the Chicago World's Fair with *The Water Engine*, a play written originally for radio but subsequently performed by the author's own St Nicholas Theatre Company in Chicago in 1977 and, in New York, at Joe Papp's New York Festival Public Theatre the following year. Subtitled 'A Fable', it is a comic-strip drama which tells the story of a man, Charles Lang, who invents an engine which is fuelled only by water. It is the perfect American invention: free energy to fuel the American machine; something for nothing. To Mamet it is a fable about the common person and the institution. Paraphrasing Tolstoy, he wrote that, 'We have it somehow in our nature ... to perform horrendous acts which we would never dream of as individuals, and think if they are done in the name of some larger group, a *state*, a *company*, a *team*, that these vile acts are somehow magically transformed, and become praiseworthy.'[38] In that sense it is a variation on the theme of *American Buffalo* and the still-to-be-written *Glengarry Glen Ross*.

Once news of the invention leaks out, Charles Lang finds himself threatened by the criminal agents of the industry which that invention will displace. Eventually, indeed, he and his sister are killed by the agents of monopoly capitalism. However, this is less an anticapitalist tract (a form which, in keeping with its 1930s setting, it partly parodies) than an exploration of myth and, as he has said, 'The only profit in the sharing of a myth is to those who participate as storytellers or as listeners, and this profit is the shared experience itself, the *celebration* of the tale, and its truth.'[39]

The plot identifies divisions of class and money power. It dramatises the fate of the individual, isolated, threatened, excluded by those who have commandeered American enterprise. But the form—a radio play, a public fable—asserts the opposite. It joins together actors and listeners as collaborators in a common world. The human contract denied by institutions which absolve themselves of human responsibility is reinvented by a theatre (in this case a radio drama) which relies on the survival both of communality and a shared sense of justice for its effect. The particular drama, moreover, turns on what Mamet insists is an instinctive distrust of the institution, a distrust which indicates a shared apprehension of the world. As he explained in a note to the published version, the result of a play which was presented partly realistically and partly as a self-conscious radio production, is 'a third reality, scenic truth which dealt with radio not as an electronic convenience, but as an expression of our need to create and to communicate and to explain—much like a chainletter'.

The stage version retains the radio station conventions of the time, the drama being partly enacted in front of microphones. The action intercuts between the studio, a lawyer's office and the World's Fair. The voice of a chain-letter—mixing promises and threats—is intercut with that of a soapbox speaker analysing national decline, an elevator operator whose staccato statements offer an ironic commentary on the action, and a newspaperman—truth-teller and myth-maker combined. In effect he stages a debate about an America which is scarcely less fictional than the characters who implicitly define it. As the soapbox speaker remarks, 'Where is America? I say it does not exist. And I say that it never existed. It was all but a myth. A great dream of avarice ... The dream of a Gentleman Farmer.'[40] The Fair itself is a fiction, a myth of American progress which, like the other competing myths in the play, emphasises the evident need for story.

There is an irony, however, unstated but present. The company which presents this radio drama is itself a part of the commercial world which it indicts. Indeed a companion piece, *Mr Happiness*, added to the Broadway production, features a radio agony aunt, close kin to Nathanael West's Miss Lonelyhearts, who, following an apparently sincere and humane programme of advice to the lovelorn and the suffering, most of whom are trying to absolve themselves of responsibility for their lives, ends up with a sales pitch for his book.

Mamet wrote *Lakeboat* in 1970. It was a decade before it was staged. It is a cross between an early O'Neill sea play and a series of sketches from Chicago's Second City. A play in twenty-eight scenes, it offers an impressive account of shipboard life on a Great Lakes boat as seen through a series of conversations. These slowly create a portrait of the private lives of those for whom the society of the ship becomes an image of a wider world. The language is frequently banal or self-cancelling. Thus one sailor, whose job it is to make sandwiches, remarks that 'I don't want to make these sandwiches ... Not that I mind it. I just fucking hate making sandwiches.'[41] When a crew member fails to turn up one of the characters insists that he knew him but 'Not overly well.' By the end he is asserting that he 'knew him *very* well ... very well'. Another sailor denounces the missing man as a 'gambling degenerate' while celebrating the purity of the racetrack. A former cook is described as 'not married' by a man who thirty seconds later insists that he is or has been. Their language is by turns bathetic and obscene—the Mafia being a 'very property-oriented group' and women 'soft things with a hole in the middle'. But beneath the male camaraderie and pointless banter is another world. Slowly we learn that one sailor is divorced, while another, who has a blind mother and a father killed by drink, is himself suffering pains which lead him to consider suicide, admissions which ring no response from his colleagues. They are more interested in the fantasies they elaborate from the movies or the dramas which they invent for themselves. When not developing their sexual fantasies they construct a story to account for the missing member of their crew. In the course of the play he becomes in turn a derelict gambler robbed by a prostitute, a high-spending gambler attacked by the Mafia and a man who has to be silenced by the FBI. He is injured or, more likely, killed. There is no evidence for any of this. The reductive truth is that he had overslept and missed the sailing. The fictions which they elaborate, and which they subsequently abandon without regret, are their protection against boredom. Like Beckett's tramps they pass the time by talking.

Mamet's plays tend to be predominantly male. There are no women in *Lakeboat*, as there are none in *Duck Variations, American Buffalo, A Life in the*

Theatre or *Glengarry Glen Ross*. They have, however, a parodic relationship to that equally male tradition of American writing which celebrated the independent, self-defining individual, creating an identity out of his encounter with the natural and social world. In Mamet's plays the men enact ironic versions of these encounters. Cooper's forests have become real estate developments, Melville's open sea a lakeboat sailing on an endlessly repeated voyage around domestic ports.

It is that absence of women and still more the differing needs and perceptions of men and women that he chose to address with *The Woods*. Another two-hander, it concerns the relationship between Nick and Ruth, a relationship which is slowly exposed not so much through action or plot as language. Ruth, sensitive, anxious to cloak sexual need with a sentimental vocabulary, speaks in a free-verse form. Her speeches are lyrical, over-extended as she tries to construct a world out of words, displacing Nick's blunt physicality into language. *The Woods*, Mamet insists, is a play about intimacy but it is, for the most part, about failed intimacy, a will for connection which is frustrated. Nick's response to Ruth's romanticism, her desire to reshape her world linguistically, is a series of blunt, prosaic interjections. The rhythm of the play is a mirror of its theme as Nick resists the sentimental, thrusting through Ruth's protective chatter and carefully elaborated fantasies with reiterative interjections, brief spasms of language. From time to time she succeeds in pulling him into her world and briefly his prose is reshaped as verse, but for the most part his speeches barely extend beyond a few sentences. Ruth has twice as many lines as Nick and many of his are little more than monosyllables, blunt and resistant. Something is plainly breaking up. Their relationship is collapsing and she tries to hold it together with a nervous flow of words, to hold truth at bay. Her comments range from the banal—'our *appetites* are just the body's way to tell us things we may need'[42]—to the revelatory, as her fears about the relationship bubble to the surface in seemingly random remarks about male aggression. She is increasingly desperate to accommodate herself to a situation which she instinctively resists: 'It all is only things the way they are.'[43]

She looks for permanency, continuity. She deals in symbols—rings, bracelets—which bind people together, and a natural world which she sees as validating their relationship. She explores the past because 'This is the best / This is the best thing two people can do. / To live through things together. If they share what / they have done before.'[44] She asks him to tell her a story because, as she later promises, 'I will tell you a story ... a bedtime story.'[45] She presents herself as lover, child, mother, offering reassurance, comfort and love. He counters with stories of violence and betrayal. On the rare occasion he does appear to share her vision, imagining himself living happily with someone, protected from the elements, she is absent.

Afraid to broach the question of their relationship, to acknowledge her fear that it has failed to engage him, she speaks elliptically: 'sometimes things are different than the way you thought they'd be when you set out on them. This doesn't mean that, *you* know, that they aren't ... that they aren't ... Wait. Do you know what I mean?'[46] Her repeated appeals—'Do you understand me? ... Do you know what I mean? ... Do you know what I mean? ... Do you know what I mean? ... Do you know what I meant?'—simply break on his intransigence. Indeed, in a parody of her need for contact he launches on a crude sexual assault, forcing her to abandon the gentility of her protective language: 'You tore 'em, will you hold on, for chrissakes?'[47] In terms of the basic rhythm of the play this is a moment of defeat for Ruth. Increasingly desperate, she is reduced to bizarre legalism: 'If you come up here with me, that means you are ... when you come up here that means you are committed ... If you are a man. Because I am your guest.' Nick's response is to underline a central truth of the play: 'You talk too much.'[48]

Her next attempt to secure the commitment which she craves is to give him an inscribed bracelet which announces her love. He declines it. Desperate, she falls back on narrative: 'I'm telling you this story.'[49] The image she offers is of aliens who appear on earth simply because their absence has created a need which can only be satisfied by their appearance. Once again he refuses the metaphor. She now becomes the rationalist; he the one belatedly aware of emotional truth.

In this third and final scene the balance of power has shifted. Her decision to leave gives her momentary advantage. Frustrated, he strikes her. In a spasm of guilt and regret he reveals that his brutally simplistic approach to their relationship had been rooted in a fear of his own emotional vulnerability. He confesses to being confused by his own need for a companionship which goes beyond mere physicality. In moving his characters outside the cityscape, which is the context for many of his plays, he strips them of social role. What interests him here is the gulf which exists between male and female experience, language and needs. Set, very deliberately, against a background of the natural world ('Down in the City everything is vicious ... I come up here, I see things'),[50] it strips them of their posturing. Nick, indeed, seems driven almost to the borders of breakdown. Slowly his language is infiltrated by metaphor, shaped into the verse which, until then, had characterised Ruth's speeches. For what is probably the first time he speaks of love rather than sex. The play ends as Ruth begins to tell a story, a story of two lost children who cling to one another for comfort, a story in which the two characters also come together. The evidence of their contact lies in his urging her to continue the story. The play ends with three words which project the story and their relationship forward: 'The next day ... '. His fear of death, repeatedly expressed in the play, is neutralised, Scheherazade-like, by story, and the relationship on which story depends.

Duck Variations is in fourteen scenes, as is *Reunion*. *Sexual Perversity in Chicago* is in thirty-four, *Lakeboat* twenty-eight, *A Life in the Theatre* twenty-six and *Edmond* twenty-three. Experiences are presented in a series of vignettes, revue-style acts ending in a blackout. In part this is a product of his Chicago experience of Second City ('My first plays were a bunch of dramatic blackouts. For a long time I wrote very episodic plays as if I'd been forever fixed by the six-minute blackout'),[51] but beyond that it says something about the structure of experience in these plays, an experience marked by discontinuities, radical incompletions and isolated moments. The plays discover patterns which are invisible to the characters themselves. If the scenes are short, so are the speeches. More often than not there is a staccato rhythm to his work, with dialogue consisting of abbreviated bursts of language. Character dominates plot, which is in turn compressed into dramatic images. As he said at the time of the first production of *Glengarry Glen Ross*:

> There are two kinds of plays that I've been writing for the past fifteen years. One of them is an episodic play, one which is done in a lot of short takes, short scenes, where one sees various aspects of the lives of these people and where there is perhaps very little causal connection given the audience between one scene and the next. And it's true that in those plays there isn't a lot of plot. There's a spine to them; there's a certain progression but these are basically one-act plays. The difference between a one-act play and a two-act play deals with the development of character, the change of character. I think that those episodic one-act plays deal with the revelation of character and there is in most of them very little plot. On the other hand the plays that I've written that are traditionally structured, that have a two or three-act structure, have a lot of plot in them. It's just that the subject of the action is one that we're used to seeing as a traditional plot.[52]

Edmond, produced in 1982, managed to be both episodic and concerned with the development of character. Described by Mamet as a play he likes about a city—New York—which he does not, it is, as he has said, 'very, very spare, with words of one syllable, kind of harsh'. He was, he explained, 'rather surprised' that he had written it. It is a play, in his view, about a man who is looking for a place where he can be saved. Asked whether it might not be a play about death he replied, 'Maybe it is. It is about a man resigning. In every scene he casts off more and more of the veil of the world.'[53]

Overwhelmed by the pointlessness of his daily existence and of a marriage that has lost its meaning, he sets off on a personal odyssey, looking for experience which will cut through the banality of his life, stimulate a sensibility dulled to the point of torpor. Like Nathanael West's Lemuel Pitkin, in *A Cool Million*, he is systematically abused and deceived but, unlike Pitkin, he fights back, screaming invective at a woman on the subway, beating a pimp-turned-mugger and murdering a waitress after a brief sexual encounter. It is a journey stimulated, as elsewhere in Mamet's work, by a confidence trickster, one of many in the play. A fortune-teller, whose words have the same plausibility as those of the salesmen in *Glengarry Glen Ross*, the supposed clairvoyant of *The Shawl* or the accomplished tricksters of *House of Games*, assures him of the special status and significance in which he wishes to believe. Her analysis of Edmond's alienation is accurate enough: 'The world seems to be crumbling around us. You look and you wonder if what you perceive is accurate. And you are unsure what your place is. To what extent you are cause and to what an effect ... '[54] Once again, though, the perception of need is merely a prelude to deceit. Edmond's experiences lead him not from naivety to knowledge but from ignorance to self-defeat as he himself becomes a false teacher, parading banalities as truth.

For Dennis Carroll, in his book on Mamet, the final scene indicates Edmond's new-found vulnerability and personal growth as he forges a new relationship with his black cell-mate, a relationship which he sees as 'clearly an authentic one marked by genuine rapport, a fact underlined by a dialogue which moves in consonant images'. The ending, in which the two men kiss and go to sleep in separate bunks, he sees as indicative of 'deep love and affection'.[55] It is hard to agree. The relationship is based on an act of homosexual rape, which is an inversion of his own earlier sexual aggression, while the space between the two men is emphasised not only by the separate bunks but by the rhetorical distance between them, with Edmond quoting Shakespeare and the black prisoner reduced to echoing his words ('There is a destiny that shapes our ends ... PRISONER: Uh-huh ... EDMOND: Rough-hew it how we may. PRISONER: How'er we motherfucking may')[56] or developing theories about spacemen or crazy gurus blessed with second sight. The play ends as they swap banalities: 'Do you think we go somewhere when we die? / I don't know, man. I like to think so. / I would, too. / I sure would like to think so. / Perhaps it's Heaven. / I don't know. / I don't know either but perhaps it is. / I would like to think so. / I would, too.'[57] It is a dialogue which resembles nothing in the play so much as its opening: ('The girl broke the lamp. / Which lamp? / The antique lamp. / In my room? / Yes. / Huh.').[58] The circle is closed.

Edmond is Mamet's *Woyzeck*, with the city playing the same role as in Buchner's play and the central action once again the stabbing to death of a woman. The question which hangs over *Woyzeck*, moreover, is the one with which *Edmond* opens; is its protagonist a free agent or the victim of a logic that escapes him? The most bleak of Mamet's plays, it presents a world in which hell is not so much other people as the degradation of human relationships into soulless transactions. In a series of variations on a theme Edmond visits a clipjoint, a peepshow, a pimp and a brothel. The dominant realities are money and sex. We see him in the lobby of a hotel, in a subway station, a coffee house, the doorway of a mission, the interrogation room of a police station. He is always passing through, temporary, unrooted, in the anteroom of life. In a sense that is the condition of most of Mamet's characters as they ricochet off one another in a search for something that can seldom find its way into words. In fact the language of *Edmond* is not quite as spare as Mamet remembers it being, but when characters do elaborate beyond a simple question or statement it is to become articulate in the language of self-deceit as they offer hand-me-down advice as wisdom or elaborate theories born out of paranoia. The need for human contact, the desire to penetrate the mysteries of experience, is as apparent here as in any of his plays, but where elsewhere we are allowed to glimpse the survival, no matter how vestigial, of other values, here they are corrupted at source. Perhaps Mamet's surprise at having written the play comes from a recognition that *Edmond* is indeed harsher than anything else he has created.

For those in the American theatre Hollywood has always stood as an image of success and corruption. Mamet feels much the same ambivalence, speaking of it, as does one of his characters in *Speed the Plow*, as a sink of iniquity, while rejoicing in its possibilities.

The dialogue in *Speed the Plow* is a blend of cant and hypocrisy; the characters are self-serving and cynical. They look for material reward but flavour private ambition with the language of public responsibility. They want credit for sustaining the very values which they betray. Bobby Gould is a Hollywood executive charged with approving scripts for production. Faced with a pretentious script by a well-known author, on the one hand, or a 'buddy movie' featuring a star lured from another studio on the other; he has no difficulty in deciding on his priorities. The deal is brought to him by a long-time associate, Charley Fox, who holds a 24-hour option. It nearly comes unstuck, however, when a temporary secretary trades her sexual favours in a bid to support the 'art movie'. Fox rescues his deal by forcing her to confess her strategy to Gould, who had convinced himself that she acted out of love or at least respect.

It is patent that both films are devoid of redeeming features. The one, written in a witheringly mannered prose, is a post-nuclear fantasy about the regeneration of mankind by radiation; the other is a formula movie whose details interest no one precisely because its success is guaranteed by its adherence to formula. This is not, in other words, a question of art versus the market, integrity betrayed by venality. *Speed the Plow* is a comic play whose humour is generated by characters who switch from self-serving cant to arrogant honesty with breathless speed. Thus, Gould sentimentalises over the fact that theirs is a 'People Business', that 'people ... Are what it's All About', only to add, 'It's *full* of fuckin' people.'[59] It is, indeed, the very speed of these changes of direction in the levels of discourse which is the basis of Mamet's comic method: 'If you don't have principles', explains Gould, 'then each day is hell, you haven't got a compass. All you got is "good taste"; and you can shove good taste up your ass and fart "The Carnival of Venice".'[60] That disjunction functions, too, at the level of character. Karen, his secretary, appeals to '*principles*', wishes to 'Talk about purity' while planning to screw her way to influence. Gould, meanwhile, plans to screw her to win a $500 bet. The fun is to watch three confidence tricksters each determined to trick each other. Bobby Gould, arch manipulator, is himself manipulated in every sense by his secretary. His evident need to be loved for himself rather than for his influence makes him vulnerable to those who realise how to exploit that need, in just the same way as does Hollywood itself, whose buddy movies are a celebration of that very need to believe in the significance and value of friendship and love which make the exploitation of that need possible.

In *The Day of the Locust* Nathanael West used Hollywood for his satire on an America in the process of moral implosion, as did F. Scott Fitzgerald in *The Last Tycoon*. In both books character has collapsed into role, art been debased into commerce, principles traded on the open market. In both books, Hollywood, in pandering to grosser appetites, had become an image of a debased American dream. *Speed the Plow* lacks West's paranoia and anger, his apocalypticism, as it does Fitzgerald's sense of tragedy, of the final curtain being rung down on the liberal dream and on an art which could no longer sustain itself in the face of corruption. Aside from a brief assault by Fox on Gould, it lacks the violence of West's and Fitzgerald's novels. But there is a sense here, as in those works, of real need met by artificial satisfactions, of dreams colonised by commerce, of sexuality become simple currency, of language drained of its function. Life, in *Speed the Plow*, is aestheticised; it becomes a badly plotted script. But as ever in Mamet's plays there is a countercurrent: an irrepressible energy to the characters, a wild inventiveness to their dialogue and a persistent confidence that drives them. And though that energy is neurotic, that inventiveness paranoid and that confidence shot through with irony, we are never quite left, as we are in West's book, with apocalypse or, as we are in Fitzgerald's, with a planned entropy. For West, life as pure performance was life denying itself. For Mamet, performance retains a more positive quality which if it cannot quite redeem can at least fascinate.

'I hope that what I am arguing for, if I'm arguing for anything', Mamet has said,

> finally and lately has been an *a priori* spirituality, saying 'let's look at the things that finally matter: we need to be loved, we need to be secure, we need to help each other, we need to work.' What we're left with at the end of the play or the end of the day is, I hope, courage to look at the world around you and say, I don't know what the answer is but I'm going to try to reduce all of my perceptions of the terror around me to the proper place. After all is said and done we're human beings and if we really want to we can find a way to get on with each other, if we have the great, almost immeasurable courage to be honest about our desires and to not institutionalise and abstract our relationships to each other.[61]

Challenged to confess to a certain sentimentality in such a view he pleaded guilty but insisted, with equal conviction, that there is no alternative.

There is little sign of sentimentality, however, in *Oleanna* (1993) which is, first and foremost, a study of power. The particular circumstances of the battle between the characters, John and Carol, is provided by a university in which he is a professor and she a student. Institutional authority comes up against gender politics: the language of political correctness impacts on that of a presumed liberal humanism. Such was the sensitivity of the issues, indeed, that the play was frequently received by partisan audiences dividing along gender lines.

Carol, apparently bemused by her studies, comes to see her professor. Her language is confused and confusing. She, seems to have only the most tenuous grasp not only of the course but of human relationships. The professor, meanwhile, is preoccupied with his own affairs. His marriage seems under pressure. He is buying a new house and awaiting confirmation of his tenure. The conversation between the two is interrupted by the telephone. For his part he does little more than offer a few mildly patronising remarks, placing an apparently consoling and, it seems, avuncular hand on her shoulder, a gesture whose ambiguities fuel the dramatic confrontation of the second act. She seems to fail to understand what he is telling her, or respond to his attempts to put her at her ease.

In the second act she returns, her language and attitude transformed. She is now aggressively confrontational, retrospectively interpreting his earlier gesture as an assault and deploying the jargonised language of militant feminism. The play ends with his marriage and career in ruins as, in a spasm of violence, he strikes out at the woman who has destroyed him, thereby apparently validating her accusations.

The playwright Paula Vogel regarded this as such a partisan piece that she set herself to create a work in which audiences' sympathies would be genuinely equally divided: *How I Learned to Drive*. It is certainly true that the faults are not evenly divided. Carol plainly speaks a language which is not her own. She over-interprets words and actions and pursues her quarry with what she sees as detachment but what, in truth, seems closer to vindictiveness. For his part, John is unprofessional, patronising, remiss in his duties, but scarcely worthy of an attack which is plainly disproportionate. This, however, is not the point. The play is not designed as a delicate balancing act but an exploration of the mechanisms of control.

Both characters possess power. John's derives from his role as a teacher and from the knowledge he possesses. Carol's is based on an authority derived from her gender at a moment when that is invested with social and political force. The battleground on which they meet, however, is largely linguistic. Each deploys his or her own jargon to which they seek to make the other subject. With the exception of the ambiguous physical gesture of the first act and the physical assault that concludes the second, the battle is waged entirely at the level of language. It is that which shapes them as it defines the nature of their relationship. They are both the victims of language and its arch-manipulators.

The vulnerabilities of each are exposed obliquely, as much through John's one-sided conversations on the telephone and Carol's baffled circularities as through directly confrontational linguistic encounters. *Oleanna* is a deeply disturbing play not simply because it touched on an issue that was genuinely dividing society at the time or even because, like Miller's

The Crucible, it inverts the power relationship between youth and age, thereby destabilising normative values, but because it is a reminder of the power of interpretation, of the fact that language defines the nature of the real and hence human relationships. It was a point that Mamet had made in another context in *Sexual Perversity in Chicago* and *The Woods*. In the latter, a man and a woman see the world differently, deploy different images, encode language differently, using that language to ensnare or distance one another, to close off the avenue to true intimacy, an intimacy which both, in different ways, fear. They inhabit different experiences. Language may appear to be shared but is, finally, not wholly transitive. There are no true dialogues but simply overlapping privacies. In a world in which reciprocity carries implications of a feared mutuality, words are weapons or shields in an undeclared war. Beyond the immediate politics of the play, then, is a more profound irony, a deeper sense of dismay. As in *Sexual Perversity in Chicago*, men and women meet across an apparently unbridgeable divide, a gulf reflected at the level of language and, in part, created by language.

In one of his essays, Mamet asks whether all communications between men and women are negotiations. The answer is 'yes'. *Oleanna* is a flawed negotiation not least because, as he has also remarked, society has fallen apart and nobody knows what they should be doing. That anxiety is clear in *Oleanna*. Carol and John step out of their roles but fail to discover others that satisfy.

In the London production, Harold Pinter chose to begin the play with the song from which the title is derived: 'Oh, to be in Oleanna—that's where I would rather be. Than be bound in Norway and drag the chains of slavery.' It is a song whose vision of utopia is plainly at odds with the reality of a republic whose own vision of perfection has foundered. Mamet's fragmented speeches provide a correlative for a society whose dialogue with itself is flawed. It is not just that below the surface the old Adam survives, that American images of a new Eden sit uneasily alongside a manifestly fallen mankind, but that something has disappeared from American life. These characters are now rootless people for whom the old maps no longer apply. They are adrift. John is not destroyed by Carol. He is already insecure in his relationship to the world. Carol is neither a victim nor an avenging harpie. She genuinely does not understand the world in which she moves and eagerly grasps at anything that seems likely to render it into her hands. The power that both seek and deploy is no more than a sublimated desire to feel that they command their lives. The irony is that to exert that power is to lose what they most seek, some sense of consolation, harmony and peace.

There is a kind of power working, too, in Mamet's next play, *The Cryptogram*, which opened in London in 1994. This power derives from suppressed knowledge, from truths withheld, from betrayals. Things are coming to an end—a friendship, a marriage, a young boy's innocence. The ground is moving beneath the feet of those whose assurances are now slowly destroyed. A three-way conversation between a boy, his mother and a family friend, circles around a vacant centre. The boy's father is absent. Father and son are due to go on a trip to the woods. The clothes are packed. Everything is ready, except that there is a tension in the room that seems to have no point of reference. The boy cannot sleep, indeed hears voices. His mother is tense. Everyday objects seem to acquire disproportionate and obscure significance. A teapot is dropped, a blanket is torn, either now or in the past. A knife is flourished. Every effort at normalising the situation fails. The conversations are fragmented, the characters never quite engaging with one another, each with his or her own unexpressed fears. The words 'spilt', 'broken', 'torn', punctuate the action as though there were, indeed, a code to be read. In the distance is the Second World War (the events occur in 1959), a correlative for present anxieties.

There is a sense that they are all in thrall to something over which they like to believe they have no control. Thus the male friend insists that 'things unfold ... independent of our fears of them'.[62] But he, it turns out, has a vested interest in promulgating such an idea, as if his own treachery were in some way unwilled or inevitable.

In fact, we slowly learn, he has lent his hotel room to the woman's husband, thus facilitating the adulterous affair that has led to his decision to abandon the family. Her response—'Things occur. In our lives. And the meaning of them ... is not clear'[63]—is in part a genuine expression of the gnomic nature of experience and in part a defensive response, a distancing of herself from an all too clear betrayal.

The play ends with each wrapped in his or her own privacies, unable to reach out. The male friend, an ageing gay, is sent spinning back to the isolation of his hotel room home. The boy's mother prepares to move on, still unable to make sense of what has happened. The boy himself, in some ways the true centre of the play, edges closer to psychosis. He has witnessed without seeing, heard without understanding. Aware that the fixed points of his existence have been removed, alert, indeed, from the very beginning, to a feeling of insecurity he nonetheless could not earth in true meaning, he looks for a consolation he is plainly not going to be afforded.

The Cryptogram, which would seem to have a clearly autobiographical dimension, Mamet himself being the product of a broken home, is a spare, elliptical, disturbing work. Its indirections indicate the existence of a black hole to be detected only by the effect it has on those drawn to the very edge of self-extinction. That corrosion of communality which has characterised all his work here moves beyond the proto-families of *American Buffalo* and *Glengarry Glen Ross* into the very family itself, the family about which he had, perhaps, been speaking all along.

The Old Neighborhood (1997) which followed—three linked plays, two of which had been written and, indeed, published some time before—served to underline his sense of a community long since decayed, of relationships which have thinned to transparency.

Apart from anything else, *The Old Neighborhood* is evidence of Mamet's increasing fascination with the nature of Jewish identity, and though the decade and century ended with his Wildean comedy *Boston Marriage* (1999), it is that aspect of his career that was becoming most evident, as he broadened his work to include novels and poetry. A novel, *The Old Religion* (1997), centred on a Jew framed for a murder in 1913 in Georgia. In the course of the book he slowly finds his way back to his faith, losing his life but discovering the meaning of that life. Mamet's work now included not only a movie, *Homicide* (1991), in which a policeman finds his way back to his Jewish identity, a television film, *Lansky*, which explored the Jewish roots of a Mafia figure and a volume of poetry, *The Chinaman* (1999), which includes a poem called 'Song of the Jew', but also coffee-table, richly illustrated books called *Passover* (1996) and *Bar Mitzvah*(1999). The writer who had first appeared a quarter of a century earlier as the author of plays exploring the collapse of language, community, the moral self, now stood as an essayist, theatre and film director, screenwriter, poet and novelist increasingly concerned, as individual and artist, with the nature of faith and the Jewish self.

There is in David Mamet's work a yearning for that very sense of trust denied by every betrayal he documents. His characters are the victims of the language they speak, evidence of the paranoia they express. But somewhere, at the very heart of their being, is a sense of need which is the beginning of redemption. Their words may snap, like so many brittle shards, under the pressure of fear or greed; they may anxiously try to adjust themselves to the shape of myths and fantasies, deny or exploit the desire for companionship. Deep down, however, below the broken rhythms of speech, beyond the failed gestures at contact, is a surviving need for connection. The plays enact the failure of that urge but are, in their very being, an announcement of its possibility. Their energy is generated by that ambiguity.

NOTES

1. Mario Vargas Llosa, 'Latin America: Fiction and Reality', in *Modern Latin American Fiction: A Survey*, ed. John King (London, 1987), p. 5.

2. David Mamet, *the Water Engine* (New York, 1978), p. 64.

3. Vargas Llosa, 'Latin America', p.5.

4. João Ubaldo Ribeiro, *An Invincible Memory* (London, 1989).

5. David Mamet, *Writing in Restaurants* (London, 1988), p. 27

6. *Ibid.*, p.24.

7. Dennis Carroll, *David Mamet* (London, 1987), p. 27.

8. See Daniel Bell, *The Coming of Post-Industrial Societ* (London, 1974), p. 168.

9. *Ibid.*, p. 488

10. David Mamet, *The Shawl and the Prairie Du Chien* (New York, 1985), p. 5.

11. Michael Billington, 'Dream Sequence: David Mamet talks to Michael Billington', *The Guardian*, 16 Feb. 1989.

12. *Ibid.*

13. Mamet, *Writing in Restaurants*, p. 11.

14. *Ibid.*, p.21.

15. *Ibid.*, p. 30.

16. *Ibid.*

17. *Ibid.*, p. 21.

18. *Ibid.*, p. 105.

19. Interview with the author.

20. David Mamet, *American Buffalo, Sexual Perversity in Chicago and Duck Variations* (London, 1978), p. 35.

21. Interview with the author.

22. *Ibid.*

23. *Ibid.*

24. *Ibid.*

25. *American Buffalo*, pp. 6, 7.

26. *Ibid.*, p. 74.

27. *Ibid.*, p. 41.

28. Interview with the author.

29. *Ibid.*

30. *Ibid.*

31. *Ibid.*

32. David Riesman, *Thorstein Veblen: A Critical Interpretation* (New York, 1953), p. 187.

33. Mamet, *Writing in Restaurants*, p. 19.

34. *Ibid.*, p. 30.

35. *Ibid.*, p. 36.

36. *Ibid.*, p. 69.

37. *Ibid.*, p. 111.

38. *Ibid.*, p. 19.

39. *Ibid.*, pp. 107–8.

40. Mamet, *The Water Engine*, p. 64.

41. David Mamet, *Lakeboat* (London, 1981), p. 36.

42. David Mamet, *The Woods* (New York, 1979), p. 8.
43. *Ibid.*, p.10.
44. *Ibid.*, p. 23.
45. *Ibid.*, p. 39.
46. *Ibid.*, p. 54.
47. *Ibid.*, p. 59.
48. *Ibid.*, p.63.
49. *Ibid.*, p. 73.
50. *Ibid.*, p. 96.
51. Interview with the author.
52. *Ibid.*
53. *Ibid.*
54. David Mamet, *Edmond* (New York, 1983), p. 16.
55. Carroll, *David Mamet*, p. 103.
56. Mamet, *Edmond*, p. 100.
57. *Ibid.*, p. 106.
58. *Ibid.*, p. 17.
59. David Mamet, *Speed the Plow* (New York, 1987), pp. 21–2.
60. *Ibid.*, p. 45.
61. Interview with the author.
62. David Mamet, *The Cryptogram* (New York, 1995), p. 31.
63. *Ibid.*, p. 78.

David Kennedy Sauer

Oleanna *and* The Children's Hour:
Misreading Sexuality on the Post/Modern Realistic Stage

Lillian Hellman's *The Children's Hour* (1934) and David Mamet's *Oleanna* (1992) confront similar problems: both deal with difficult-to-verify sexual accusations, and both were consequently banned or protested when first staged.[1] Both are written by Jewish playwrights who moved easily back and forth between stage and film and who directed their own productions. Both are set in schools, but the line between home and school is blurred; both deal with female students and with accusations against teachers; both deal with sexual accusations, which by definition are murky and matters of perception. Yet both employ the conventions of realism, which require that the hidden secrets be revealed by the end of the play. So, from the outset, the clarity of the realistic form is potentially at odds with the sexually ambivalent content.[2] As a result, critical response is deeply divided over these plays, producing particularly vituperative attacks on both playwrights. More importantly, however, the two playwrights are deeply linked by the common approach of attacking the objectivity of the audiences who make judgments on their plays. Both problematize the possibility of making objective judgments and thereby question the very foundation of the realistic conventions that they seem to espouse.

This paper examines one source of divided response: two confessional scenes, one modernist and realistic, the other postmodern realism. In

From *Modern Drama* 34, no. 3 (Fall 2000). © 2000 by the University of Toronto.

essence, I want to distinguish between a modernist confession marked by a key feature of modernism, dualistic ambiguity, and the postmodern confession constructed in terms of multivalent indeterminacy.[3] On the basis of this difference, I distinguish postmodern realism from the earlier modernist realism with which it may be confused.

The two kinds of realism are easily confused, and with good reason. These two plays, as representatives of the different forms of realism, superficially look the same—especially if viewed in the realistic form of filmed adaptations. But in theatrical performance there are substantial differences between them. Modernist realism works in dualistic alternatives: Is Martha lesbian or not? Out of such questions, audiences are trained to construct binaristic themes: appearance versus reality; art versus nature; and so on. These are derived from the view of reality that is hierarchical, with outer life (appearance) as less important than inner life (reality). Acting styles are constructed to embody both inner and outer person in a layered effect so that audiences can read both levels of character. At the end of the modernist realistic play there is closure and full revelation of the hidden or inner realities.

David Mamet usually puts his plays in just such a context, so that audiences tend to respond to them as they have been trained to do by modernist realism. But his works are postmodern, not modern, and, as a result, there are often substantial misunderstandings of his plays, as they are read in the wrong context. For Mamet, as a representative postmodern, there is no weighting of inner over outer; indeed, Mamet requires his actors to abandon any attempt to imply some inner depths—they should simply stick to the surface. As a result, the old themes of modernism disappear: there is no distinction between appearance and reality; both are the same, since everything is on the surface. There is no conflict between art and nature: nature is not a separate thing but, rather, a part of the artificially constructed human idea of reality—formed largely by mass media presentations of nature in books, films, television, and photographs. As a consequence, there is no closure as in modernist realism—no full revelation of the buried secrets so that the audience feels it knows the full truth as it has interpreted it by reading the signs all along. For example, contrast the revelation of the meaning of incest and the death of the infant at the end of *Desire Under the Elms* (1924) with the conclusion of *Buried Child* (1979), in which Tilden's appearance with the dead body is overdetermined with meanings—no one of which is particularly authorially privileged. Current representations of realism in the drama tend to see modernist and postmodernist as the same, and this article is an attempt to clarify the difference.

As an example of a critical work that blurs the differences between the two realisms, consider William Demastes's *Beyond Naturalism: A New Realism in American Theatre*, which sees contemporary dramatists as simply "infusing realism with fresh and contemporary perspectives of the world around them", (7). On a more profound level, W.B. Worthen, in *Modern Drama and the Rhetoric of Theatre*, sees no significant distinction between earlier and postmodern writers in terms of rhetorical effect; he privileges the audience as outside and objective viewers of the action. After citing a number of dramatists who seem to work in the modernist realistic tradition (August Wilson, Beth Henley, Brian Friel, David Storey, Marsha Norman, Neil Simon), Worthen notes the influence on others by

> aggressively antirealistic modes like absurd theater, happenings, the theater of Brechtian alienation, poor theater, and indeed by conceptions of pace, temporality, and dramatic organization reintroduced to the stage from video and film. The bizarre and unexpected turns of plot, unusual mises-en-scène, or oblique and refractory language characteristic of David Mamet, Harold Pinter, Sam Shepard, Maria Irene Fornes, and other playwrights like them often seem to signal an effort to reshape the project of realistic theatricality. In many respects, though, this drama capitulates to the categories of meaning and interpretation found in earlier realistic modes, especially the classic dialectic between character and environment, still visible in the drama, in production practice, and in the figuration of an audience. (82)

As much as I admire Worthen's book, my article is designed to take issue with this statement and to demonstrate how Mamet's realism differs from that of modernists such as Hellman.[4]

For that reason I am using *The Children's Hour* as an example of modernist realism that is familiar. The problems it poses for criticism, in my view, result from postmodern readings backward that fail to appreciate the differences between earlier figurations of realistic drama and postmodern understandings. Nevertheless, the concept of postmodern realism has not previously been recognized or defined, so, after considering how *Oleanna* sets up the problems of this different kind of realism, the remainder of the essay is devoted to examining Mamet's approach and theory in order to construct a definition of postmodern realistic drama.

Martha's confession at the end of *The Children's Hour* has created considerable critical debate. Eric Bentley states unequivocally that "one of the teachers *is* Lesbian" (74).[5] C.W.E. Bigsby, however, takes a much more neutral approach: "Martha does indeed confess that she had loved her friend with something more than the affection of a friend" (275). He seems to be walking a line between Bentley and the view of Richard Moody that Martha's is a "hysterical confession" that results from her sense that "she's ruined their lives" (54).

The problem with Martha's final revelation is the way in which it is expressed. Her declaration of love for Karen is ambiguous:

> *Martha* I love you that way—maybe the way they said I loved you. I don't know. (*Waits, gets no answer, kneels down next to Karen*) Listen to me! [...] You've got to know it. I can't keep it any longer. I've got to tell you how guilty I am.
>
> *Karen* [*deliberately*] You are guilty of nothing.
>
> *Martha* I've been telling myself that since the night we heard the child say it; I've been praying I could convince myself of it. I can't, I can't any longer. It's there. I don't know how, I don't know why. But I did love you. I do love you. I resented your marriage; maybe because I wanted you; maybe I wanted you all along; maybe I couldn't call it by a name; maybe it's been there ever since I first knew you –
>
> *Karen* [*tensely*] It's a lie. You're telling yourself a lie. We never thought of each other that way.
>
> *Martha* [*bitterly*] No, of course *you* didn't. But who says I didn't? I never felt that way about anybody but you. I've never loved a man—[*Stops. Softly.*] I never knew why before. Maybe it's that. (104–5)

Starting with Martha's opening words, the declaration can be read as unequivocal: "I love you that way. [...] You've got to know it. [...] But I did love you. I do love you. [...] I never felt that way about anybody but you." Yet if one reads against the grain, the speech is stammered out with uncertainty: six "maybe" qualifiers, three "I don't know" disavowals. It must leave the audience confused—there both is and isn't a revelation at the end; is Martha lesbian or isn't she?

This initial critical question has given way to a more deeply theoretical rift over this play. Is it an insensitive treatment of an awkward coming-out by a heterosexual writer, as Mary Titus argues? Or is it, rather, a problem of the realist's inability to convey lesbianism in language, to express something that can only be represented by suppression, as Anne Fleche proposes? At issue is the whole concept of realistic form and its inability to deal with issues that cannot be simply and directly articulated.

Fleche clearly delineates the structural problems that the realistic undergirding of Hellman's play necessitates:

> [Martha's] discovery that Mary's misbehavior actually constitutes a sustained performance with very sophisticated implications is a reminder that realism relies on such belated discoveries, and that these surprises are made possible by realistic characters' inability to see themselves. (22)

The double problem of realism is "belated discoveries" that result from "characters' inability to see themselves." Adding the complication of latent lesbianism doubles the problem. It is difficult to know, since the revelation comes only at the end of the play, whether the belated discovery is real or whether it is self-induced based on Martha's lack of self-understanding.

The underlying premise of this debate is found in Catherine Belsey's discussion of "classic realism," which argues that the conventions of realism require the enigma to be revealed at the end so that the reader feels the power of knowing all as outside observer and judge of the work.[6] Hellman indicates her own felt need to create this kind of closure: "The play probably should have ended with Martha's suicide: the last scene is tense and over-burdened. I knew this at the time, but I could not help myself. I am a moral writer, often too moral a writer, and I cannot avoid, it seems, that last summing-up" ("Introduction" viii–ix).

In Hellman's view, the play's focus was on the lie, not the lesbianism: "It's the results of her [Mary's] lie that make her so dreadful—this is really not a play about lesbianism, but about a lie. The bigger the lie the better, as always" (qtd. in Gilroy 25). For Hellman's purpose, the realistic moral ending is conveyed by Mrs. Tilford's announcement that Mary has lied. To make that tragic, the consequences of the lie had to be irreversible; the announcement immediately follows Martha's suicide. To motivate Martha's suicide, her confession is necessary. But the confession can be read two ways: either as the recognition of a repressed lesbian desire or as a consequence of the instability the lie creates.

Realistic plays, however, do not resolve all ambiguities—even though the main enigma is revealed. Belsey's example was drawn from Sherlock Holmes; Barthes's example, which she followed, from Balzac. But realistic playwrights, working in a much shorter, more compact form, leave space for actors and directors to create their own interpretations.

Herman Shumlin's original 1934 production of *The Children's Hour*
stressed lesbianism; Hellman's own direction in 1952 changed the emphasis:
"To my mind, the theme of Lesbianism is less this time and what comes out
stronger is the power of a lie and what it can do to people when it has even
one little ounce of truth" (qtd. in Lederer 26). But the point is that the actor
must decide how to play Martha. She could be played as lesbian, as Shirley
MacLaine played her in William Wyler's 1962 film; or not, as in his earlier
1936 version, *These Three*. Either way would work.

Lee Strasberg seems to make this very point about acting as he explains
to an actress that she is getting hung up on which choice to make as an actor,
rather than going forward with the action:

> You say you have to jump out of the way of the car. You say you
> want to know which way. Does it matter whether you jump this
> way or that way? Not at all. The problem is not how you jump or
> where you jump. The problem is only, Do you stand still or do
> you jump: Once you decide to jump, jump. You'll find different
> ways, and you'll find that they are all right so long as they carry
> you out of the way of the car. (193)

In the view of the master of the traditional (modernist, realistic) American
Method, the key for the actor is to avoid ambiguity, since she will become
confused with multiple intentions. Rather, she must choose one way of
playing or the other; "they are all right," so which choice is made is not as
important as making a single choice. The same is true, by extension, with the
actress playing Martha. In the original modernist realistic context, she must
simply choose which way to play the character.

For the actor playing Carol in Mamet's *Oleanna*, however, there are
none of the clear-cut character choices offered. Instead, the creation of the
character seems deliberately constructed in terms of gaps or leaps. The most
notable is between the inarticulate, "slow leaner" Carol of the limited
vocabulary in Act One to the articulate and controlling Carol of Acts Two
and Three. What causes the change in outlook, in vocabulary, in confidence?
The actor (and audience) are given no answer to the transformation, and
frequently they simply construct their own interpretations (often focusing on
"the group") in the absence of any authorial direction.

To understand Mamet, however, one must realize that his playwriting
approach is to challenge the audience (and actor) with such unresolved
lacunae. Matthew C. Roudané, in *American Drama Since 1960*, has given an
excellent analysis of what I am calling postmodern realistic form as a series

of "gaps" in the realistic veneer that should be used as the basis for any analysis of *Oleanna*:

> Mamet returns to a world in which the gaps between words and deeds remain. The play is theatrically powerful precisely because its author never fills in such gaps. Instead, the theatergoer thinks, Is Carol framing John? Are her accusations legitimate? Is Carol simply the first to have the courage to challenge a patronizing and, perhaps, womanizing male teacher? Is John so much a part of an inherently misogynistic world that he is blithely unaware that his well-meaning actions are in fact highly sexist? Mamet invites the audience to respond to these and many other issues [...]. (173)

This passage makes clear that the questions of meaning that are often raised concerning this play are precipitated not by the answers that Mamet gives to these questions but, rather, by the way the play avoids asking or answering them. As a result the audience, assuming the play to be realistic, fills in the gaps for the playwright, with sometimes quite forced or bizarre results.

To see how these gaps work on an audience, consider Francine Russo's essay from the *Village Voice*, which alternates between an attempt to see the play objectively, as an equal contest, and her gut feeling that it is all women-bashing:

> Alternate programs were printed, half showing a male figure with a target on his chest, the other half with a female sporting the same bull's eye. A contest of perception. [...] But it was always a rigged game. There's been a lot of smart analysis of this play to prove it's weighted on both sides, but to experience *Oleanna*, you need to bring your nose as well as your intellect. The on-its-head world Mamet's written *reeks* of woman-hating, and his directorial choices spew a mean-spirited, unwholesome smog over the proceedings on and off-stage. (96–97)

This jump within one paragraph, which begins with the marketing strategy of the programs, then leaps to her perception, demonstrates the kind of back-and-forth moves that Russo makes. Her language and diction provide a microcosm of the whole controversy.[7]

Yet despite her view of Mamet's hidden purpose of beating and rejecting women, Russo just as quickly acknowledges the objective reality of the characterization of Carol, as well as the *gaps* in the narrative:

> But Carol is at best insufferable, at worst antiseptically evil. She's a cipher, a trick card, an either/or. You can project anything you like upon her, as the critics have. Can you see *Oleanna* as "a tragedy of language," as the *Voice's* Michael Feingold does? Yeah, you can. Can you make a case, as John Lahr does in *The New Yorker*, that it's about "the awful spoiling power of envy disguised as political ideology"? Why not? These interpretations are built partly on character, and viewers can just jot what they like in the character blank. The *Times's* David Richards concedes Mamet "is not exactly playing fair" and "forces us to chart our own path through the play with only our speculations and prejudices to guide us." Sure. Leave some pieces out of a puzzle and people will fill in the holes. A good Rorschach test, perhaps, but hardly proof of literary merit. (97)

This excerpt clearly depicts what Mamet has given—a puzzle with missing pieces—and yet what Russo has made of it is clear from the earlier passages. Russo is evidently aware of the existence of the gaps, and yet she can't help herself from constructing her view of Carol, which she knows is a projection of her own psyche, a Rorschach test. This is most honest. Her quotations from the other major reviewers make clear the variety of conflicting responses that the play elicits. The quotation from David Richards comes closest to my view that the play forces the audience to project its own prejudices onto the characters, as Russo does in her essay.

I believe that Mamet encourages the audience to misinterpret the play as Russo does by presenting it as a seemingly realistic construction, which can then be interpreted by realistic rules. When the audience applies those rules, instead of objectivity there is subjective prejudice, which is mirrored in each person's own interpretation. Thus Mamet's gaps allow the audience to experience something like what Russo experiences: an externalization of its own fears and prejudices, a recognition that the characters are not at all what one thinks they are. The framework that one assumes determines how the object is seen and understood. The objective reality of the characters in *Oleanna* cannot be seen except through one framework or another—so it is one's own frameworks that one confronts when watching the play. As John notes early in the play, "Well, you see? That's what I'm saying. We can only interpret the behavior of others through the screen we [...] Through the screen we create" (19–20). There is at least a double irony in this line: John says it condescendingly to Carol, as if she alone misunderstands him because of faulty screening. But the irony is developed in the second act, when the tenure committee accepts her construction of the first-act episode, so that Carol's "screen" becomes the dominant. An added level of irony, however, is that the audience too interprets the play as a whole "[t]hrough the screen we create."

Carol's confession scene in *Oleanna* is a key example of Mamet's use of gaps in the narrative. Scarcely noticed by critics,[8] the confession is central to constructing a more favorable view of Carol. Deborah Eisenstadt, who played Carol in Mamet's production on the stage and in film, indicated the centrality of the final-act climax in a conversation after her presentation at the David Mamet Society session of the MLA in 1996. The concluding first-act moment is crucial because it comes just after John puts his arm around her to console her, when it seems Carol is about to entrust John with her deepest and most painful secret:

John	Sshhhhh. Sshhhhh. Let it go a moment. (*Pause*) Sshhhhh ... let it go. (*Pause*) Just let it go. (*Pause*) Just let it go. It's all right. (*Pause*) Sshhhhh. (*Pause*) I understand ... (*Pause*) What do you feel?
Carol	I feel bad.
John	I know. It's all right.
Carol	I ... (*Pause*)
John	What?
Carol	I ...
John	What? Tell me.
Carol	I don't understand you.
John	I know. It's all right.
Carol	I ...
John	What? (*Pause*) What? *Tell* me.
Carol	I can't tell you.
John	No, you must.
Carol	I can't.
John	No. Tell me. (*Pause*)
John	It's all right.
Carol	I'm ...
John	It's all right.
Carol	I can't talk about this.

John	It's all right. Tell me.
Carol	Why do you want to know this?
John	I don't want to know. I want to know whatever you ...
Carol	I always ...
John	... good ...
*Carol*ᴸ	I always ... all my life ... I have never told anyone this ...
John	Yes. Go on. (*Pause*) Go on.
Carol	All my life ... (*The phone rings.*) (*Pause.* JOHN *goes to the phone and picks it up.*)
John	(*into phone*) I can't talk now. (37–38)

Contrast Martha's last-act confession with Carol's. Instead of ambiguity, Carol's confession is expressed almost entirely in negatives: "I can't" (three times); "I didn't" (three times); "never," "not"; and the direct statements are "I feel bad [...] I'm bad." But, since there is no positive assertion, her secret remains hidden. As soon as she begins, "All my life ...," she is cut off by the telephone call, and John leaves her hanging. When Act Two opens, she has brought her complaint to the tenure committee, and that issue consumes the last two acts.

This confessional scene differs markedly from the more complete modernist version. It has the familiar postmodern markers: it is fragmented, continually interrupted, and ultimately aborted. This much one might expect in postmodernism. If the scene is understood through realistic conventions, the audience is given continual hints here of some deep dark secret that Carol has hidden inside. But, unlike the modernist confession, this one never reveals to the audience the secret in the character's heart, and, in this case, no allusion is ever made back to this secret.[9] Thus the postmodern author is no longer the authority that predetermines interpretation. In this open-ended situation, there is no evidence that Mamet had anything more in mind to explain Carol's secret. Actor, Audience, and Author are all left with only the text, and no subtext, to interpret.

In the play, Mamet evades revealing/writing Carol's secret when the final telephone interruption of Act One informs us that all the frustrating calls were a ruse to get John to the surprise party. The trick has also been played on the audience—"there are those who would say it's a form of aggression [...] A surprise" (41).

And yet, this aborted confession is central to the meaning and experience of the play. It certainly was for me when I saw Mamet's production at the Kennedy Center with Eisenstadt and William H. Macy—I thought John had led Carol on shamelessly to reveal her innermost secret, and then, as she started to confess, he just abandoned her and left for his party. As I saw the performance, it was not quite sexual abuse, but it was certainly some form of student abuse. What is important is not *what* her secret was but John's total lack of recognition of her vulnerability in being about to reveal it.

That concluding confession of Act One is set up by the moments of physical touching that precede it. The blocking reveals a shift of power, as demonstrated in the Lincoln Center Library videotape of the New York production with Macy and Rebecca Pidgeon. In the first act, *he* is in total control of the movement. My sense is that where she first lands is her place, the place of powerlessness: the bench inside the door, stage right, farthest from his desk. This is established from the outset when he takes a chair and places it just across from the bench right. But he doesn't offer her a seat— she takes the bench as he first sits in the chair. At other times he moves the straight wooden chair around the set, sometimes to sit opposite her, sometimes to place it center and put her in the middle. However it works, he is in control of the space, and usually she is stage right, near the entrance/exit, ready to flee. He is physically identified with the desk, again his place of power, but he never sits at it in any conventional way. He leans against the front of it, stands behind it to answer the phone and talk, and actually sits on it. In the second act, to demonstrate the reversal of power, *his* first place to sit is on her bench. She takes the chair and sits opposite him. Physically this makes clear the psychological change in power and position that has happened between the two acts.

The critical ingredients in the blocking of Mamet's production, however, are the moments of physical touching. The crucial moment clearly defines John's view of Carol. He is joking about the tenure committee finding out his own "dark secret," essentially that he is unworthy of the position, as his family has told him in the past. She wants to know what the secret is, and he dismisses it laughingly. She quickly shifts ground to ask about her grade, but the telephone rings. After that interruption, he goes toward her; both are standing, and she backs up until she has nowhere left to turn—between the two benches stage right. She then turns away toward the door, and they freeze momentarily, with their backs to the audience, as he puts his arm around her shoulders. The stage direction in the published script reads

(He goes over to her and puts his arm around her shoulder.)
NO! *(She walks away from him.)* (36)

When this happens in the videotaped production, she jumps and turns quickly away under his arm. At this point, he asks, "What do you feel?" and the meaning is highly ambiguous. This line fits his affective approach to education, contending that Carol cannot learn because of how she feels: "I think you're *angry*, I ... " (7); "I think you're angry. Many people are" (12). And he later asserts that "I feel I must fail" predetermines failure.

But the feelings she has had when he put his arm around her may be quite different. That was the sense I got. "I feel bad." "I ... I ... I don't understand you." "I ... What? What? *Tell* me. I can't tell you." "I'm bad [...] I can't talk about this [...] I always ... all my life ... I have never told anyone this ... " (37–38). When she is about to tell him this secret, they seem to have reached a place of real confiding and understanding. Then the telephone rings, the party is announced, and he leaves. He never notices what happened; seemingly the physical touch has aroused something in her, something she is about to confess for the first time, but he simply ignores all of her feelings, and the act ends.

Clearly John just doesn't get it—he never sees anything sexual about the contact, but the moment does have some effect on her that he ignores. And when he pleads, at the start of the second act, "What have I done to you? How can I make amends?" he sounds convincing, but he has no clue what he's done. More importantly, the audience has no clue either; the incident is never alluded to again, and the confession is aborted, incomplete. The apparent buried secret of realism is never revealed.

Such a moment is a good example of the difference between Mamet's postmodern drama and the earlier realists'. There is no need for the actor playing Carol to supply a subtext here, as she would have done if playing Martha. Instead, the actor can play the lines exactly as written, without adding any subtext to reveal hidden secrets to the audience.

The actor playing the role of Martha, and the director of *The Children's Hour*, would conventionally need to make a decision about Martha's lesbianism: is she or isn't she? The audience of realism is encouraged to think that it can know the secrets of the inner self when it watches the play, picks up the hints from the actor, and learns the complete truth at the end of the play: the enigma must be revealed.

This completed circuit is best represented by Elin Diamond in *Unmaking Mimesis*, where she presents the completed circuit as she examines how Freud's "new therapy and the new theater depend on exploring and exposing the woman with a past" (15):

Realism is more than an interpretation of reality passing as reality; it *produces* "reality" by positioning its spectator to recognize and verify its truths: this escritoire, this spirit lamp affirms the typicality, the universality of this and all late Victorian bourgeois drawing rooms. Human signification is no less teleological. The actor/signifier, laminated to her character/signfied, strenuously seeks admission to the right class of referents. (4)

This does not mean, of course, that playwright and audience are always in perfect communication. For example, in *The Children's Hour*, Hellman came to discover that audiences overreacted and saw the child as totally villainous, not at all what she envisioned:

On the stage a person is twice as villainous as, say, in a novel. When I read that story I thought of the child as neurotic, sly, but not the utterly malignant creature which playgoers see in her. I never see characters as monstrously as the audiences do—in her case I saw her as a bad character but never outside life. It's the results of her lie that make her so dreadful [...] (Gilroy 25)

Audiences, clearly, interpret the play in dualistic terms, seeing children as either monsters or innocents; Hellman had a more sophisticated understanding, but the audience reads the play in simple binary terms.

The actor, too, goes beyond these simple oppositions. Diamond examines the complexity of early realistic acting:

Testimony of the density of her performance comes from [Elizabeth] Robins's own memoir, *Ibsen and the Actress*, in which she retroactively fleshes out [...] exactly as though she were writing a psychoanalytical case study—filling in the gaps which the play leaves ambiguous: Lovborg's sensuality "made her [Hedda's] gorge rise ... the man who had wallowed in filth must not touch Hedda Gabler." What Robins creates here is an ontological alternate "that no critic ... ever noticed"—which was precisely Konstantin Stanislavsky's goal in the "psychotechnique" that he formalized after years of acting in the plays of Ibsen and Chekhov. An actor "after a long and penetrating process of observation and investigation" creates "an inner life," a "subconscious" for his/ her character. (29–30)

Robins's process of filling in the gaps and eliminating ambiguities is precisely the technique that subsequently evolved for realistic plays, beginning with Ibsen. The attempt of the actor is to make a clear and consistent reading, as it is the endeavor of the audience to pick up the hints and decode a consistent interpretation of its own, eliminating ambiguities.

By contrast, Mamet's approach to acting, like his approach to writing, is not to fill in the past history of the character and enact an inner life on stage; quite the opposite, as he argues in *True and False*:

> The Method got it wrong. Yes, the actor is undergoing something on stage, but it is beside the point to have him or her "undergo" the supposed trials of the character upon the stage. The actor has his own trials to undergo, and they are right in front of him. They don't have to be superadded; they exist. His challenge is not to recapitulate, to *pretend* to the difficulties of the written character; it is to open the mouth, stand straight, and say the words bravely— adding nothing, denying nothing, and without the intent to manipulate anyone: himself, his fellows, the audience. (22)

For the Mamet actor, Carol in this instance, the approach to the confession cannot be the conventional, Method-based, realistic assumption of an inner life to the character. Instead, character is all on the surface, and the actor need only deliver the lines. This kind of confession is truly ambivalent, or multivalent. In such a case, the actor sends no signals to the audience of the hidden inner life. The audience is left to puzzle out its own interpretation of the character, with no direction from the actor, as *True and False* indicates:

> The actor does not need to "become" the character. The phrase, in fact, has no meaning. There *is* no character. There are only lines upon a page. They are lines of dialogue meant to be said by the actor. When he or she says them simply, in an attempt to achieve an object more or less like that suggested by the author, the audience sees an *illusion* of a character upon the stage. (9)

Just as the actor need not become the character or fill in the "subtext," so too the Mamet audience need not look for hidden meanings, the inner life of the characters, as was necessary in modernist realism.[10] The focus of the play is, then, in part, to hold a mirror not to nature, as a realist would have done, but to the audience itself, making clear how its own preconceptions are mirrored in the way the characters and action are understood.

The function of ambiguity in modernist realistic drama, therefore, seems to be to give space for the actor to make choices. It also leaves space for the discerning reader, or viewer, to perceive a larger view than that of the more didactic, single-minded reader. The result still privileges the audience, giving it the sense of objectivity and perception of the grand narrative. In the decentered ambivalence of the postmodern dramatist, however, that place of actor and audience privilege is gone. Both audience and actor are given merely the words on the page, and any construction of depth, subtext, or inner life is a construction of the actor/audience, rather than of the play itself. The play, instead, like the reality it seeks to present, is constructed of indeterminacy and mocks any attempt to reduce it to neat choices or ambiguities.

Attempts to interpret *Oleanna* by the standards and approaches of modernism can only lead to frustration. Limiting critical choices to the simple either/or of modernist ambiguity results in the critic's having to choose between Carol and John and to build a case around one choice. But the ambivalence of indeterminacy requires that much greater space be left open in interpreting the postmodern work. Characters' motives are not fully knowable, as they are in the revealed-secret form of modernist realism—in *The Children's Hour*, for example. And the interpreter must recognize that postmodern characters are not fully knowable. If the critic can accept this fact, then a different kind of appreciation of the art of the dramatist will result.

Mamet argues in *True and False* that the actor continually wants to have certainty, assurance, and relies on a method in order to feel secure with her interpretation. Mamet rejects this approach because it limits the possibilities and excludes the spontaneous, the indeterminate, from performance:

> The skill of acting is not the paint-by-numbers ability to amalgamate emotional oases—to string them like pearls into a performance (the Method). Nor is it the mastery of syntax (the academic public speaking model). The skill of acting is like the skill of sport, which is a physical event. And like that endeavor, its difficulty consists to a large extent in being much simpler than it seems. Like sports, the study of acting consists in the main in getting out of one's own way, and in learning to deal with uncertainty and being comfortable being uncomfortable. (19–20)

The skill of the interpreter must be the same: not imposing one's own framework and explanation of character motivation to create a consistent interpretation but, rather, "getting out of one's own way" to allow the "uncertainty" of understanding to emerge fully.

Worthen, by contrast, argues that realism as a theatrical form places the audience in a position of objectivity from which its judgment of the characters can give certainty because they are seemingly untainted by the audience's own prejudices and presupposed frameworks:

> The spectator is cast as an impartial observer, construed outside and beyond both the drama and the theatrical activities— including his or her attendance, participation—that produce it. Staging *drama* that often insists on the pervasive determination of an environment metonymically reduced to the drawing-room box, realistic *theater* suppresses the theatrical environment as both cause and explanation of the drama's meanings or our interpretation of them. (20–21)

But in both of Mamet's theatrical productions, in New York and Washington, *Oleanna* was produced in a fragmentary set, a raised platform with a desk, three chairs, and two benches. The signal this set sends to the audience is that imagining it as "John's office" already requires the complicity, the participation, of the audience. Like the set, the characters, too, are fragmentary; what the audience adds to make them into whole beings becomes its own creation. Objectivity and impartiality are left behind, and the conclusion of the play prods the audience to recognize that its own projections are what it has seen. The characters remain, in Mamet's phrase, "only lines upon a page" (*True and False* 9).

The difference, then, between modernist realist work like *The Children's Hour* and postmodern fragmented work like *Oleanna* is much greater than would appear on the surface. The difference is between text and context. In the ambiguous modernist text there is an implied authorized interpretation, or alternate interpretations, which the actor then delivers and which the audience decodes (assuming that its objectivity ensures that the judgment it makes is entirely its own). Thus all three work in a kind of harmony, or, ideally, there is a potential direct communication between author and actor, actor and audience.

Jean-François Lyotard, in *The Postmodern Condition*, declares at the outset that the condition of the modern (as opposed to the postmodern) is this idea of shared communication based on a set of common assumptions:

> I will use the term *modern* to designate any science that legitimates itself with reference to a metadiscourse of this kind making an explicit appeal to some grand narrative, such as the

dialectics of Spirit [i.e., Hegel], the hermeneutics of meaning [i.e., Freud], the emancipation of the rational or working subject, or the creation of wealth [i.e., Marx]. (xxiii)

These grand narratives of Hegel, Freud, or Marx are built upon the Hegelian dialectic and struggle of mighty opposites, thesis and antithesis, base and superstructure, conscious and unconscious. They create a framework for communication; authorial intention is discovered/fulfilled by actors, who then communicate it to an audience that decodes it at the other end. Lyotard continues,

For example, the rule of consensus between the sender and addressee of a statement with truth-value is deemed acceptable if it is cast in terms of a possible unanimity between rational minds: this is the Enlightenment narrative, in which the hero of knowledge works toward a good ethico-political end—universal peace. (xxiii–iv)

In Hellman's drama, this enlightenment concept of working toward "a good ethico-political end" is especially evident in her direction of *The Children's Hour* as a commentary on the House Un-American Activities Committee hearings before which she had been summoned.

By contrast, the point of Lyotard's work is that there are no more overarching narratives that unite all knowledge: "I define *postmodern* as incredulity toward metanarratives" (xxiv). One of the starting points for his examination of the postmodern is the way in which realism is continually critiqued by the avant-garde, exposing its hidden assumptions:

It is not my intention to analyze here in detail the manner in which the various avant-gardes have, so to speak, humbled and disqualified reality by examining the pictorial techniques which are so many devices to make us believe in it. Local tone, drawing, the mixing of colors, linear perspective [...] the avant-gardes are perpetually flushing out artifices of presentation which make it possible to subordinate thought to the gaze and to turn it away from the unpresentable. (79)

In my view, Mamet's *Oleanna* functions like Lyotard's avant-garde, "flushing out artifices of presentation." While at first glance the play seems realistic, in fact it is not—instead it exposes the hidden ideological assumptions of realism.

William H. Macy made the point clearly in an interview with Liane
Hansen on National Public Radio during the Washington run of *Oleanna*:

> David's point of view, and I believe he's exactly right, is there it is,
> it's on the page, it's right in front of you. You don't need to know
> any back story. And I always find it fascinating that audiences
> come in to this play and because it's such a hot button issue, and
> they bring so much anger to the party that they have a tendency
> to want to interpret the play. They can't accept what they see
> before their very eyes. They want to figure it out. (Macy and
> Eisenstadt)

The audience that Macy describes is misreading the play. Indeed, the whole
point of *Oleanna*, as I understand it, is to bring the audience to the
recognition that it is, in fact, (mis)reading—interpreting based on what the
audience brings to the theatre itself, its own mental baggage.

In the interview Liane Hansen points out that when audiences exit
from the Kennedy Center Theater, they see in the lobby a large blackboard
with ushers taking votes under signs: "Is he right"; "She was wronged";
"Could it really happen." What is this? Years later, in a discussion at the
Mamet at Fifty Conference held at UNLV in 1998, Macy noted that it was
the Theater's idea to put up the blackboard. But surely he and Mamet had
approved this. What does the blackboard imply? First, it announces to the
audience that, as the *Oleanna* film poster declared, "Whichever side you
choose, you're wrong"; clearly, some people will sympathize with John, some
with Carol, and seeing that fact on the blackboard problematizes the
response for anyone. It is a post facto way to get the audience to confront the
postmodern point of the play—that it is our own stereotypes we see on stage,
not what is really there. The even more ironic middle question–"could it
really happen?"—is about realism: does the audience take this play as if it
were reality?

Without seeing the point of the survey, Megan Rosenfeld reported on
the experiment in *The Washington Post*. The night she attended,

> 61 percent of those who voted thought he was right, compared
> with a week long average of 79 percent. Thirty-nine percent
> thought she was wronged, compared with the average 21 percent.
> And only 85 percent said something like this could really happen,
> compared with the normal 96 percent. (B4)

Percentages vary depending on the audience; matinee audiences voted with John much more strongly than evening audiences—and all thought it could really happen. But the key to this publicity stunt/poll is that, as an audience member, I was shocked at how many disagreed with me. The decentering of the audience, of interpretation, happened, for me, in the moment when I confronted the blackboard.

In the indeterminate postmodern play, there are different contexts in which different audience members read the text. The result is that the play *Oleanna* is not about John and Carol, the characters, so much as it is about how we read John and Carol. If we assume that we "know" Carol in an objective and unbiased way, as we are led to think we "know" Martha in *The Children's Hour*, we are in error. Carol's innermost secret is never revealed, and so any interpretation made of her is necessarily a subjective, not objective, construction. She is not, finally, knowable in the complete sense that realistic characters are.

Why would Mamet withdraw from an author's power and authority over his text? Macy provides his answer as he gives his truth:

> They [the audience] just can't accept what they see before their very eyes. They want to figure it out, well, what's the angle. They just can't accept that it's a professor who is very full of himself and is biting the hand that feeds him, when it comes to the educational system and the university. (Macy and Eisenstadt)

I think Macy is close to Mamet's point here—but in fact it is the system itself that subverts and distorts the people within it. When the professor has control and power, he is distorted by the system; when the student has it, she is distorted as well. The fault is not in the individual psychology of each character, as it would have been in modernist realism, but, rather, in the system as a whole.[11]

NOTES

1. Katherine Lederer notes three main controversies: "*The Children's Hour* was kept before the public eye much longer than any other Hellman play [...] because of news articles about (1) its being banned in Boston, Chicago, and London; (2) the failure of the Pulitzer Prize committee even to attend a performance; and (3) the difficulties attendant on retitling and rewriting the film version to gain the approval of the Hays Office, the then-all-powerful Hollywood censorship board" (22). Arthur Holmberg explains that when *Oleanna* "premiered last October in Cambridge, Mass.

[...] Mamet was attacked by people on both sides of the sexual battlefront. 'Your play is politically irresponsible,' one female student challenged the playwright. 'You don't take a position. Your political statement is wrong.' [...] 'As a playwright,' Mamet answered the student, 'I have no political responsibility. I'm an artist. I write plays, not political propaganda. If you want easy solutions, turn on the boob tube. Social and political issues on TV are cartoons; the good guy wears a white hat, the bad guy a black hat. Cartoons don't interest me. We are living through a time of deep transition, so everyone is unsettled. I'm as angry, scared and confused as the rest of you. I don't have answers'" (94).

2. This is, essentially, the argument that Anne Fleche makes regarding *The Children's Hour* in "The Lesbian Rule."

3. The terms are key critical perceptions of their times. In 1930 William Empson's *Seven Types of Ambiguity* made the earlier term a cornerstone of modernist interpretation. Ihab Hassan takes "indeterminacy" to be crucial to postmodernism (41). He supports this claim by citing Geoffrey Hartman's assertion that "contemporary criticism aims at the hermeneutics of indeterminacy" (41).

4. I find support for this attempt in Ruby Cohn's recognition of the differences in British drama articulated in *Retreats from Realism in Recent English Drama*. She, however, does more work in tracing the divergences from classic realism in contemporary plays and does not probe the theoretical reasons for the differences. Una Chaudhuri, in *Staging Place*, begins by contrasting early modernist playwrights' experiments with Place (Ibsen, Strindberg) and then, in the rest of the book, implicitly contrasts what I am calling postmodern dramatists. My focus on realism is clearly related to one sense of place that she examines with substantial sophistication.

5. Other critics agree with him: Doris V. Falk is even more certain, misinterpreting the facts to support her reading: "Martha, has indeed loved Karen 'that way,' and in fact, the aunt's accusation was true" (39–40). In point of fact, Lily never makes this accusation. R.C. Reynolds follows Falk: "Martha admits that even though she never revealed her feelings to Karen or anyone else, the charges are true" (133). Hellman states the facts clearly in an interview with Fred Gardner: "one of the girls, suspecting herself of lesbian desires, not lesbian acts, but lesbian desires, and thus feeling that the charge made against her had some moral truth, although no actual truth, kills herself" (110).

6. See Belsey 354–70. The centrality of Belsey's argument is indicated by Dolan (43).

7. Academic critics fall into the same trap of filling in the gaps on their own. For example, Roger Bechtel fills in the gap of "the Group" to produce his view of Carol: "If Carol does have some feeling of compassion for John, and the scene seems to indicate she does, she cannot exercise it because it is no longer her prerogative to do so. She no longer speaks or acts as an individual, but only as an agent of the Group. The Group has subsumed her identity into its own, and she has become as rigid and unforgiving as it must be" (39). Even Steven Ryan, who otherwise takes the most balanced approach to the play, seems to be inventing his own script when he extrapolates his view of the effect of the group on Carol: "John is the proverbial last straw in her academic life, the catalyst who drives her into the arms of he 'group,' who minister to her bewilderment by providing a comfortable illusion of certainty that renders her confusion about the academic world completely comprehensible" (396).

By contrast, Marc Silverstein's Marxist analysis of the play attacks Mamet for a perceived attack on feminism through Carol: "[...] Carol's actions suggest that women aspire to the logocentric mastery that feminism attacks in patriarchal culture. The play transforms the feminist call for women to fashion their voice(s) into an aggressive urge either to silence men or to grant them a voice only on condition they speak to affirm the woman's Word (Carol offers to retract her charges if John signs a self-condemning statement *written by her 'group'*)" (111–12). More stridently, Carla McDonough also takes Mamet to task as she fills in gaps and constructs Carol as "a vicious harpy out to destroy her professor's livelihood, life, and soul. Her penchant for willfully misunderstanding John's well-intentioned, if highly befuddled, gestures and words provides a convincing argument that sexual harassment charges are bogus and that political correctness is to blame for disrupting an otherwise comfortable, if somewhat paternalistic, system" (96). The hyperbole here, depicting Carol as out to destroy John's "soul," indicates the degree to which the writer has filled in a scenario of her own.

8. Only Ryan takes notice of the import of this moment: "Apparently, Carol is prepared to trust John with her most personal secrets, but the telephone [...] suddenly rings again. At this crucial moment in the play, John turns away from Carol's pain. [...] Ironically, John's attempts to secure his new house—in conversations that actually have nothing to do with that house—will cost him his career" (398).

9. Stephen Watt makes the point that the drama of the 1920s "was strongly influenced by notions of subjective depth," citing Joel Pfister's *Staging Depth* in support of the assertion. By contrast, Watt observes, in "contemporary plays, human subjectivity is cast in migratory (horizontal) terms quite different from those informing the vertical, or depth, model" (23). This discovery leads Watt to his conclusion that contemporary drama has to be examined in a larger artistic, political, and economic context than was necessary with the depth model, in which character itself was the basis of analysis.

10. Philip Auslander makes clear that postmodern (Derridean) concepts of character and actor differ substantially from earlier theories.

> We often praise acting by calling it "honest" or "self revelatory," "truthful"; when we feel we have glimpsed some aspect of the actor's psyche through her performance, we applaud the actor for "taking risks," "exposing herself." One example must stand for many: Joseph Papp was recently quoted as saying: "With Brando in 'Streetcar' or Olivier in 'The Entertainer,' the actor exposed himself in such a way that it was a kind of revelation of the soul." With what authority can such a statement be made? As semiotists who have studied acting have discovered, the performing actor is an opaque medium, an intertext, not a simple text to be read for "content." We arrive at our perception of a performance by implicitly comparing it with other interpretations of the same role (or with the way we feel the role should be played), or with our recollection of the same actor in other roles, or with our knowledge of the stylistic school to which the actor belongs, the actor's private life, etc. If our perception of the actor's work derives from this play of differences, how can we claim to be able to read the presence of the actor's self back through that performance? (60)

11. I have made a similar argument about Mamet's implication that the system is the cause of the corruption in *Glengarry Glen Ross* in "Marxist Child's Play."

WORKS CITED

Auslander, Philip. "'Just Be Your Self': Logocentrism and Difference in Performance Theory." *Acting (Re)Considered: Theories and Practices.* Ed. Phillip B. Zarrilli. London: Routledge, 1995. 59–68.

Bechtel, Roger. "P.C. Power Play: Language and Representation in David Mamet's *Oleanna.*" *Theatre Studies* 41 (1996): 29–48.

Belsey, Catherine. "Constructing the Subject: Deconstructing the Text." *Feminist Criticism and Social Change: Sex, Class, and Race in Literature and Culture.* Ed. Judith Newton and Deborah Rosenfelt. London: Methuen, 1985. Rpt. in *Contemporary Literary Criticism: Literary and Cultural Studies.* Ed. Robert Con Davies and Ronald Schleifer. 3rd ed. New York: Longman, 1994. 354–70.

Bentley, Eric. "Lillian Hellman's Indignation." *The Dramatic Event: An Amercan Chronicle.* Boston: Beacon, 1956. 74–77.

Bigsby, C.W.E. *A Critical Introduction to Twentieth Century American Drama, Volume One: 1900–1940.* Cambridge: Cambridge UP, 1982.

Bryer, Jackson R., ed. *Conversations with Lillian Hellman.* Jackson: UP of Mississippi, 1986.

Chaudhuri, Una. *Staging Place: The Geography of Modern Drama.* Ann Arbor: U of Michigan P, 1995.

Cohn, Ruby. *Retreats from Realism in Recent English Drama.* Cambridge: Cambridge UP, 1991.

Demastes, William W. *Beyond Naturalism: A New Realism in American Theatre.* New York: Greenwood, 1988.

Diamond, Elin. *Unmaking Mimesis: Essays on Feminism and Theater.* London: Routedge, 1997.

Dolan, Jill. "'Lesbian' Subjectivity in Realism: Dragging at the Margins of Structure and Ideology." *Performing Feminisms: Feminist Critical Theory and Theatre.* Ed. Sue-Ellen Case. Baltimore: Johns Hopkins UP, 1990. 40–54.

Empson, William. *Seven Types of Ambiguity.* London: Chatto, 1930.

Falk, Doris V. *Lillian Hellman.* New York: Ungar, 1978.

Fleche, Anne, "The Lesbian Rule: Lillian Hellman and the Measures of Realism." *Modern Drama* 39 (1996): 16–30.

Gardner, Fred. "An Interview with Lillian Hellman." Bryer 107–23.

Gilroy, Harry. "The Bigger the Lie." Bryer 24–26.

Hartman, Geoffrey. *Criticism in the Wilderness: The Study of Literature Today.* New Haven, CT: Yale UP, 1980.

Hassan, Ihab. *The Postmodern Turn: Essays in Postmodern Theory and Culture.* Columbus: Ohio State Up, 1987.

Hellman, Lillian. *The Children's Hour.* New York: Knopf, 1934.

———. "Introduction." *Four Plays by Lillian Hellman.* New York: Random, 1942. vii–xiv.

Holmberg, Arthur. "The Language of Misunderstanding." *American Theatre* 9.6 (1992): 94–95.

Lederer, Katherine. *Lillian Hellman.* Boston: Twayne, 1979.

Lyotard, Jean-François. *The Postmodern Condition: A Report on Knowledge.* Trans. Geoff Bennington and Brian Massumi. Minneapolis: U of Minnesota P, 1984.

Macy, William H., and Deborah Eisenstadt. "David Mamet's 'Oleanna' Raises Question of Harassment." Interview with Liane Hansen. *Weekend Edition/Sunday.* National Public Radio. 2 May 1993.

Mamet, David. *Oleanna.* New York: Pantheon, 1992.

———. *True and False: Heresy and Common Sense for the Actor.* New York: Pantheon, 1997.

McDonough, Carla J. *Staging Masculinity: Male Identity in Contemporary American Drama.* Jefferson, NC: McFarland, 1997.

Moody, Richard. *Lillian Hellman—Playwright.* New York: Pegasus, 1972.

Pfister, Joel. *Staging Depth: Eugene O'Neill and the Politics of Psychological Discourse.* Chapel Hill: U of North Carolina P, 1995.

Reynolds, R.C. *Stage Left: The Development of the American Social Drama in the Thirties.* Troy, NY: Whitston, 1986.

Rosenfeld, Megan. "Exit Audience, Arguing: A Poll on Mamet's Uneven Battle of the Sexes." *Washington Post* 30 Apr. 1993: B1+.

Roudané, Matthew C. *American Drama Since 1960: A Critical History.* New York: Twayne, 1996.

Russo, Francine. "Mamet's Traveling Cockfight." *The Village Voice* 29 June 1993: 96–97.

Ryan, Steven. "*Oleanna*: David Mamet's Power Play." *Modern Drama* 39 (1996): 392–403.

Sauer, David Kennedy. "The Marxist Child's Play of Mamet's Tough Guys and Churchill's *Top Girls*." *David Mamet's 'Glengarry Glen Ross': Text and Performance.* Ed. Leslie Kane. New York: Garland, 1996. 131–56.

Silverstein, Marc. "'We're Just Human': *Oleanna* and Cultural Crisis." *South Atlantic Review* 60.2 (1995): 103–20.

Strasberg, Lee. *Strasberg at the Actors Studio: Tape Recorded Sessions.* Ed. Robert H. Hethmon. New York: Viking, 1965.

Titus, Mary. "Murdering the Lesbian: Lillian Hellman's *The Children's Hour.*" *Tulsa Studies in Women's Literature* 10 (1991): 215–32.

Watt, Stephen. *Postmodern/Drama: Reading the Contemporary Stage.* Ann Arbor: U of Michigan P, 1998.

Worthen, W.B. *Modern Drama and the Rhetoric of Theater.* Berkeley: U of California P, 1992.

RICHARD BRUCHER

Prophecy and Parody in Edmond

Gregory Mosher, David Mamet's longtime collaborator, remarked a few years ago that what was great about Eugene O'Neill was that he could "*see* the culture.... O'Neill couldn't write a line of dialogue if you put a gun to his head, but he sure looked out at America, and he said at the turn of the century, 'We blew it. It doesn't work. The American Dream failed. It's a tragedy, America'" (Kane 236–37). Mosher invokes O'Neill to make a claim for clairvoyance in *Edmond*, Mamet's 1982 play about (in Mamet's words) "a man trying to discover himself and what he views as a sick society" (Schvey, "David Mamet" 94). According to Mamet, the play addresses the social consequences of a capitalistic dream that has nothing left to exploit. "'All those considerable talents that the white race has been living by since the birth of Christ and before, the emotionlessness, the viciousness, and the acquisitiveness that have sustained them, they now turn against each other ... '" (Leahey 3). In this version of the American Dream turned nightmare, Edmond Burke, a middle-class white executive, leaves his wife to seek validation among New York's conmen and whores. They cheat him and beat him, until he turns on a pimp who tries to mug him. Beating the black man mercilessly liberates Edmond; he picks up a waitress and gets the sex he's wanted, but then he kills her in a panicky dispute about honesty. He finally achieves peace in jail, after being sodomized by his black cellmate. Mosher contends that what seemed

From *Gender & Genre: Essays on David Mamet*, edited by Christopher C. Hudgins and Leslie Kane. © 2001 by Christopher C. Hudgins and Leslie Kane.

horribly exaggerated in 1982 turned out to be an accurate prediction of the racial strife at Bensonhurst and the "exploding hatred" of the 1980s (Kane 236).

Edmond has not been a popular or well understood play. Its characters' racism, misogyny, and homophobia are calculated to offend; and its attitude toward its protagonist is delightfully ambivalent. A 1982 reviewer remarked that Mamet "clearly sees [Edmond] as representative of an abused underclass" (Gussow C17), a notion that suggests the play's sustained irony. In partial defense of Edmond's homicidal degradation, Mamet has cited Jung's contention that sometimes society, not the individual, is sick (Schvey, "David Mamet" 94). On another occasion, with what I suspect was some disingenuousness, Mamet asked a hostile critic, a woman, "'Didn't you feel any compassion for [Edmond]?'" (Dean 188). Yet despite the sympathy he invests in Edmond, Mamet makes his protagonist highly culpable. As a middle-class white man, Edmond is heir to the American Dream and its fallout, a naive but by no means innocent victim of his race's success. As an Irish-American, Edmond Burke may be a fairly recent achiever of the dream, but that affirms the play's disturbing prophecy. The racial and ethnic violence for which Bensonhurst has become a code word can be read as white backlash against black predation in white neighborhoods. However, in Bensonhurst, Brooklyn, in 1989, Yusuf Hawkins, the young black man killed by whites, was innocent of criminal intent. He was looking for a used car in the wrong neighborhood (DeSantis passim). Backlash against intrusion becomes indistinguishable from racism, an expression of violent primitivism lurking beneath the surface of what purports to be a civilized society.

The persuasiveness of *Edmond*'s clairvoyance—its ability to see contemporary America so clearly that it seems prophetic—derives in part from its ironic affirmation of prophecies made by earlier social theorists and its witty appropriation of conventions used by earlier playwrights. The cultural degradation *Edmond* depicts can be traced to the breaking of social contracts that Edmond's namesake prophesied two centuries ago. According to Edmund Burke, the conservative political philosopher, "liberty without wisdom and without virtue ... is folly, vice, and madness ... " (373).[1] But if *Edmond* the play seems to insist on the consequences of violating Burke's principles of social order, Edmond the character seems to operate according to the premises of one of Thorstein Veblen's new aristocrats, parodic heir to the elite order presumably championed by Burke the conservative philosopher. Edmond's reversion to violence can be as easily associated with Veblen's leisure class as with Edmund Burke's anarchists and New York's predators. Veblen observes that fair-haired Europeans are particularly prone to reversion to barbarism.

It is a matter of common notoriety that when individuals, or even considerable groups of men, are segregated from a higher culture and exposed to a lower cultural environment, or to an economic situation of a more primitive character, they quickly show evidence of reversion toward the spiritual features which characterize the predatory type; and it seems probable that the dolicho-blond type of European man is possessed of a greater facility for such reversion to barbarism than the other ethnic elements with which that type is associated in the Western culture. (136)

Mamet has called *Edmond* "a morality play about modern life" (Schvey, "David Mamet" 94), a description with which many of its commentators would agree. As a morality, "it reveals with a frightening explicitness Mamet's apocalyptic vision of a society bent upon self-destruction" (Schvey, "Power Plays" 99). But as one reviewer noted in 1982, "Where conventional morality plays (or even moralistic ones) attempt to soothe or educate, *Edmond*, until its final, oddly blissful scene, is a continuous affront," making it seem "like a grotesque parody of a morality play" (Kissel 160). In 1982, *Edmond* tended to be described, even by those who liked it, as "a brutish, unsparing" play, one "squeezed ... almost dry of humor and color" (Gussow C17). In its New York revival in the fall of 1996, at Mamet's Atlantic Theater, *Edmond*'s violence seemed less shocking than in 1982 (because of Bensonhurst?); but its tone and attitude still divided viewers. One 1996 reviewer noted a "seriously comic interpretation that [gave] new credence to a much maligned play" (Brantley C13). Yet charges of implausibility have persisted. Edmond's "descent, from collected man in a conservative suit to ferocious killer, feels forced," another critic complained. His "transformation at the end is not credible," and his "sophomoric conversation about life's meaning" with his black cellmate is "weak" (Greene 12).

The problem with the charges of implausibility is not that they seriously undervalue *Edmond*. Rather, they betray a yearning for a naturalism or psychological realism that would offer a full accounting of Edmond's journey into squalor, crime, self-discovery, and redemption. *Edmond* supplies no such reliable causality. "And you are unsure what your place is," a Fortune Teller assures Edmond in the opening scene, "To what extent you are cause and to what an effect" (scene 1, 16). Her remark, calculated to aggrandize her client, poses the play's dilemma fairly well, but Edmond never seems to get it. He may see how his savaging experience can be construed as an effect of a civilization that has lost its bearings. "Do you want to live in this kind of world?" (scene 11, 51), he justifiably wails at a hotel clerk who refuses to help him after he's been beaten and robbed. His incarceration may appeal to his liberal sense of inevitability. "You know, I always thought that *white* people should be in prison....To be with black people," he remarks naively to his cellmate just before he is sodomized (scene 20, 90). But he never quite sees how he may also be cause. Consequently, the psychological justification for his murdering Glenna, the waitress he picks up, may be difficult to perceive. The situation is absurd, a moment of high cultural satire rather than of psychological clarity or melodramatic plausibility. Similarly, the philosophizing between Edmond and his cellmate, leading up to their goodnight kiss that ends the play, fails to resolve matters because Mamet intends the talk to be superficial and disconcerting. What appears to be sophomoric, a barely credible parable of the achievement of racial and sexual harmony, is parodic, a travesty of the sort of recognition we expect to experience in moralities and tragedies. *Edmond*, for all its nasty seriousness, may be another of Mamet's oblique comedies. That is, Mamet offers a scathing indictment of late-twentieth-century American society, and perhaps even the possibility of a middle-class tragedy, except that he keeps turning the play back in on itself, distancing us from Edmond as self-conscious victim, and so deflecting the tragic gesture with ironic comedy.

At least that's a proposition I'd like to test by looking at several of *Edmond*'s scenes in light cast by Veblen's *The Theory of the Leisure Class* (1899) and by *The Hairy Ape* (1922), another play, despite O'Neill's subtitle, that almost no one credits as a comedy. Mamet's fondness for Veblen is well known. Veblen's skepticism about social progress and his insistence that capitalist behavior is essentially irrational and hedonistic—"an almost atavistic phenomenon reflecting not so much the cool prudence of bourgeois man as the residual habits of primitive societies" (Diggins 18)—resonate in *Edmond*. So does Veblen's deadpan, high comic style inform the sustained irony of Mamet's observations of late-twentieth-century yuppie ennui. The O'Neill connection is more tenuous. I don't mean to offer *The Hairy Ape* as a rival source for *Edmond*, although the two models for *Edmond* most often cited—Georg Buchner's *Woyzeck* (1836) and Georg Kaiser's *From Morn to Midnight* (1912/1916)—have also been cited as influences on *The Hairy Ape*.[2] I would like to invoke the Emersonian license implicit in a remark on intertextuality by Stanley Cavell: "When a given text is claimed to work in the light, or in the shadow, of another—taking obvious extremes, as one of a given work's sources or as one of its commentaries—a measure of the responsibility of such a linking is the degree to which each is found responsive to the other, to tap the other, as for its closer attention" (1).

Whether or not Mamet had O'Neill's early radical play in mind when he wrote *Edmond*, the two plays tap one another responsively.[3] Both plays use episodic structures to reveal absurdly causal worlds and to satirize inhuman modern life, and both plays invoke and resist naturalistic determinism as a way to explore will and culpability. Both plays pursue paradoxical impulses to rediscover roots in nature and to belong to human communities, impulses presented with particularly American notions of privilege. Part of the mutual responsiveness, then, has to do with O'Neill's ability to "*see* the culture," as Mosher put it. O'Neill thought *The Hairy Ape* was "a surprisingly prophetic play. Not superficially, about labor conditions," he wrote Lawrence Langner in 1941, "but about Man, the state we are all in of frustrated bewilderment." The war in Europe affirmed for O'Neill that "we have certainly failed to 'belong' and then unlocked the cage and turned the Gorilla loose." O'Neill thought the play's symbolism and meaning would be clearer in 1941 than in 1922. "Very few got it then," he complained to Langner (Bogard and Bryer 522).

Incidental cultural and sociological details may have proved more prophetic than universals. Yank champions his labor as a vital force, dismissing as irrelevant the class of owners and their factotums, but conversion to diesel engines on the ocean-going liners would soon make stokers extinct. By converting Yank from a Liverpool Irishman to a New York tough, O'Neill capitalized on a cult of male primitivism and anticipated problems of mobility and assimilation that dominated American culture in the twentieth century.[4] Certainly Yank anticipates Mamet's boisterous, baffled males, both in their need to belong and in their obscenity, which is usually vented at women when social pressures become strong and dislocating. Yank's animus toward "Fif' Avenoo" mannequins—"Bums! Pigs! Tarts! Bitches!" (scene 5, 209)—is only slightly less vicious than Edmond's rage against a woman in the subway who views him as a pervert when he gets nostalgic about his mother's hat: "I'm *talking* to you ... What am I? A *dog*? I'd like to slash your fucking *face* ... " (scene 13, 58). Yank's eventual envy for the gorilla in the zoo—"Youse can sit and dope dream in de past, green woods, de jungle and de rest of it" (scene 8, 230)—echoes back to us in Edmond's conversation in a bar. "I'll tell you who's got it *easy*," a Man explains. "The niggers....Northern races *one* thing, and the southern races something else. And what *they* want to do is sit beneath the tree and watch the elephant. (*Pause.*) And I don't blame them one small bit" (scene 3, 22–23). Remarks from the beginning of *Edmond* seem to pick up where *The Hairy Ape* leaves off, as Yank's existentialism collapses into the Man's wistful, casual racism. This example illustrates my idea that the plays respond to one another's anxieties in particularly apt and disturbing ways. Especially interesting, in this context, is the relationship between comic-ironic form and the characters' "not getting it," notably in the plays' controversial final scenes.

The subtitle of *The Hairy Ape*—"A Comedy of Ancient and Modern Life in Eight Scenes"—suggests O'Neill's intended universalism and reflects the "tone of hard-boiled irony" he cultivated as a hedge against the sentimentalism to which Smitty was prone in the earlier sea plays (Engel 54–55). But O'Neill was not being purely ironic or coy, as if we are to understand "tragedy" for "comedy." Comic form pervades the play, especially in Bergson's sense of the mechanical encrusted upon the human. Dehumanization is most explicit in the ape-like stokers' robotic movements and metallic choruses—as if this is the mechanical encrusted upon the subhuman. Mechanization pervades Yank's words and gestures, too, even as he asserts his dominance over machines and men. Yank boasts of his union with steel, and his crudely sexual language suggests that shoveling coal has displaced his urge to have sex with women. "Dat's de stuff! Let her have it! All togedder now! Sling it into her! Let her ride! Shoot de piece now! Call de toin on her! Drive her into it! Feel her move!" Yank chants, shoveling, "*His voice rising exultantly in the joy of battle*" (scene 3, 189). The stokehole scene offers a lurid "condemnation of the whole structure of machine civilization, a civilization which succeeds only when it destroys the psychological well-being of those who make it possible" (Winter 196). Still, the scene reproves Yank for so willingly perverting his own vitality. Yank would do well to heed Bernie Litko's advice to his friend Danny Shapiro (in Mamet's *Sexual Perversity in Chicago*): "Dan, Dan ... don't go looking for affection from inanimate objects" (53).

Disjunctions between characters' assumptions about control and what actually happens to them create comic, alienating effects and patterns in *The Hairy Ape*, subverting romantic and melodramatic conventions, and preventing us from sentimentalizing the action. The sight of Yank, furious in the stokehole, knocks Mildred unconscious and out of her liberal posing. The sight of her—a ghostly sign of his own expendability—emasculates Yank, although he's slow to understand the effect her shock ("Oh, the filthy beast!" 192) has on him. He will eventually glean some irony in his condition. "Sure dere was a skoit in it—but not what youse mean, not dat old tripe" (scene 6, 213), he says by way of accounting for how he lands in jail. Initially, though, Paddy's sarcastic rendering of the perverted romance baffles Yank: "And there was Yank roarin' curses and turning around wid his shovel to brain her.... 'Twas love at first sight, divil a doubt of it!" (scene 4, 197). Paddy's mocking enrages Yank, precipitating a beating that initiates a recurring pattern of physical and psychological humiliation. All hands pile on Yank as he rushes for the door, "*and, after a fierce struggle, by sheer weight of numbers*," the stokers bear him to the floor (scene 4, 201 s.d.). In subsequent scenes Yank is "*clubbed to the pavement and fallen upon*" (scene 5, 210 s.d.) for inconveniencing a Gentleman at a bus stop, hosed down (and probably straight-jacketed) in jail for inciting a riot (scene 6), and tossed into the street, "*with gusto and éclat*" (scene 7, 225 s.d.), for seeming to be a police informant at a Wobblies' local. The sequence isolates Yank poignantly, taking him deeper and deeper into his existential angst. "Say, where do I go from here?" he asks a cop, in "*a vague mocking tone*," after his ejection from the union hall, to which the cop answers, "Go to hell" (scene 7, 227). The humiliating pattern is nonetheless comic in its redundancy (a manifestation of his mechanization), comic in its irony (he's supposed to be so tough), and comic in its exasperating wrongheadedness. By the time Yank arrives at his rendezvous with destiny at the zoo, he has tried four times to secure his place in the world by avenging himself on that skinny, white-faced tart; and he has been beaten up and tossed in jail or out on the street four times for his efforts.

The routinization of the action contributes to the bizarre quality of the final scene at the zoo. Yank has tried valiantly to "tink" and to discover a language that articulates his increasing alienation. Yet he has misread the situation every time, and so has learned almost nothing, except, perhaps, to seek affection from animate objects. But he offends the gorilla, too, whom he wishes to befriend and liberate. His language, groping back toward Paddy's lyrical evocation of an idyllic life on the sea, envies the gorilla's natural primitivism. Mockery in Yank's voice insults the gorilla, and it kills Yank for it, tossing him, in a now familiar gesture, to the floor of the cage. Perhaps Yank has achieved peace, as O'Neill's closing stage direction suggests; but it's not a peace in which an audience can take solace. The gorilla's opportunism, shuffling "*off menacingly into the darkness*" (scene 8, 232 s.d.), Yank's contributory aggression, his mocking tone, and his objectifying himself as a side-show attraction—all mitigate against the empathy associated with Aristotelian (or even working-class) tragedy. One of the great things about *The Hairy Ape* is not that O'Neill dared to make a tragic hero out of a stoker, but that he resisted the urge.

This may be a way of agreeing with Joel Pfister's recent, controversial reassessment of O'Neill's art as a staging of middle-class cultural identity for middle-class audiences. Although appreciative of O'Neill's depiction of working conditions in *The Hairy Ape*, Pfister aruges that "O'Neill's deep interest seems to be in creating a working-class seaman who has been converted to professional-managerial-class angst" (119). Even so, there's little flattery in the transmutation because Yank, like the original critics and audiences (who according to John Styan probably identified with Mildred [107–108]), never quite gets it. He's a "bonehead," the Secretary of the Wobblies says (scene 7, 225), and so the analogy insults managers as well as workers. The point I wish to carry over to *Edmond* is that resistance to tragic empathy keeps the social criticism alive. "[A] dollar more a day ... and cauliflowers in de front yard—ekal rights—" (scene 7, 225) won't fix Yank for Jesus, but neither will nostalgia for the good old days in the jungle. Nor will the brute power Yank still celebrates in the gorilla, and with which the gorilla kills him.[5]

Mamet tests this premise in *Edmond*, using comic-ironic devices similar to those deployed by O'Neill. Edmond Burke is the sort of egotistical, alienated "professional" that Yank, in Pfister's arguments, is supposed to represent. Yet I doubt if Edmond would "get it." He might identify with Yank's sense of victimization—"I ain't on oith and I ain't in heaven ... I'm in de middle ... takin' all de woist punches from bot' of 'em" (scene 8, 230–31)—but it's less likely that he would see the irony in the failure of Yank's primitive strength. As Christopher Bigsby has argued, Edmond imagines his reversion to primitivism to be therapeutic (103). Beating the Pimp liberates him from 30 years of racist guilt and gets him laid, to boot, which is more than Yank manage. It's as if this beating solves for Edmond the centuries-old problem of Hamlet's liberal paralysis, an anomie Yank tries to overcome with physical power. "That fucking nigger comes up to me, what am I fitted to do.... Thirty-four years fits me to sweat and say he's underpaid.... Eh? That's what I'm fitted to do. In a mess of intellectuality to wet my *pants* while this *coon* cuts my *dick off* ... eh? Because I'm taught to *hate*" (scene 16, 68).

The beating, though, is highly problematic. Edmond presumably beats the Pimp because the attempted mugging is one too many violations. Civilization, as Edmond thinks he understands it, has collapsed. He has just been rebuffed by the woman in the subway, with whom he tried to make human contact: "My mother had a hat like that" (scene 13, 58). Her refusal to be drawn into his nostalgia replays the rebuff he received from the Hotel Clerk. She regards Edmond as strange, perhaps demented, and certainly dangerous, especially after he grabs her and threatens her with his survival knife. His response to her fear only affirms her suspicions: "Is everybody in this town *insane?* ... Fuck you ... fuck you *all* ... I don't *need* you ... I worked all my life!" (scene 13, 59). It's not clear what kind of dispensation Edmond expects to receive for that last assertion; it's as if he's back in the bar, insisting on his privileges as one who has accepted his white, middle-class, professional responsibilities and now expects to be ratified for it. That truculent plea carries Edmond into his encounter with the Pimp, who gains Edmond's confidence only to break their implied contract by taking Edmond's money without supplying the agreed-upon service (Tuttle 159). Scene 14, then, enacts both white, middle-class anxiety and its fantasy of revenge, but it does so on a professional as well as a moral and ethical frontier. Edmond has been soliciting sex for money, and he may be violating his own professional code by inhibiting the Pimp's work. In any case, and in a replay of the subway-hat scene, Edmond's righteousness quickly turns vicious: "You *fuck*. You *nigger*. You dumb *cunt*," he screams as he kicks the man (scene 14, 65). The Pimp becomes the scene's baffled victim: "Hold on.... I ... I ... Oh, my God ... "(64).

Obviously this scene shows how savagery can lurk in all of us and that Edmond may be as bad as his predators. That ambivalence perfectly captures the "exploding hatred" of Bensonhurst and Howard Beach; it nails an audience's ambivalence, too, as we delight in Edmond's rebellion and recoil at his extra kicks. But white backlash against urban predation doesn't fully account for the beating, especially as a context for the dispute over personal liberation and professional identity that results in Glenna's death. The chain of causation is indirect. The beating doesn't justify or even explain Edmond's descent into barbarity so much as it observes an anthropological phenomenon and offers an episode in Edmond's parodic self-creation. Edmond quite literally *imagines* his therapeutic liberation. Beating the Pimp frees Edmond to eschew coffee for Irish whiskey and beer, to resee his previous life as fog-bound, and to proposition the white waitress boldly. However, after sex with Glenna, he invents the beating as liberation. The story he tells Glenna, as he brandishes the survival knife, is not much like the incident we witnessed.

> I want to tell you something. Something *spoke* to me, I got a *shock* (I don't know, I got mad ...), I got a *shock*, and I spoke *back* to him. "Up your *ass*, you *coon* ... you want to fight, *I'll* fight you, I'll cut out your fuckin' *heart*, eh, I don't give a fuck ... " Eh? I'm saying, "*I* don't give a fuck, *I* got some warlike blood in *my* veins, too, you fucking *spade*, you coon...." The *blood* ran down his neck.... (scene 16, 68–69)

In one sense, Edmond is cheering himself up, aggrandizing his action, converting what appeared to be an act of frustrated rage and terror into a political act, a declaration of race pride. At the same time it is a clever act of parody, as Mamet has Edmond lay claim to the language and values of Veblen's warrior-sportsman and O'Neill's waterfront toughs, values Veblen and O'Neill have already discredited. Veblen calls this celebration of violence a "common-sense barbarian appreciation of worth or honor." This "high office of slaughter, as an expression of the slayer's prepotence, casts a glamour of worth over every act of slaughter and over all the tools and accessories of the act." Hence Edmond's pride in the acquisition of the survival knife. At the same time, common labor becomes "odious" and "irksome" (31).

Edmond kills Glenna, in effect, because she refuses to admit she's a waitress. Still trapped by the assumptions of the consumer society he thinks he has escaped, he won't allow her claim to be an actress because she's never acted before paying customers. In this sense, Glenna proves to be just as expendable as the poseur Mildred, and, ironically, in similar socio-economic terms. Anemic Mildred, by her own admission, is "a waste product in the Bessemer process" (scene 2, 183) from which her grandfather, an Andrew Carnegie avatar, made his millions. Useless and unnatural—she doesn't even like sports—Mildred disappears from the play, as if to affirm Veblen's theory of the leisure class, a class defined by its incapacity to do productive work (Veblen 24–25). Glenna, on the contrary, is a working woman, a role Edmond both denigrates and sentimentalizes. In the coffeehouse, he exhorts her to reject subservience: "you can do anything you *want* to do, you don't sit down because you're '*working*,' the reason you don't sit down is you don't *want* to sit down, because it's more comfortable to *accept* a law than question it and live your life" (scene 15, 67). In her apartment Edmond needs to behold Glenna as worker to affirm what he believes is his new commitment to living life honestly: "I loved a *woman*. Standing there. A working woman. Who brought life to what she did. Who took a moment to *joke* with me. That's ... that's ... that's ... god *bless* you what you are. Say it: I am a waitress" (scene 16, 75). Like the story of the beating, this version of their meeting distorts and sentimentalizes the scene we witnessed. Edmond rebukes Glenna for betraying her honest productivity with pretense. More fundamentally, though, he objectifies her as his prize for beating the Pimp. As warrior's booty, she too plays out a favorite Veblen metaphor for the unproductive wealthy, their possessions, and their imitators. Mamet sacrifices Glenna to his cultural analysis more ruthlessly than O'Neill expends Mildred.

Glenna demonstrates the "incentives," as Veblen calls them, for acquiring women as property: She gratifies Edmond's propensity for coercion, she verifies his prowess as owner, and she provides sexual and other utilitarian services (Veblen 52). I think it is probably this sense of "possession" that Mamet had in mind when he suggested to a British audience its centrality to dislocations in American culture. According to Carla McDonough's summation, "Mamet describes how the continuity of relations between men and women has always been upheld 'by the possession of woman' so that having women in the market place vying for equal positions in a 'man's world' seems the reason that the old value system in this country is breaking down" (197). Mamet's social criticism seems to me to be deeper, more playful, and perhaps more rueful that this summation suggests. The "old value system" is itself a travesty, a higher form of barbarism masquerading as civilized progress, as Mamet would understand from his reading of Veblen. This is not to say that male anxieties are not real, and it's not to say that the anxieties, however false the premises may be that rouse them, do not result in real violence against women. But Veblen provides a useful gloss on the gender and race issues that McDonough notes in *Edmond* (and that are similarly vexed in *The Hairy Ape*). When, after providing sex, Glenna refuses to define herself by her productive labor, but rather by creative or professional pretension, she is annihilated by Edmond's crazy reformist zeal. Her gesture toward self-preservation refutes the presumptions of consumerism that have driven Edmond from bar to peepshow to whorehouse to pawnshop. "Get out!" she shrieks. "GET OUT GET OUT! LEAVE ME THE FUCK ALONE!!! WHAT DID I DO, PLEDGE MY LIFE TO YOU? I LET YOU FUCK ME. GO AWAY" (scene 16, 77). In a now familiar pattern, Edmond displaces onto her his own rising hysteria. As "*He stabs her with the knife*," he accuses her: "Are you *insane?* Are you *insane*, you fucking *idiot?* ... You stupid fucking *bitch*.... Now look what you've blood fucking done" (scene 16, 78). The scene is terrifying in its depiction of the hazards of reading feel-good-about-yourself manuals and of consenting to casual sex, and yet it's absurd in its logic. Is being a waitress who studies acting an offense against society (or art?) punishable by death? The enormity of the act never dawns on Edmond. His presumptuousness contributes to the scene's sardonic humor, as the play sacrifices Glenna to its analysis of primitivism, solecism, and professional prerogative. This is what I meant earlier when I suggested that this murder scene, building on painful comic disjunction, succeeds as travesty and social satire rather than as psychological analysis or melodrama.

The impulse toward primitivism and the critique of middle-class anxiety come full circle in the play's final scene, although how we're to take the scene is much debated. Dennis Carroll, for example, argues that

Edmond's "new-found vulnerability ... indicates further growth in him." His relationship with his cellmate, although begun in rape, is now "marked by genuine rapport" (103). Characteristic of the play's ambivalence, there appears to be some truth in this. "Every fear hides a wish" (scene 20, 89), Edmond remarks hopefully to his cellmate when he first arrives in jail; by the end of the scene Edmond will be sodomized. Edmond—misogynist, racist, and homophobe—becomes "wife" to his black cellmate; and he seems, by the end of the play, to be reasonably happy with his turn in fortune. His language loses its hostility and obscenity, which implies some personal and social progress. I'm tempted to say that the final scene in prison replays and "improves" O'Neill's ending to *The Hairy Ape*. Edmond's affectionate goodnight kiss with his black cellmate recalls and transcends Yank's murderous embrace in the zoo cage with the gorilla, suggesting that the primitivism is domesticated rather than loosed. It's characteristically bold and witty of Mamet to literalize O'Neill's metaphors to confront and transcend late-twentieth-century racial and homosexist fears.

The ending of *Edmond*, however, resonates well beyond *The Hairy Ape*, although it, too, can be said to mock its protagonist the way Yank's encounter with the gorilla mocks him. As Christopher Bigsby has argued, banal philosophical musings, of the sort popular in the 1970s, hardly compensate for the radical circumscription Edmond's life has undergone. Desiring freedom, he's achieved prison, where sodomy "happens" (scene 21, 94; Bigsby 107).[6] This may be a morality play in the manner of Marlowe's *Edward the Second*, with its sardonic, deeply disturbing insistence on poetic justice. And yet it's *Hamlet*, that great, troubled document of secular humanism, to which *Edmond* seems parodically to aspire at the end. "There is a destiny that shapes our ends," Edmond muses, "Rough-hew them how we may." "How e'er we motherfucking may," the Prisoner adds (scene 23, 100). Perhaps Edmond has "adopted a Hamlet-like position of acceptance" (Schvey, "Power Plays" 100), but what strikes me is how un-Hamletlike the posture is. "Divinity" shapes Hamlet's end (5.2.10); and that signals, at least in a traditional humanistic reading, his acceptance of and responsibility to a moral order beyond himself. Edmond and the Prisoner cast about for some "destiny" to shape their ends, in effect exonerating themselves. Edmond expresses some remorse for killing Glenna, but he never quite assumes responsibility for the act. "I think I'd just had too much coffee," he explains to his estranged, unsympathetic wife (scene 19, 87). "O Hamlet, what a falling-off was there" (1.5.47), we might say with the Ghost of King Hamlet. Travestying Hamlet's recognition doesn't make a strong case for providential redemption. About the best Edmond and the Prisoner can do is hope that someone understands—"Some whacked-out sucker. Somewhere. In the Ozarks?"—and admit that maybe *they* (we) are the animals (scene 23, 102, 105). That is not a lot of progress in the 60 years that separate *Edmond* and *The Hairy Ape*, let alone in the four centuries that separate *Edmond* and *Hamlet*.

If *Edmond* did see the early 1980s so clearly that it predicted the exploding hatred of the middle- and late-1980s, it seems to me to be less willing to prophesy lasting reconciliation. Its parodic attention to earlier texts—by Veblen, O'Neill, and Shakespeare, in my brief analysis—underscores the human propensity for self-delusion that makes reconciliation so necessary and difficult. That admission, I suppose, places me with those who read *Edmond* pessimistically, as Mamet's journey to the heart of darkness.[7] Nonetheless, I wish to recognize a serious comic technique at work in the play that resists wishful thinking and melodramatic gloom. Echoes of Veblen and O'Neill help us see that *Edmond's* problems are not the product, in any simple way, of recent encroachments by women, blacks, and others into the provinces of white males. Admittedly, the *Edmond-Hairy Ape* connection may be far-fetched. As a pair, though, the plays analyze problems of identity and belonging in American society that arc over the entire century. *Edmond* literalizes the middle-class angst that finds incipient expression in O'Neill's alienated stoker. (The recent Wooster Group production of *The Hairy Ape* in New York gave astonishing expression to Yank's energy and diminishing power, as if he were one of Mamet's street people.) Both plays create persistently materialist environments that account for their characters' baffled rage and yet also reveal them to be surprisingly culpable for not understanding more clearly their choices within those environments. *The Hairy Ape* and *The Theory of the Leisure Class* are part of the cultural critique that *Edmond* reexamines, and comic-ironic dramatic form—comedy of ancient and modern life—is crucial to that enterprise. These texts tap one another as if for closer attention, especially in these times of rampant, self-deluding capitalist behavior.

NOTES

This essay is dedicated to the memory of John Sekora.

    1. Jon Tuttle, in "'Be What You Are'" (158), and Henry I. Schvey, in "Power Plays" (101), discuss Edmund Burke's presence in *Edmond*.

    2. C.W.E. Bigsby discusses the *Woyzeck* influence in *David Mamet*, 103–04, as does Schvey ("Power Plays" 100–101), and a number of reviewers. Jon Tuttle makes a persuasive case for *From Morn to Midnight* in "'Be What You Are'" (158–9).

3. Marcia Blumberg argues that *"Edmond* traces the O'Neillian dive to the gutter" but associates Edmond with Edmund Tyrone (107).

4. Jon Curry discussed this socio-economic issue and the pertinence of *The Hairy Ape* in "'Men of an Entirely Different Grade': O'Neill's Laborers," a paper presented at the Conference on O'Neill's People, Boston, MA, May 12, 1995. On the masculine primitive, see James A. Robinson, "The Masculine Primitive and *The Hairy Ape*," and Carla J. McDonough, "Every Wish Hides a Fear."

5. Although the program notes don't verify it, it appeared to me that in the recent (Spring 1997) Wooster Group production of *The Hairy Ape* in New York, Kate Valk, who played Mildred Douglas, re-appeared in a monkey-fur coat to play the gorilla. It was a witty detail in this brilliant interpretation, directed by Elizabeth LeCompte.

6. Bigsby uses Christopher Lasch's *The Culture of Narcissism* (1979) effectively to contextualize Edmond's solecism in *David Mamet* (101–10).

7. Tuttle invokes Conrad's *The Heart of Darkness* in "'Be What You Are.'" Schvey, "Power Plays," and Bigsby are also persuasive on the darkness of *Edmond*.

WORKS CITED

Bergson, Henri. "Laughter" (1900). *Comedy*. Ed. Wylie Sypher. Garden City, NY: Doubleday Anchor, 1956.

Blumberg, Marcia. "Eloquent Stammering in the Fog: O'Neill's Heritage in Mamet." *Perspectives on O'Neill: New Essays*. Ed. Shyamal Bagchee. Victoria, BC: U of Victoria P, 1988, 97–111.

Bogard, Travis, and Jackson R. Bryer, eds. *Selected Letters of Eugene O'Neill*. New Haven: Yale UP, 1988.

Brantley, Ben. "In Mamet's 'Edmond,' a Man on Empty." *New York Times* October 2, 1996: C13–C14.

Burke, Edmund. *Reflections on the Revolution in France*. Harmondsworth, England: Penguin Books, 1969.

Carroll, Dennis. *David Mamet*. New York: St. Martin's, 1987.

Cavell, Stanley. "Macbeth Appalled (I)," *Raritan* XII:2 (Fall 1992): 1–15.

Dean, Anne. *David Mamet: Language as Dramatic Action*. Rutherford and Madison, NJ: Fairleigh Dickinson UP, 1990.

DeSantis, John. *For the Color of His Skin: The Murder of Yusuf Hawkins and the Trial of Bensonhurst*. New York: Pharos Books, 1991.

Diggins, John P. *The Bard of Savagery: Thorstein Veblen and Modern Social Theory*. New York: Seabury Press, 1978.

Engel, Edwin A. *The Haunted Heroes of Eugene O'Neill*. Cambridge: Harvard UP, 1953.

Greene, Alexis. "Theatre Reviews." *Theater Week* 10:12 (October 21 1996): 12–13.

Gussow, Mel. "Stage: Mamet Explores the Fall of 'Edmond,'" *New York Times* June 17, 1982: C17.

Kane, Leslie. "Interview with Gregory Mosher." *David Mamet: A Casebook*. Ed. Leslie Kane. New York: Garland, 1992, 231–47.

Kissel, Howard. "'Edmond.'" *Women's Wear Daily* October 28, 1982; reprinted in *New York Theatre Critics Reviews* 43 (1982): 160.

Leahey, Mimi. "David Mamet: The American Dream Gone Bad." *Other Stages* (November 4, 1982): 3.

Mamet, David. *Edmond*. New York: Grove, 1983.

———. *Sexual Perversity in Chicago and The Duck Variations*. New York: Grove, 1978.

McDonough, Carla J. "Every Wish Hides a Fear: Unstable Masculinity in Mamet's Drama." *Theatre Journal* 44:2 (May 1992): 195–205.

O'Neill, Eugene. *The Hairy Ape*. *"Anna Christie," The Emperor Jones, and The Hairy Ape*. New York: Vintage, 1972.

Pfister, Joel. *Staging Depth: Eugene O'Neill and the Politics of Psychological Discourse*. Chapel Hill: U of North Carolina P, 1995.

Robinson, James A. "The Masculine Primitive and *The Hairy Ape*." *The Eugene O'Neill Review* 19:1 & 2 (Spring & Fall 1995): 95–109.

Schvey, Henry I. "David Mamet: Celebrating the Capacity for Self-Knowledge." *New Theatre Quarterly* 4:13 (February 1988): 89–96.

———. "Power Plays: David Mamet's Theatre of Manipulation." *David Mamet: A Casebook*. Ed. Leslie Kane. New York: Garland, 1992, 87–108.

Shakespeare, William. *Hamlet*. Ed. Edward Hubler. New York: New American Library, 1963.

Styan, J. L. *Modern drama in theory and practice, volume 3: Expressionism and epic theatre*. Cambridge: Cambridge UP, 1981.

Tuttle, Jon. "'Be What You Are': Identity and Morality in *Edmond* and *Glengarry Glen Ross*." *David Mamet's "Glengarry Glen Ross": Text and Performance*. Ed. Leslie Kane. New York: Garland, 1996, 157–69.

Veblen, Thorstein. *The Theory of the Leisure Class*. Ed. C. Wright Mills. 1899; New York: New *American Library, 1953*.

Winter, Sophus Keith. *Eugene O'Neill: A Critical Study*. New York: Russell & Russell, 1934.

LINDA DORFF

Reinscribing the "Fairy": The Knife and the Mystification of Male Mythology in The Cryptogram

> You take a knife, you use it to cut the bread, so you'll have strength to work; you use it to shave, so you'll look nice for your lover; on discovering her with another, you use it to cut out her lying heart.
> —*Huddie Ledbetter, quoted in David Mamet,* Three Uses of the Knife

Although *The Cryptogram* (1994) appears to make a departure from the male-centered worlds of David Mamet's earlier plays, representing his first domestic drama in which the defining figure of patriarchy—the father—is notably absent, the play nevertheless engages in an obsessively enigmatic examination of the myths that construct Mamet's worlds of men. In an interview on *The South Bank Show*, Mamet remarked that until recently, he had felt that "the domestic scene was best left to anyone else but me, that it wasn't the fit subject for drama" (*South Bank Show*), until he realized that *American Buffalo* (1975) was "really just a family play—it is a play about a father and a mother and a little kid" (*SBS*). If *American Buffalo* is to be understood as a family play, then it would seem more precise to say that it is a metadramatic attempt to define the family in terms of male mythology, to the exclusion of women. *The Cryptogram* engages in a similar attempt, which is far subtler, for it is disguised as the inverse of *American Buffalo*: in the manner of Mamet's con-game drama and cinema, it pretends to be a family play, set—not in a place of business—but in a family home. By subtracting

From *Gender & Genre: Essays on David Mamet*, edited by Christopher C. Hudgins and Leslie Kane. © 2001 by Christopher C. Hudgins and Leslie Kane.

243

the (heterosexual) patriarch, it masquerades as a drama of Others, focusing on a woman, a gay man, and a child. But rather than exploring marginalized identities as alternative subjects of drama, the characters negotiate their relationships to each other through a system of mythical objects that refer to the absent father, positioning him as the (present) subject of the play. The play's minimalist action is driven by the characters' attempts to decode the mythologies attached to these objects, but this hermeneutic activity is blocked at every turn. Legends about the father encoded in one of these objects—the knife—are revealed to be false, exposing his respective betrayals of his son, his wife, and his friend. But the heterosexual male mythology for which he stands is reinscribed at the play's end with invective that is all too reminiscent of Ricky Roma's indictment of Williamson at the end of *Glengarry Glen Ross* (1983) as he calls him "you stupid fucking *cunt*.... You *fairy*.... You fucking *child* ... " (96–97). It is as if Mamet has made visible these male-to-male terms of abuse in the physical form of the characters of *The Cryptogram*, who aim similar invectives at each other.[1] This reinscription of misogynist, homophobic verbal abuse is, at best, disturbing, precisely because it is mystified through insoluble cryptograms that ultimately serve to affirm and, therefore, to recirculate the fictions of male mythology.

Until recently, most scholars and audiences have tended to take quite a different view of Mamet's plays, praising them as critiques and exposés of the "world of men" (*Glengarry* 105). In this vein, Hersh Zeifman claims that in *American Buffalo* and *Glengarry Glen Ross*, "Mamet makes use of this exploration of 'the gendered perspective' for specific thematic ends: a dramatic world in which women are marginalized to the point of literal exclusion provides *in itself* the most scathing indictment imaginable of the venality and corruption of American business" (124). A few critics, however, have taken issue with such interpretations in response to Mamet's plays of the 1990s. While Mamet claims to have represented an "even-handed" (McDonough 101) view of sexual harassment in *Oleanna* (1992), for example, Carla J. McDonough disagrees, arguing that "Mamet's play stacks the deck, perhaps unconsciously on Mamet's part, in favor of his male character, effectively shutting down the possibility of real exposé by its lack of character development in regard to the female character" (95). Indeed, it would seem that plays such as *Oleanna* and *The Cryptogram* are moving away from the critique-exposé direction of his earlier "world of men" drama and shifting instead toward attempted defenses of the belief systems with which Mamet's men identify.

The ideological systems that I identify as male mythology are fictional systems by which males in a social order construct the gender "male" as a subject identified with the phallus. According to Lacan's "mirror stage" (2), in which gendered identity is formed, the biological penis is equated in the symbolic order with the phallus, which (Lacan claims) organizes all cultural information, especially language (66). As Jill Dolan has observed, when the phallus is seen as the structural determinant for meaning in language, women are relegated to a position outside discourse, for "the phallus is exchanged [only] between men" (12). This phallic (symbolic) exchange is highly visible in Mamet's earlier drama, in which male-to-male conversation is privileged and women are relegated, in *Sexual Perversity in Chicago* (1974), to the status of "inanimate objects" (53). Inasmuch as Mamet is a master manipulator of the symbolic order at the linguistic (aural) level, producing litanies of phallic obscenity, his plays also activate a chain of visual signification that obsessively presents objects/props as symbols of the phallus. These include the knives in *Edmond* (1982), *The Shawl* (1985), and *The Cryptogram*. In these plays, the knife is used as a phallus that literally and figuratively penetrates feminized Others—women, children, and gay men—in order to establish gendered difference and, thereby, power over them.

As a symbolic system, the function of male mythology extends beyond structuring gender identification to shaping the ontological constructions of a culture. In her work on male subjectivity, Kaja Silverman locates a "dominant fiction," which "not only offers the representational system by means of which the subject typically assumes a sexual identity, and takes on desires commensurate with that identity, but forms the stable core around which a nation's and a period's 'reality' coheres" (41). Silverman points out that the dominant fiction of sexual difference based upon the equation of the penis with the phallus is largely unconscious, emphasizing the degree to which a society's collective belief in what is real depends upon repression of the fact that the penis (or male gender) does not always equal the phallus (a position of authority). In noting that "classic male subjectivity [identity formation] rests upon the denial of castration" (44), Silverman could be describing the unconscious anxiety that motivates so many of Mamet's male characters. Certainly, when one of his male characters loses power, he immediately unleashes a string of misogynist or homophobic invective at another character—as if to accuse the Other of being castrated and, thereby, to deny his own castration, or lack of authority.

In order to reinforce this denial of castration, Mamet shrouds his *allegiance to* and *belief in* male mythology in mysticism, disguised in the forms of dramatic con games and linguistic conundrums. In linking Mamet's writings with those of the leaders of men's movements such as Robert Bly, David Savran notes that the writings of both evidence a strong sense of "'mystery' in male bonding" (186). While mysticism of this type would seem to be grounded in a desire to refer to an authoritative male subject, thereby (theoretically, at least) producing a stable image of a male self, Savran notes a seeming inability in the writings of Bly to enact such a mystical conjunction. In Bly's *Iron John* (1990), Savran locates "a failure, despite its repeated attempts, to produce anything resembling a stable, integral and full male subject, one based on presence (as opposed to absence), on hardness (as opposed to flaccidity). Rather, masculinity is continually figured as a *lack*, and the phallus as an elusive and mysterious commodity" (174). This emphasis upon failure and absence (two of the fundamental schema for denoting the father in *The Cryptogram*) are cloaked by Mamet in mysticism, in order to maintain belief in the fictional equation between the penis and phallus.

This mysticism is manifest in the generalized concern with cryptography (a method of concealing information), which lies at the core of much of Mamet's drama. In Mamet's earlier plays, male mythology is concealed and finally revealed through metaphors of con games, poker, and business deals. In *The Cryptogram*, however, as in his other plays of the 1990s, the method of concealment becomes increasingly mystical in form and context, frustrating both characters' and audiences' attempts to decode the cryptograms. Unlike Poe's story "The Gold Bug" (1843), which employs a cryptogram with the purpose of demystifying popular myths,[2] these cryptograms defy solution, as the play's characters repeatedly complain, "It's all such a mystery" (21). Clues to Mamet's mystification of male mythology in *The Cryptogram* appear in an essay published five years prior to its 1994 production, in *Some Freaks*, "Kryptonite: A Psychological Approach," which examines the Superman myth. Mamet figures Kryptonite as Superman's secret, which, if revealed, will bring about his destruction. It is not an accident, I would like to suggest, that Kryptonite and Cryptogram are phonetically similar. If Kryptonite is Superman's secret—which, if revealed or decoded, can destroy the myth of his super-masculine powers—then the cryptograms in the play also carry the power to deconstruct male myths. Mamet writes, "Only Kryptonite cuts through the disguises of wimp and hero, and affects the man below the disguises. And what is Kryptonite? Kryptonite is all that remains of his childhood home. It is the remnants of that destroyed childhood home, and the fear of those remnants, which rule Superman's life"(178).

In Mamet's language, Kryptonite becomes an imaginary knife that "cuts" not only the "wimp" disguise but also that of a "hero," suggesting the castrating force that destroys the patriarchal family home staged in *The Cryptogram*. In his admission that "Superman comics are a fable, not of strength, but of disintegration" ("Kryptonite" 178), Mamet would seem to suggest that male myths are constructed—not to celebrate strength, which is an illusion—but to protect the weakling (at least on the symbolic level) from association with castration. The attempt to protect the weakling extends, in Mamet's all-male-cast plays, to the banishment of women, who, as McDonough has noted, are marginalized in "offstage space" due to a male "fear of femininity" (72), a fear that, as David Radavich has observed, is frequently manifested in homophobia (46–47).

Male mythology in Mamet's plays is deeply conflicted, for while his characters will go to any lengths to avoid intimacy—coded as femininity/castration—with each other, yet they long for it. In his essay, "In the Company of Men," Mamet writes that:

> Men ... get together to bitch. We say, "What does she *want?*" And we piss and moan, and take comfort in the fact that our fellows will, at some point, reveal that, yes, *they* are weaklings, too, and there's no shame in it. This is the *true* masculine equivalent of "being sensitive." No, we are *not* sensitive to women, but we are sensitive to our own pain, and we can recognize it in our fellows. What a world. (87)

The revelation that "*they* are weaklings, too,"—that is, the breaking of the mythic code of Machismo, which Zeifman identifies as superior male strength and cunning (125)—may take place only in the company of men, as if it were a secret that straight white men alone know. Robert Vorlicky theorizes that the "virile myth" (*Act Like a Man* 17) of masculinity restricts individualization and demands avoidance of such self-disclosing dialogue (*ALM* 16), as if to attempt to produce a hegemonic "real" behavior that corresponds seamlessly with the mythology.

Although *The Cryptogram* would appear to deconstruct the seams between the "real" and the mythic through its revelation of the father's various betrayals, the mystification of male mythology is so romantically and so nostalgically embedded in the play's *logos* that it becomes a sort of hymn to the phallic (symbolic) order. This mysticism is encoded in two dramaturgic systems of the play: it first appears through linguistic coding in which characters seem to communicate with each other about the absent father in a shorthand lingo that is loaded with oblique allusions to a metaphysical plane that is impossible for them, or the audience, to decode. On a second level, the action of the play seems to be driven by the characters' vain attempts to decode a collection of objects connected with the father. On the first, linguistic level, the conversations between Donny, Bobby's wife, John, her son, and Del, their gay male friend, center obsessively on Bobby's absence. John's repeated question, "When is Dad coming home?" (38), constructs the father's absence as the central cryptogram of the play. As Del, who functions as the surrogate father/husband—a stand-in for "Dad" in the first part of the play—attempts to allay John's anxiety, he only seems to fuel it, for he cannot offer him any solutions to the puzzle:

Del: What does it mean "I could not sleep"?
John: ... what does it mean?
Del: Yes. It means nothing other than the meaning you choose to assign to it. (4)

Lines like these early in the play function as a warning that linguistic signification is random, subject to an infinite multiplicity, problematizing both the characters' and audiences' ability to extract definite (symbolic) meanings from the dramatic situation. Yet in the text for the play, which is not seen by the audience, Mamet emphasizes certain words and phrases with capitalization, quotation marks, and italics, as if to indicate that they bear significant meanings. When Del refers to John and his father's camping trip to the woods that John is looking forward to the next day, for example, the "T" in the word "Trip" (4) is capitalized, as is the "W" in "woods" (4), signaling the importance to John of this father-and-son outing. To the reader, these capitalized words appear to be a code referring to a male myth, which John confirms when he acknowledges that "it's something. To go out there" (5). This "something," however, is not able to be explicated by John, Del, or Donny.

While Mamet frequently places such emphasis on words in his writing, this linguistic coding is particularly significant when it refers to such male myths, for it points to big ideas that men cannot articulate when together, for it would be considered to be a femininized activity. In his essay "In the Company of Men," Mamet derides the notion of "male bonding [as] an odious phrase meant to describe an odious activity" (87). In its place, he celebrates "hanging out" and "spending time with the boys" in places and activities like "The Lodge, Hunting, Fishing, Sports" (88), capitalizing the first letters as if to fill The Lodge with mystical male meaning. Indeed, such big ideas would suffer from verbal definition, interfering with what Mamet identifies as the ideal way for men to be together, having "That Fun Which Dare Not Speak Its Name" (87). This obvious allusion to Lord Alfred Douglas's description of male homosexuality substitutes "fun" for the all-too-vulnerable word "love," which is verboten in the lexicon of male mythology. In fact, as Eve Kosofsky Sedgwick points out, Douglas's description[3] comments upon the societal investiture in maintaining ignorance and secrecy in "public speech" when referring to nearly *any* type of male-to-male form of intimacy (74). The appropriation of Douglas's 1894 phrase, restated in Mamet's 1990s capitalization-code, expresses a flip dismissal of homosexual implications about male bonding. Radavich has documented the ways in which homophobic dismissals in Mamet's male-cast plays, such as *American Buffalo* and *Glengarry Glen Ross*, begin with "homosexual slander" (50) (homophobic name-calling) and escalate into "'homosexual panic'" (54) as men try to protect themselves from the "threat of emasculation" (51) by absent women and other men. Within the all-male universe of these earlier plays, homophobic dismissals may be contextualized as logical extensions of a heterosexual male mythology, and, therefore, may be construed as critiques of such.

The Cryptogram, however, with its openly gay man, a woman, and a child, stages a different world—one in which the audience might reasonably expect discourse patterns to shift away from heterosexist male mythology. But as verbal cryptograms are exchanged it becomes clear that they nearly all refer back to the absent patriarch, establishing an offstage straight man and his mythology as the present and controlling subject of the play. Del, Donny, and John are cast as—to borrow *Sexual Perversity's* reference to women— "inanimate objects" (53). As an extension of their objectified status, the three are preoccupied by a collection of objects in the attic, all of which symbolize the father. These objects are essentially family mementos—a photograph, a stadium blanket, and a knife. They are, effectively, antiques, for they no longer have any functional use. In *The System of Objects*, Jean Baudrillard[4] observes that, while functional objects fulfill a utilitarian purpose in the present time, "antiques refer to the past giv[ing] them an *exclusively* mythological character. The antique object no longer has any practical application, its role being merely to *signify*" (74).

Baudrillard theorizes that antiques may signify mythology on two levels, both in terms of a "nostalgia for origins" (76) and as an "obsession with authenticity" (76). He notes that "authenticity always stems from the Father: the Father is the source of value here. And it is this sublime link that antiques evoke in the imagination, along with the return journey to the mother's breast" (77). Certainly, the motivation behind the fascination with objects in *The Cryptogram* lies in the nostalgia for origins embodied by stories about the father. But this nostalgia and the accompanying desire for authenticity—that is, *proof of the truth* of these stories—is continually frustrated.

While the play's aborted dialogue attempts to interpret the narrative meaning of the family's past, it focuses obsessively upon the "mass of things" (42) in the unseen attic, gesturing at Harold Pinter's play *The Collection* (1962). As Mamet's most obvious linguistic influence, Pinter's language continually frustrates the desire of the spectator or characters to understand an authentic story, or myth. Perversely, Pinter's play refers only once to the objects named in its title:

> James: Hawkins was an opera fan too. So's whatsisname. I'm a bit of an opera fan myself. Always kept it a dead secret. I might go along with your bloke to the opera one night. He says he can always get free seats. He knows quite a few of that crowd. Maybe I can track old Hawkins down and take him along too. He's a very cultivated bloke, your bloke, quite a considerable intelligence at work there, I thought. He's got a collection of Chinese pots stuck up on the wall, must have cost at least 1500 a piece. Well, you can't help noticing that sort of thing. (67)

The Chinese pots themselves bear very little significance to the play's meaning, other than the connotation of orientalism that they place upon the object—"the bloke"—to whom James refers. Rather, it is the *idea* of the collection of useless objects that function as antiques to which James responds. They function *only* on the symbolic level and to James they signify the quantitative wealth of the "bloke." James also reads their qualitative signs, but does so by implying that the "bloke" is homosexual, or at least a feminized (castrated) man through code words such as "opera fan." (which James must maintain as a "secret" identity) and "that crowd" (i.e., "knowledge" of the queer opera crowd). When James says "You couldn't say he wasn't a man of taste" (67), Pinter employs a double negative to confuse the audience's ear, while allowing James to give a dubious compliment. Ironically, he tells his wife that by sleeping with the "bloke," "by accident," she has "opened up a whole new world" (67) for him, implying that he has some homoerotic interest in the "bloke." This "accident," like Pinter's play itself, experiments with the randomness of plot, character construction, and symbology. Mamet, to a large degree, adopts Pinter's project in *The Cryptogram*, indicated when Del says that things mean "nothing other than the meaning you choose to assign to [them]" (4).

As if to search for the father, or the family's authenticity, Donny sends John up the prominent staircase to "see if you find any things up there" (13). The staircase, which is the only part of the set that gestures at the attic, would seem to be a ladder up to the higher allegorical meanings one might assume are attached to the attic's store of antiques. Donny has found a photograph in the attic that she shows to Del, saying, "Isn't it funny? Though? The things you find?" (17). Rather than prompting memory, however, as an authentic antique might, the photograph of Bobby, Donny, and Del before the child's birth causes Del to repeatedly claim that "I don't remember" (31), severing his connection with the family's past, as well as fracturing his present identity within it. Although Del recognizes that he is wearing Bobby's shirt in the photo—a sign that could point either to his male bonding with Bobby or to his role as a surrogate husband to Donny—he distrusts it, remarking that "photography is ... very seductive"(23).

Like the photograph, the blanket is also an antique that refers to the family's past, confusing the bond between mother and child, who argue about when it was torn, or when its ability to signify the unity of the family was broken. Speaking from offstage, Donny calls out:

> *Donny*:   It was torn long ago. You can absolve yourself.
> *John*:   ... I *thought* that I tore it.
> *Del*:   But you see, in reality, things unfold ... independent of our fears of them.
> *John*:   I don't know what you mean.
> *Del*:   Because we *think* a thing is one way does not mean that this is the way this thing must be. (30–31)

When Del explains that "in reality, things unfold," he echoes Mamet's ontological idea, which recurs in several plays and films, that "things change" at random, independent of human narratives or attempts at myth-making.[5] In *The Cryptogram*, the "things" that change are expressed on two metadramatic levels: first, circumstances change in the father's absence, altering the structure of the family and their relationships. This is made apparent in the secondary level, in which the meanings of the objects change, in that they no longer possess the ability to signify patriarchal origin or authenticity. The photograph and the stadium blanket function as hypercoded stage props on a theatricalist level, detached from dramatic meaning. Their ability to signify meanings about the family's origin has been lost and they become, not cryptograms, but vacuous conundrums. The Others in the play, however, cling to their desire to make symbolic sense of the props.

Unlike the photograph and the blanket, which metadramatically question the audience's ability to understand the family's history, the knife, which is the play's most central prop, deludes characters and audience into believing that it carries decipherable meanings. When Donny asks Del if he knows the "Meaning" (64) of the knife, if he knows "what it's for" (65), he gives a simple answer: "To cut things" (65), as if it were merely a utilitarian object with only a practical, everyday use. The phrase "to cut things" could establish the knife as a phallic metaphor that both literally and symbolically penetrates "things," enacting a form of rape that could also be murder. This is certainly the case in Eugene Ionesco's *The Lesson* (1951), in which a Professor tutors a Pupil in an absurdist repetition of "knife ... kni ... fe ... " (73) as he brandishes a knife at her.[6] This repetition builds until he stabs her and she falls onto a chair, *"legs spread wide"* (75), as if she has been raped, as well as murdered, by the knife. Ionesco's stage directions allow the director a choice between *"a big knife, invisible or real"* (73), recalling Macbeth's "dagger of the mind, a false creation" (2.2.38). If an imaginary knife is used, the action becomes focused almost entirely upon the lack of meaning in the word "knife," and the rape-murder becomes a theatricalist abstraction that illustrates the power of language to murder; as the Professor observes, "the knife kills" (74). The knife, then, signifies language itself in Ionesco's play, and, in the Maid's estimation, "philology leads to crime"(76). This formulation could be said to be the underlying logic in most of Mamet's drama and cinema, in which language betrays.

In *Three Uses of the Knife: On the Nature and Purpose of Drama*, Mamet conceives of the knife as providing a "drive-to-resolution" (67) in dramatic structure. Quoting Leadbelly (also Huddie Ledbetter, see epigraph), Mamet reasons that the first two uses, "to cut the bread ... [and] to shave" (66), were to please a lover, whereas the third use, "to cut out her lying heart" (66), was to "ensure she gave her love to no one else" (67). This obvious phallic rape-murder is justified by various male mythologies that call upon men to take control of women as property. Mamet, however, veils the type of power-motivated murder symbolized by the knife in romanticism, writing that "the appearance of the knife is the attempt of the orderly, affronted mind to confront the awesome" (67). The "orderly, affronted mind" is obviously male in Mamet's lexicon, and he goes on to claim that "the awesome, the inevitable are the province of theater and religion" (67), the purpose of which "is to inspire cleansing awe" (69).

Here, Mamet seems to invoke Aristotelian notions of the positive effect of tragic purgation in order to mystify the violence encoded in male myths of the knife, imbuing it with vague religiosity. This religious mystification surrounds the recitation of a story of murder, told in the voice of a fake spiritualist medium, in *The Shawl* (1985). The male medium represents the voice as a woman's, who says that she provoked the murder by begging her lover to take her with him when he leaves: "How can you leave me in this room—clung to him, threatened, his fierce, my mistake, threatened with the ... you say that I reaped the desired result, that I won, stabbed, stabbed in the belly, ripped out with his dirk, bloodied the sheets, wiped it on the wall ... when he'd killed me" (23). The incredulous voice says that "his fierce" was "my mistake" and goes further to suggest that it was suicide, saying, "I reaped the desired result," in which she "won" a stab "in the belly." Mamet makes the equation between the knife and the phallus in the phrase "ripped out with his dirk," in which the dirk/ knife clearly stands for "dick."

In *The Cryptogram*, the knife functions as a phallic signifier of male mythology, said to be a "War Memento, with 'associations'" (87), as if to promise that it is a conduit for the father's heroic war stories. The knife is an antique, a phallic weapon of the father, which carries the weight of two male myths in the play. The first myth of the knife is recounted by Donny as a story that would seem to establish the authenticity of Bobby's masculinity, in which the knife is said to be a "combat trophy" (84), a "German Pilot's Knife" (83) that he brought back from the "War."

Donny: It's a *pilot's* knife ...
Del: ... yes. I know that ...
Donny: If he was forced to *parachute* ...
Del: Yes.
Donny: The pilot would use it to cut the *cords*. If his parachute snagged.
Del: Huh. If it snagged. On, on what?
Donny: On a tree. (65)

This reading of the knife is reminiscent of the knife in Mamet's play *Edmond*, in which the knife is identified as "*a survival* knife. G.I. Issue. World War Two"(77). In both of these plays, the stories that attach the knives to a historic war and to the notion of survival represent the symbolic, idealized level of male mythology. These speeches romanticize the past, expressing the nostalgia for origins represented by the father for whom both John and Edmond are searching.

The characters are faced with the task of decoding the meaning of this myth at greater length, however, producing a slippage between the symbolic and "real" levels. As Del reflects: "When he was forced to *abandon* his ... (*Pause.*)" (66). In the space of Del's pause, the unspoken word "family" could be inserted. He continues, "He looked for *safety*, and the knife, it cut.... It '*released* him'"(66). When Del considers Bobby's "Odd Gesture"(64) of giving him the knife as a sort of "going-away present" (64), the potential for the knife (male mythology) to release him from his family bonds becomes resonant, if unspoken, in the cryptic dialogue. Del then proceeds to tell his narrative of the gift of the knife, which is a nostalgic myth of male friendship that seems to romantically forget the myth's proscription against homosexuality. His fictional account of his fishing trip with Bobby imagines that Bobby's gift of the knife is a "sign" (68) of his symbolic initiation—as a gay man—into the world of men and its codes. He says: "It's funny for two grown men to go camping anyway. (*Pause.*) I don't care. (*Pause.*) Huh. I was born a *city* boy. (*Pause.*) (*He displays knife.*) And now I'm a Forester. (*Pause.*) I'm a Ranger ... did you know there's a Fraternal Group called the Catholic Order of Foresters?" (68).

In making up this lie about the knife, which he displays as a badge of honor, Del nostalgically reveals his own desire to become an "official" man, a member of a "Fraternal ... Order," and in doing so, exposes the nearly medieval fictions of male mythology. As Donny continues to probe for specifics, clearly disbelieving him, Del finally breaks down, violating the masculine ethos by telling the truth to an outsider—a woman. He says: "We didn't *go!* Do I have to *shout* it for you ... ? We stayed *home.* What do you *think?* He'd traipse off in the *wilds* ... with *me* ... ? To talk about *life?* Are you *stupid?* Are you *blind?* He wouldn't spend a *moment* with me. Some poor geek ... " (74). In substituting the word "geek" for "queer," Del frames his status as a homosexual in a world of straight men as being equivalent to a sideshow freak, for whom there is no possibility of being anything than Other. Their common betrayal by Bobby could (in someone else's play) unite them in a common bond of anger. But these marginalized characters are like the collection of objects in the attic who reference their identities to the male mythology of the father-subject.

This scene recalls the "mock duel" (75) in Pinter's *The Collection,* when Bill picks up a "splendid cheese knife" (72) and James grabs a "fruit knife" (74) for his attack on Bill, the gay "bloke." The knives are referred to by their utilitarian names, indicating that they are not antiques, but they nevertheless function as warlike phalluses. The metatheatricality of the "mock duel" emphasizes the symbolically homoerotic nature of their gestures and wounds, as the two ask each other if they "swallow" knives. James throws the "fruit knife" at Bill's face, missing it, but producing a "scar" (75) on Bill's hand. While Pinter appears to be more concerned with the sexual level of *The Collection* as yet another narrative to be unspun, Mamet's *The Cryptogram* seems to be fixated primarily upon the narrative mythology of the father.

With the destruction of the nostalgic myth of male friendship, Donny challenges the myth of heroic authenticity attached to the knife, revealing that it is not a souvenir from the "War," but that Bobby simply bought it "From a man. On the street. In London" (87). Similarly, in *Edmond*, the real history of the *"survival* knife," for sale in the pawn shop, is equally fuzzy, even though it is said to be the "best knife that money can buy" (57). While the war story attached to the knife in *Edmond* goes unchallenged, in *The Cryptogram*, the (apparent) truth would seem to debunk the knife's masculine "associations," severing its symbolic link with male heroism and history and decoding it as a fraudulent "story" purchased in a capitalist exchange. Donny uses Del's lack of knowledge of the "real" story as a weapon, attacking him with Mamet's arsenal of invective, calling him "You 'fairy'" (86) and "You faggot" (94), ostensibly removing him from his role as surrogate father and husband and homophobically reinscribing him as an Other on the margins of the family.

The overlapping metadramatic stories connected to the encrypted objects in the play increasingly point to its tragic end, as John questions, "Do you ever think things? ... Do you ever wish that you could die?" (78). John's "think[ing] things," in his attempts to decode the blanket and the knife, have been blocked, and he can only cling, childishly, to the meanings and outcomes he desires—his father's return and a trip to the "Cabin" (80)—that are still encoded for him in the knife's mythology. He seizes upon the knife as a symbol in his own version of a masculine "story," and, hearing "voices" (100) calling him, he constructs a fiction about why he wants it, saying that he needs it to cut the twine wrapping the blanket, as if to unravel his family's history. In the end, Del tells him to "Take the knife and go" (101), as if it were an invitation to take all of the associations with masculinity the knife carries and do the only thing he can do, which is to exit from the family and life. John's suicide seems to reverberate with one of the last lines in Clifford Odets' *The Big Knife* (1949), in which the lead male is said to have "killed himself ... because that was the only way he could live" (76).[7]

The end of *The Cryptogram* suggests that John's death occurs at a symbolic level, almost without his use of the "real" knife, but an imaginary one. In *Edmond*, also, the knife seems to wield itself as Edmond stabs Glenna, saying to her *"now* look what you've done" (78). Edmond's act of murder, that is, killing the "stupid fucking *bitch*" (78), is defended when Edmond acknowledges he "doesn't feel like a man" because his "balls were cut off ... A long, long time ago" (25). After the murder, when he claims he had the knife "for protection" from "everyone" (83), it is suggested that, suffering from castration anxiety, he could not discover that his "real" manhood/penis

resembled the symbolic phallus. He metatheatrically acts out a male myth
with the prop/knife by killing Glenna, who represents a figure of castration
in the world, which Edmond perceives as a "shit house" (71). He wants to
return to the "Theatre.... [where he may] *ask respect*" (71) for himself. As
Edmond sits in prison awaiting emasculation by homosexual rape, he says,
"Every fear hides a wish," (89), suggesting an awareness of homoerotic desire
underlying his homophobia. While *Edmond* is an expressionist journey play,
it keeps a masculine silence, as the audience is not permitted to witness the
interiors of any of its characters.

The *Cryptogram* would seem to suggest that in Mamet's drama of the
1990s there is no exit from the crippling fictions of male mythology.
Although the deconstruction of the knife's symbolic value reveals the
unstable, fictional quality of those myths, the marginalized characters of this
"family play" are so deeply invested in defining themselves in relation to the
patriarchy that the play could hardly be said to be a critique of the masculine
ethos. It is, rather, a tragedy of delimited vision that ultimately can only
continue to reinscribe those myths. At the play's end, Donny rationalizes the
failure of the myths, claiming that "Things occur. In our lives. And the
meaning of them ... the *meaning* of them ... is not clear.... But we must assume
they have a meaning. We must" (79). Despite her crucial role in exposing the
myths as lies, she can only reinvest her identity in them. Using the vernacular
of the masculine ethos, she writes Del off as "You faggot. [Like] Every man
I ever met in my life ... " (94). Del participates in this fag-bashing, saying
"Who am I? Some poor Queen. Lives in a hotel" (94), and "I'm pathetic. I
know that. You don't have to tell me. The life that I lead is trash. I hate
myself" (88). This language of self-pity and self-loathing—which is some of
the most direct, least cryptic verbiage in the play—does not seem to be
spoken by the voices of a woman and a gay man, but rather by the voice of a
heterosexual male, just as the voice of the murdered woman in *The Shawl*
emanates from the fake male spiritualist. The male voices in these plays,
speaking from behind Mamet's wizard-curtain, manifest a basic belief in male
mythology that reinscribes the woman as "cunt" and gay man as "fairy." And
that is the tragedy.

NOTES

1. Robert Vorlicky has observed that Donny's identification of Del as "You
fairy" and "You faggot" recall the labels applied to Williamson in *Glengarry Glen Ross*,
when, after he breaks the male codes of salesmanship, Roma calls him a "stupid
fucking *cunt*," a "fairy" and a "fucking *child*" (96–97)—names which could, ironically,

be applied to the characters of *The Cryptogram*. (See Robert Vorlicky, review of *The Cryptogram*, Westside Theatre, New York, May 28, 1995, in *The David Mamet Review* 2 [Fall 1995]: 3–4).

    2. For a discussion of Poe's use of cryptograms to demystify myths (as opposed to Mamet's use of them to mystify), see Terence Whalen's "The Code for Gold: Edgar Allen Poe and Cryptography," *Representations* 46 (Spring 1994): 35–57. Also see Michael Williams' "'The language of the cipher': Interpretation in 'The Gold Bug,'" *American Literature* 53 (January 1982): 646–60.

    3. Lord Alfred Douglas wrote of the "Love that Dare Not Speak Its Name" in "Two Loves," *The Chameleon* 1 (1894): 28.

    4. For a different reading of Baudrillard against Mamet, see Elizabeth Klaver's "David Mamet, Jean Baudrillard and the Performance of America," *David Mamet's Glengarry Glen Ross: Text and Performance*, Ed. Leslie Kane (New York: Garland, 1996), 171–83.

    5. See, for example, Mamet's *American Buffalo*, *Glengarry Glen Ross*, *House of Games* and *Things Change*.

    6. For studies that relate Ionesco's *The Lesson* to Mamet's *Oleanna*, see Verna Foster's "Sex, Power and Pedagogy in Mamet's *Oleanna* and Ionesco's *The Lesson*," *American Drama* 5:1 (Fall 1995): 36–50; and Craig Stewart Walker's "Three Tutorial Plays: *The Lesson, The Prince of Naples* and *Oleanna*," *Modern Drama* 40 (1997): 149–62.

    7. Clifford Odets' *The Big Knife* contains very few similarities with *The Cryptogram*. It is, by Odets' description, a "melodrama" (Rhodes) about a Hollywood actor's descent into suicide. It contains no knife or allusion to one, but in an interview with the *New York Times*, Odets explained that "the big knife is that force in modern life which is against people and their aspirations, which seems to cut people off in their best flower" (Peck). Like so many of Odets' plays, therefore, this becomes a play about the struggle of an individual against social forces, ultimately critiquing society. Arguably, that is also an aspect of Mamet's drama, although the comparison would seem to end there.

WORKS CITED

Baudrillard, Jean. *The System of Objects*. First published as *Le système des objets*. Paris: Editions Gallimard, 1968. Trans. James Benedict. New York: Verso, 1996.

Dolan, Jill. *The Feminist Spectator as Critic*. Ann Arbor: U of Michigan P, 1991.

Douglas, Lord Alfred. "Two Loves." *The Chameleon* 1 (1894).

Foster, Verna. "Sex, Power, and Pedagogy in Mamet's *Oleanna* and Ionesco's *The Lesson*." *American Drama* 5:1 (Fall 1995): 36–50.

Ionesco, Eugene. *The Lesson*. 1951. *Eugene Ionesco: Four Plays*. Trans. Donald M. Allen. New York: Grove Press, 1958, 43–78.

Klaver, Elizabeth. "David Mamet, Jean Baudrillard and the Performance of America." *David Mamet's "Glengarry Glen Ross": Text and Performance*. Ed. Leslie Kane. New York: Garland, 1996, 171–83.

Lacan, Jacques. *Ecrits: A Selection*. Trans. Alan Sheridan. New York: Norton, 1977.

Mamet, David. *The Cryptogram*. 1994. New York: Vintage Books, 1995.

———. *Edmond.* 1982. New York: Grove Press, 1983.

———. *Glengarry Glen Ross.* 1983. New York: Grove Press, 1984.

———. "In the Company of Men." In *Some Freaks.* New York: Viking, 1989, 85–91.

———. Interview. *The South Bank Show.* October 1994.

———. "Kryptonite: A Psychological Approach." In *Some Freaks.* New York: Viking, 1989, 175–80.

———. *Sexual Perversity in Chicago and The Duck Variations.* 1974, 1972. New York: Grove Press, 1978.

———. *The Shawl.* New York: Samuel French, 1985.

———. *Three Uses of the Knife: On the Nature and Purpose of Drama.* Columbia Lectures on American Culture. New York: Columbia UP, 1998.

McDonough, Carla J. "David Mamet: The Search for Masculine Space." In *Staging Masculinity: Male Identity in Contemporary American Drama.* Jefferson, NC: McFarland & Company, 1997, 71–101.

Odets, Clifford. *The Big Knife.* New York: Dramatists Play Service, 1949.

Peck, Seymour. "An Angry Man from Hollywood." *New York Times* February 20, 1949.

Pinter, Harold. *The Collection.* 1961. *Three Plays.* New York: Grove Press, 1962.

Radavich, David. "Man among Men: David Mamet's Homosocial Order." *American Drama* 1:1 (Fall 1991): 46–60.

Rhodes, Russell. Interview with Clifford Odets. *New York Herald Tribune.* May 1, 1949.

Savran, David. *Taking It Like a Man: White Masculinity, Masochism and Contemporary American Culture.* Princeton: Princeton UP, 1998.

Sedgwick, Eve Kosofsky. *The Epistemology of the Closet.* Berkeley: U of California P, 1990.

Shakespeare, William. *Macbeth. The Complete Works of William Shakespeare.* Ed. William George Clark and William Aldis Wright. New York: Grosset & Dunlap, 1864, 979–1006.

Silverman, Kaja. *Male Subjectivity at the Margins.* New York: Routledge, 1992.

Vorlicky, Robert. *Act Like a Man: Challenging Masculinites in American Drama.* Ann Arbor: U of Michigan P, 1995.

———. Review of *The Cryptogram,* dir. David Mamet. Westside Theatre: New York. May 28, 1995. *David Mamet Review* 2 (Fall 1995): 3–4.

Walker, Craig Stewart. "Three Tutorial Plays: *The Lesson, The Prince of Naples* and *Oleanna.*" *Modern Drama* 40 (1997): 149–62.

Zeifman, Hersh. "Phallus in Wonderland: Machismo and Business in David Mamet's *American Buffalo* and *Glengarry Glen Ross.*" *David Mamet: A Casebook.* Ed. Leslie Kane. New York: Garland Press, 1992, 123–35.

Chronology

1947	Born in Chicago on November 30, to Bernard Mamet, a labor lawyer, and Lenore Mamet, a teacher.
1957–58	Parents divorce.
1963–65	Attends private school and works backstage, taking small parts at Hull House Theatre. Also works at Second City.
1966–67	Attends Goddard College in Vermont for two years. Studies acting with Sanford Meisner at the Neighborhood Playhouse in New York City for 18 months. Returns to Goddard and begins writing plays.
1969	Graduates from Goddard. Works as an actor in small productions touring New England.
1970	Teaches acting at Marlboro College in Vermont. *Lakeboat*, a one-act play, is produced.
1971	Becomes part of Goddard staff, teaching acting.
1972	Along with two of his students, forms the St. Nicholas Company to produce his plays and others. *Duck Variations* is produced.
1974	Reconstitutes the St. Nicholas Company as the St. Nicholas Players in Chicago. *Sexual Perversity in Chicago* and *Squirrels* are produced.
1975	*American Buffalo* is produced.
1976	*Reunion* is produced.

1977	Marries Lindsay Crouse and later has two daughters with her, Willa and Zosia. Through wife's connections, receives first screenwriting job for the remake of *The Postman Always Rings Twice* (1981). Moves to New York, supporting himself as a playwright. *Dark Pony, A Life in the Theatre, The Revenge of the Space Pandas, or Binky Rudich and the Two-Speed Clock, The Water Engine: An American Fable, The Woods* (Mamet directs this as well), and *All Men Are Whores* are produced.
1978	*Mr. Happiness* is produced.
1979	*Lone Canoe; or, the Explorer, The Sanctity of Marriage*, and *Shoeshine* are produced.
1980	A revised *Lakeboat* is produced.
1982	The film *The Verdict* is released, for which Mamet wrote the screenplay adaptation. He receives an Academy Award nomination. *Edmond* is produced.
1983	*Glengarry Glen Ross* is produced and wins the Pulitzer Prize for Drama.
1984	*The Disappearance of the Jews* is produced.
1985	Helps found Atlantic Theater Company in New York City. *The Shawl* and *Prairie du Chien* are produced.
1986	A book of essays, *Writing in Restaurants*, is published.
1987	Film *The Untouchables* is released, for which Mamet wrote the screenplay adaptation. *House of Games* released, which he wrote and directed.
1988	Associate professor of film at Columbia University. *Speed-the-Plow* produced and wins Tony Award for best play.
1989	*Some Freaks*, a book of essays, is published. *Bobby Gould in Hell* is produced. *We're No Angels*, for which Mamet wrote the screenplay, is released.
1990	Divorces Lindsay Crouse.
1991	Marries Rebecca Pidgeon, and they have one daughter, Clara.
1992	*The Cabin: Reminiscence and Diversions*, a memoir, is published. *Glengarry Glen Ross, The Water Engine*, and *Hoffa* are released; the screenplays are written by Mamet. *Oleanna* produced. The film *Homicide* is released, for which Mamet wrote the screenplay and directed.

1994	*The Cryptogram*, written and directed by Mamet, is produced. The film version of *Oleanna* is released; Mamet also directs it. *Vanya on 42nd Street* is released; Mamet wrote the screenplay, an adaptation from Chekhov's *Uncle Vanya*. *The Village*, a novel, is published.
1995	*Passover*, a novella, is published.
1996	*American Buffalo* is released.
1997	*The Old Neighborhood* is produced. *Wag the Dog* is released, for which he co-wrote the adaptation and directed. Receives an Academy Award nomination for best adapted screenplay. *The Old Religion* and *True and False* are published.
2001	*Hannibal* is released; Mamet wrote the screenplay.

Contributors

HAROLD BLOOM is Sterling Professor of the Humanities at Yale University and Henry W. and Albert A. Berg Professor of English at the New York University Graduate School. He is the author of over 20 books, including *Shelley's Mythmaking* (1959), *The Visionary Company* (1961), *Blake's Apocalypse* (1963), *Yeats* (1970), *A Map of Misreading* (1975), *Kabbalah and Criticism* (1975), *Agon: Toward a Theory of Revisionism* (1982), *The American Religion* (1992), *The Western Canon* (1994), and *Omens of Millennium: The Gnosis of Angels, Dreams, and Resurrection* (1996). *The Anxiety of Influence* (1973) sets forth Professor Bloom's provocative theory of the literary relationships between the great writers and their predecessors. His most recent books include *Shakespeare: The Invention of the Human* (1998), a 1998 National Book Award finalist, *How to Read and Why* (2000), *Genius: A Mosaic of One Hundred Exemplary Creative Minds* (2002), and *Hamlet: Poem Unlimited* (2003). In 1999, Professor Bloom received the prestigious American Academy of Arts and Letters Gold Medal for Criticism, and in 2002 he received the Catalonia International Prize.

ANNE DEAN is the author of *Discovery & Invention: The Urban Plays of Lanford Wilson*.

DOUGLAS BRUSTER teaches English at the University of Texas, Austin. He is the author of *Quoting Shakespeare: Form & Culture in Early Modern Drama*.

TOBY SILVERMAN ZINMAN teaches at the University of the Arts in Philadelphia. She is the editor of *Terrence McNally: A Casebook* and writes frequently on contemporary drama and fiction.

DAVID RADAVICH is Professor of English at Eastern Illinois University. He is a poet, playwright, and literary critic. He has published books of poetry and a play, and has had plays produced at various theaters.

EDWARD J. ESCHE has lectured at Anglia University. He is the editor of *Shakespeare & His Contemporaries in Performance* and also of a work of Christopher Marlowe's.

MICHAEL L. QUINN had been Assistant Professor in Dramatic Theory and Criticism at the University of Washington School of Drama. He was the author of *The Semiotic Stage: Prague School Theater Theory* and also the co-author of *Staging Diversity: Plays & Practice in American Theater*.

HOWARD PEARCE is Professor of English at Florida Atlantic University. He is the author of *Human Shadows Bright as Glass: Drama as Speculation & Transformation*. Also, he is the co-editor of a book on the fantastic in literature and film.

LESLIE KANE is Professor of English at Westfield State College. She is the author or editor of numerous titles, among them *David Mamet: A Casebook*, Glengarry Glen Ross: *Text and Performance*, and *David Mamet in Conversation*. She is Editor of *The David Mamet Review*. Also, she is a co-founder of the David Mamet Society and has been president of the organization.

CHRISTOPHER W. E. BIGSBY is Professor of American Studies at the University of East Anglia. He has published more than twenty-five books on American and British theater and popular culture, among them *Contemporary American Playwrights* and *David Mamet*. He is the co-editor of *The Cambridge History of American Theatre*. Additionally, he has been a novelist and radio and television broadcaster.

DAVID KENNEDY SAUER is Professor of English at Spring Hill College in Mobile, Alabama. He has written essays on Mamet for the *David Mamet Review* and for Glengarry Glen Ross: *Text and Performance*. He has also published pieces on Shakespeare and on other dramatic subjects.

RICHARD BRUCHER is Associate Professor of English at the University of Maine. He has published essays on Mamet, O'Neill, and Miller and also has written on revenge and violence in early modern drama.

LINDA DORFF was an Assistant Professor of Theatre History, Theory, and Criticism in the School of Theatre at the University of Houston. An essay she wrote on Mamet appears in *Glengarry Glen Ross: Text and Performance*.

Bibliography

Almansi, Guido. "David Mamet, a Virtuoso of Invective." In Chéntier, Marc, ed. *Critical Angles: European Views of Contemporary American Literature*. Carbondale: Southern Illinois University Press, 1986, pp. 191–207.

Bechtel, Roger. "P. C. Power Play: Language and Representation in David Mamet's *Oleanna*," *Theatre Studies* 41 (1996): pp. 29–48.

Begley, Varun. "On Adaptation: David Mamet and Hollywood," *Essays in Theatre/Etudes Theatrales* 16, no. 2 (May 1998): pp. 165–76.

Bishop, Ryan. "There's Nothing Natural about Natural Conversation: A Look at Dialogue in Fiction and Drama." In Jurak, Mirko, ed. *Cross-Cultural Studies: American, Canadian and European Literatures: 1945–1985*. Ljubljana: English Department, Filozofska Fakulteta, 1988.

Blattès, Susan. "The Blurring of Boundaries between Stage and Screen in Plays by Sam Shepard and David Mamet." In Voights-Virchow, Eckart, ed. *Mediated Drama/Dramatized Media. Contemporary Drama in English* 7. Trier, Germany: Wissenschaftlicher, 2000.

Blumberg, Marcia. "Eloquent Stammering in the Fog: O'Neill's Heritage in Mamet. In Bagchee, Shyamal, ed. *Perspectives on O'Neill: New Essays*. Victoria: University of Victoria, 1988, pp. 97–111.

Boon, Kevin Alexander. "Dialogue, Discourse and Dialectics: The Rhetoric of Capitalism in *Glengarry Glen Ross*," *Creative Screenwriting* 5, no. 3 (1998): pp. 50–57.

Brewer, Gaylord. "Hoffa and *The Untouchables*: Mamet's Brutal Orders of Authority," *Literature/Film Quarterly* 28, no. 1 (2000): pp. 28–33.

Callens, Johan. "David Mamet," *Post-War Literatures in English* 48 (September 2000): pp. 1–21, A1–3, B1–6.

———. "Mr. Smith Goes to Chicago: Playing Out Mamet's Critique of Capitalism in *American Buffalo*," *European Journal of American Culture* 19, no. 1 (2000).

Cullick, Jonathan S. "'Always Be Closing': Competition and Discourse of Closure in David Mamet's *Glengarry Glen Ross*," *Journal of Dramatic Theory and Criticism* 8, no. 2 (Spring 1994): pp. 23–36.

Davis, J. Madison, Coleman, John. "David Mamet: A Classified Bibliography," *Studies in American Drama, 1945–Present* 1 (1986): pp. 83–101.

Dean, Anne. *David Mamet: Language as Dramatic Action. Rutherford: Fairleigh Dickinson University Press*, 1990.

Ditsky, John. "'He Lets You See the Thought There': The Theater of David Mamet," *Kansas Quarterly* 12, no. 4 (1980): pp. 25–34.

Foster, Verna. "Sex, Power, and Pedagogy in Mamet's *Oleanna* and Ionesco's *The Lesson*," *American Drama* 5, no. 1 (Fall 1995): pp. 36–50.

Gale, Stephen H. "David Mamet: The Plays, 1972–1980." In Bock, Hedwig, ed; Wertheim, Albert, ed. *Essays on Contemporary American Drama*. Munich: Hueber, 1981, pp. 207–24.

———. "The Plays of David Mamet." In *Essays on Modern American Drama*. Munich: Max Heuber, 1981, pp. 207–23.

Gidmark, Jill B. "Violent Silences in Three Works of David Mamet," *Midamerica* 25 (1998): pp. 184–92.

Goggans, Thomas H. "Laying Blame: Gender and Subtext in David Mamet's *Oleanna*," *Modern Drama* 40, no. 4 (Winter 1997): pp. 433–41.

Goist, Park Dixon. "Ducks and Sex in David Mamet's Chicago," *Midamerica* 18 (1991): pp. 143–52.

Goldensohn, Barry. "David Mamet and Poetic Language in Drama," *Agni* 49 (1999): pp. 139–49.

Greenbaum, Andrea. "Brass Balls: Masculine Communication and the Discourse of Capitalism," *Journal of Men's Studies* 8, no. 1 (Fall 1999): pp. 33–43.

Haedicke, Janet V. "Decoding Cipher Space: David Mamet's *The Cryptogram* and America's Dramatic Legacy," *American Drama* 9, no. 1 (Fall 1999): pp. 1–20.

Heller, Janet Ruth. "David Mamet's Trivialization of Feminism and Sexual Harrassment in *Oleanna*," *Midamerica: The Yearbook of the Society for the Study of Midwestern Literature* 27 (2000): pp. 93–105.

Henson, Philip. "Against Tribalism: The Perils of Ethnic Identity in Mamets' Homicide," *CLIO* 31, no. 3 (Spring 2002): pp. 257–77

Hubert-Leibler, Pascale. "Dominance and Anguish: The Teacher-Student Relationship in the Plays of David Mamet," *Modern Drama* 31, no. 4 (December 1988): pp. 557–70.

Jacobs, Dorothy H. "Working Worlds in David Mamet's Dramas," *Midwestern Miscellany* 14 (1986): pp. 47–57.

Joki, Ilkka. "David Mamet's Drama: The Dialogicality of Grotesque Realism." In Shepherd, David, ed. *Bakhtin: Carnival and Other Subjects*. Amsterdam: Rodopi, 1993, pp. 80–98.

———. "Mamet, Bakhtin, and the Dramatic: The Demotic as a Variable of Addressivity. Turku: Åbo Akad., 1993.

Kane, Leslie, ed. *David Mamet's* Glengarry Glen Ross: *Text and Performance*. New York: Garland, 1996.

Kane, Leslie. "'In Blood, in Blood Thou Shalt Remember': David Mamet's *Marranos*," *Yearbook of English Studies* 24 (1994): pp. 157–71.

———. *David Mamet: A Casebook*. New York: Garland, 1991.

———. "Time Passages," *The Pinter Review: Annual Essays* (1990): pp. 30–49.

Kim, So-im. "Sexual Myths in David Mamet: *Sexual Perversity in Chicago* and *Edmond*," *Journal of English Language and Literature* 42, no. 4 (Winter 1996): pp. 899–922.

Kim, Yun-cheol. "Degradation of the American Success Ethic: *Death of a Salesman*, *That Championship Season*, and *Glengarry Glen Ross*," *The Journal of English Language and Literature* 37, no. 1 (Spring 1991): pp. 233–48.

King, Thomas L. "Talk and Dramatic Action in *American Buffalo*," *Modern Drama* 34, no. 4 (December 1991): pp. 538–48.

Kolin, Philip C. "David Mamet's *Duck Variations* as a Parody of a Socratic Dialogue," *American Drama* 9, no. 1 (Fall 1999): pp. 21–32.

———. "David Mamet's *Writing in Restaurants*: A Primary and Secondary Bibliography," *Analytical & Enumerative Bibliography* 2, no. 4 (1988): pp. 160–67.

———. "Performing Scripts in David Mamet's *Speed-the-Plow*," *Notes on Contemporary Literature* 28, no. 5 (November 1998): pp. 5–6.

Lublin, Robert I. "Differing Dramatic Dynamics in Stage and Screen Versions of *Glengarry Glen Ross*,"*American Drama* 10, no. 1 (Winter 2001): pp. 38–55.

Lundin, Edward. "Mamet and Mystery," *Publications of the Mississippi Philological Association* (1988): pp. 106–14.

MacLeod, Christine. "The Politics of Gender, Language and Hierarchy in Mamet's *Oleanna*," *Journal of American Studies* 29, no. 2 (August 1995): pp. 199–213.

McCarthy, Gerry. "New Mythologies: Mamet, Shepard and the American Stage," *Connotations* 6, no.3 (1996–1997): pp. 354–68.

McDonough, Carla J. "Every Fear Hides a Wish: Unstable Masculinity in Mamet's Drama," *Theatre Journal* 44, no. 2 (May 1992): pp. 195–205.

Merlin, Bella. "Mamet's Heresy and Common Sense: What's True and False in 'True and False,'" *New Theatre Quarterly* 16, no. 3 (63) (August 2000): pp. 249–54.

Nelson, Jeanne-Andrée. "A Machine Out of Order: Indifferentiation in David Mamet's *The Disappearance of the Jews*," *Journal of American Studies* 25, no. 3 (December 1991): pp. 461–72.

———. "So Close to Closure: The Selling of Desire in *Glengarry Glen Ross*," *Essays in Theatre* 14, no. 2 (May 1996): pp. 107–16.

———. "*Speed-the-Plow* or Seed the Plot? Mamet and the Female Reader," *Essays in Theatre* 10, no. 1 (November 1991): pp. 71–82.

Németh, Lenke. "Miscommunication and Its Implication in David Mamet's *Oleanna*," *B. A. S.: British and American Studies* (1997): pp. 167–76.

Omer, Ranen. "The Metaphysics of Lost Jewish Identity in David Mamet's *Homicide*," *Yiddish* 11, nos. 3–4 (1999): pp. 37–50.

Pearce, Howard. "'Loving Wrong' in the Worlds of Harold Pinter's *Moonlight* and David Mamet's *Cryptogram*," *Journal of Dramatic Theory and Criticism* 15, no. 1 (Fall 2000): pp. 61–79.

Peereboom, J. J. "Mamet from Afar." In Debusscher, Gilbert and Henry I. Schvey, Henry I., eds. *New Essays on American Drama*. Amsterdam: Rodopi, 1989.

Piette, Alain. "The Devil's Advocate: David Mamet's *Oleanna* and Political Correctness." In Maufort, Marc, ed. *Staging Difference: Cultural Pluralism in American Theatre and Drama. American University Studies XXIV: American Literature.* New York: Peter Lang, 1995, pp. 173–87.

———. "In the Loneliness of Cities: The Hopperian Accents of David Mamet's *Edmond*," *Studies in the Humanities* 24, nos. 1–2 (June–December 1997): pp. 43–51.

Porter, Thomas E. "Postmodernism and Violence in Mamet's *Oleanna*," *Modern Drama* 43, no. 1 (Spring 2000): pp. 13–31.

Price, Stephen. "'Accursed Progenitor': Samuel Beckett, David Mamet, and the Problem of Influence," *Samuel Beckett Today* 2 (1993): pp. 77–85.

Radavich, David. "Man among Men: David Mamet's Homosocial Order," *American Drama* 1, no. 1 (Fall 1991): pp. 46–60.

Roudané, Matthew C. "Public Issues, Private Tensions: David Mamet's *Glengarry Glen Ross*," *South Carolina Review* 19, no. 1 (Fall 1986): pp. 35–47.

Ryan, Steven. "*Oleanna*: David Mamet's Power Play," *Modern Drama* 39, no. 3 (Fall 1996): pp. 392–403.

Schaub, Martin. "Magic Meanings in Mamet's *Cryptogram*," *Modern Drama* 42, no. 3 (Fall 1999): pp. 326–27.

Schlueter, June and Elizabeth Forsyth. "America as Junkshop: The Business Ethic in David Mamet's *American Buffalo*," *Modern Drama* 26, no. 4 (December 1983); pp. 492–500.

Silverstein, Marc. "'We're Just Human': *Oleanna* and Cultural Crisis," *South Atlantic Review* 60, no. 2 (May 1995): pp. 104–20.

Storey, Rober. "The Making of David Mamet," *The Hollins Critic* 16, no. 4 (1979): pp. 1–11.

Thompson, Terry. "Revealing Illusions in David Mamet's *The Shawl*," *Notes on Contemporary Literature* 16, no. 2 (March 1986): pp.. 9–10.

Tomc, Sandra. "David Mamet's *Oleanna* and the Way of the Flesh," *Essays in Theatre* 15, no. 2 (May 1997): pp. 163–75.

Weber, Myles. "David Mamet in Theory and Practice," *New England Review: Middlebury Series* 21, no. 2 (Spring 2000): pp. 136–41.

Worster, David. "How to Do Things with Salesmen: David Mamet's Speech-Act Play," *Modern Drama* 37, no. 3 (Fall 1994): pp. 375–90.

Zeifman, Hersh. "Phallus in Wonderland: Machismo and Business in David Mamet's *American Buffalo* and *Glengarry Glen Ross*." In King, Kimball, ed. *Modern Dramatists: A Casebook of Major British, Irish, and American Playwrights*. New York, NY: Routledge, 2001, pp. 167–76.

Zinman, Toby Silverman. "So Dis Is Hollywood: Mamet in Hell." In King, Kimball, ed. *Hollywood on Stage: Playwrights Evaluate the Culture Industry*. New York: Garland, 1997, pp. 101–12.

Acknowledgments

"*Sexual Perversity in Chicago*" by Anne Dean. From *David Mamet: Language as Dramatic Action*: 51–84. © 1990 by Associated University Presses, Inc. Reprinted by permission.

"David Mamet and Ben Jonson: City Comedy Past and Present" by Douglas Bruster. From *Modern Drama* 33, no. 3 (September 1990): 333–346. © 1990 by the University of Toronto. Reprinted by permission.

"Jewish Aporia: The Rhythm of Talking in Mamet" by Toby Silverman Zinman. From *Theatre Journal* 44, no. 2 (May 1992): 207–216. © 1992 by The Johns Hopkins University Press. Reprinted by permission.

"Man among Men: David Mamet's Homosocial Order" by David Radavich. From *Fictions of Masculinity: Crossing Cultures, Crossing Sexualities*, edited by Peter F. Murphy: 123–136. © 1994 by New York University. Reprinted by permission.

"David Mamet" by Edward J. Esche. From *American Drama*, edited by Clive Bloom: 165–177. © 1995 by Lumiere Co-operative Press Ltd. Reprinted by permission.

"Anti-Theatricality and American Ideology: Mamet's Performative Realism" by Michael L. Quinn. From *Realism and the American Dramatic Tradition*,

edited by William W. Demastes: 235–254. © 1996 by the University of
Alabama Press. Reprinted by permission.

"Plato in Hollywood: David Mamet and the Power of Illusions" by Howard
Pearce. From *Mosaic* 32, no. 2 (June 1999): 141–156. © 1999 by *Mosaic*.
Reprinted by permission.

"Gathering Sparks" by Leslie Kane. From *Weasels and Wisemen: Ethics and
Ethnicity in the Work of David Mamet*: 227–260. © 1999 by Leslie Kane.
Reprinted with permission of Palgrave.

"David Mamet: All True Stories" by C. W. E. Bigsby. From *Modern American
Drama, 1945–2000*: 199–236. © 2000 by Cambridge University Press.
Reprinted with the permission of Cambridge University Press.

"*Oleanna* and *The Children's Hour*: Misreading Sexuality on the Post/Modern
Realistic Stage" by David Kennedy Sauer. From *Modern Drama* 34, no. 3
(Fall 2000): 421–441. © 2000 by the University of Toronto. Reprinted by
permission.

"Prophecy and Parody in *Edmond*" by Richard Brucher. From *Gender &
Genre: Essays on David Mamet*, edited by Christopher C. Hudgins and Leslie
Kane: 61–76. © 2001 by Christopher C. Hudgins and Leslie Kane.
Reprinted with permission of Palgrave.

"Reinscribing 'the Fairy': The Knife and the Mystification of Male
Mythology in *The Cryptogram*" by Linda Dorff. From *Gender & Genre: Essays
on David Mamet*, edited by Christopher C. Hudgins and Leslie Kane:
175–190. © 2001 by Christopher C. Hudgins and Leslie Kane. Reprinted by
permission.

Index